PERFORMING
MARGINALITY

Humor in Life and Letters Series

A complete listing of the books in this series can be found online at
http://wsupress.wayne.edu

General Editor
Sarah Blacher Cohen
State University of New York, Albany

Advisory Editors
Joseph Boskin
Boston University

Alan Dundes
University of California, Berkeley

William F. Fry, Jr.
Stanford University Medical School

Gerald Gardner
Author and lecturer

Jeffrey H. Goldstein
Temple University and London University

Don L. F. Nilsen
Arizona State University

June Sochen
Northeastern Illinois University

PERFORMING
MARGINALITY
Humor, Gender, and Cultural Critique

JOANNE R. GILBERT

WAYNE STATE UNIVERSITY PRESS   DETROIT

Library of Congress Cataloging-in-Publication Data

Gilbert, Joanne R., 1962–
    Performing marginality : humor, gender, and cultural critique / Joanne R. Gilbert.
        p. cm. — (Humor in life and letters series)
Includes bibliographical references and index.

    ISBN 0-8143-2803-2 (pbk. : alk. paper)
    1. Stand-up comedy.   2. Women comedians—United States.   3. American wit and
humor.   4. American wit and humor—History and criticism.   5. Women—Humor.   I. Title.
II. Series: Humor in life and letters.
    PN1969.C65G55 2004
    792.7'082—dc22

2003017665

Some material in chapter 4 appeared previously in "Feminist Criticism" by Joanne
Gilbert and Roderick P. Hart in *Modern Rhetorical Criticism*, 2nd ed., edited by
Roderick P. Hart, published by Allyn and Bacon, Boston, MA. ©1997 by Pearson
Education. Reprinted by permission of the publisher.
Some material in chapters 4 and 5 is taken from "Performing Marginality:
Comedy, Identity, and Cultural Critique" by Joanne Gilbert, *Text and Performance
Quarterly* 17, no. 4.

∞ The paper used in this publication meets the minimum requirements of the
American National Standard for Information Sciences—Permanence of Paper for
Printed Library Materials, ANSI Z39.48–1984.

To my first teachers,

Doris (1931–1996) and Lawrence Gilbert,

whose loving lessons about gender, humor, and power

continue to serve me well

If you were a boy, having a sense of humor meant . . .
pouring salt on the head of the girl who sat in front of you
so it would look as though she had dandruff.
If you were a girl, having a sense of humor meant
laughing when someone poured salt on your head.

Ann Beatts

It is the inability of the critical tradition to deal with
comedy by women rather than the inability of women to
produce comedy that accounts for the absence of
critical material on the subject.

Regina Barreca

CONTENTS

Acknowledgments ix

Introduction xi

CHAPTER 1
Humor, Power, and Marginality 1

CHAPTER 2
The Question of Genre 41

CHAPTER 3
Female Comics: Talking the Talk 73

CHAPTER 4
Female Comics: Walking the Walk 95

CHAPTER 5
The Politics of Performing Marginality 137

Conclusion 169

Notes 181

Works Cited 205

Index 221

ACKNOWLEDGMENTS

Like any human endeavor, this project would not have been possible without the assistance and support of many wonderful people. First and foremost, I would like to thank my family: my parents, the late Doris Gilbert and Lawrence Gilbert, without whose love and support, both emotional and material, this book would never have come into being; my incredible husband, best friend, and soulmate, Mike Bishop, whose love and nurturing is the true lodestone of my life; my daughter, Wren, and my stepdaughter, Sarah, who have exhibited patience and goodwill far beyond their years; and Dan, Scott, and Sherry Gilbert and Lee and Ned Bishop, whose good counsel and unflagging support continue to sustain me.

I am fortunate indeed for the professional guidance I have received throughout this process, and I am extremely grateful to many: Paul Gray, who first asked me to consider the history of stand-up comedy and who, along with Richard Cherwitz, Roderick Hart, Lynn Miller, and Janet Staiger, read and contributed immeasurably to the earliest drafts of this work; Arthur Evans, whose belief in this project was instrumental in its completion; the numerous individuals who responded both informally and formally to my ideas at academic conferences and in other contexts; the several anonymous reviewers whose thoughtful feedback strengthened this manuscript considerably; and my intrepid students, who gave me the highest compliment they could by doing their assigned reading.

I am truly blessed to have the continuing support and goodwill of the following people: Tim Cage and John Capecci, who make me laugh like nobody else; Vanessa Beasley, Alison Rieber, Michelle Ronda, and Claire Van Ens, the smartest, funniest "sisters" I could ever have; Dennis Grady, Alan Hall, and Bryan Taylor, whose gifts transcend the years and miles; the late Robert Hopper (aka "Dr. Calypso"), whose songs were truly balm for the soul; Mary Banski, as much for her unique and irreverent performance of marginality over the years as for her eleventh hour rescue during the completion of this project; Carol Bender, Elizabeth Cameron, Nick Dixon, Catherine Fobes, Anne Lambrecht, Susan Root, Laura Von Wallmenich, and the late Roseanne Hoefel, whose generosity of mind and spirit have helped me more than they know; and Lawrence Rosenfeld, mensch and mentor, who long ago taught me that humor and research go hand in hand. All of these individuals have taught, by example, the true meaning of the word *friendship*.

The initial research for this investigation would not have been possible without the resources provided by Carol Diesel and Ed Smith. Additionally, the administration of Alma College provided a sabbatical leave that permitted me to attend to revisions at a crucial juncture. I would also like to acknowledge Darlene Hantzis, who first asked me to write about female comics in 1989. Finally, I must thank the people whose technical expertise has made this process both bearable and possible: Barb Tripp for her formatting prowess; Kristi Trinkle for her critical last-minute logistical assistance; Jane Hoehner for providing a smooth transition for my manuscript during a time of personnel change at Wayne State University Press; Robin DuBlanc for her thoughtful and meticulous copyediting; Adela Garcia for her wisdom, flexibility, and willingness to answer just one more question; Sarah Blacher Cohen; and the marketing staff at Wayne State University Press for their interest, insight, and energy. For all of the guides on this journey, I am extremely grateful.

Joanne R. Gilbert
Alma, Michigan
May 2003

INTRODUCTION

When I was doing stand-up comedy in New York City during the late 1980s, I used the following joke in my act: "New York has really toughened me up—the other day a guy came up to me in the street and said, 'Yo, bitch!' and I said, 'Hey, hey, hey—that's *stupid* bitch to you!'" Both male and female audience members liked this joke. Why? Because the punch line is a surprise? Because laughing about gender differences is cathartic? Because deliberate self-deprecation is actually subversive? "D, all of the above?" Perhaps men and women laughed at the joke for different reasons. Perhaps different women laughed at the joke for different reasons. The answer here is not nearly as important as the questions it raises: Why? Why is a woman making fun of herself broadly considered funny? Who is the true "butt" of the joke? And, most important, when a woman is paid for putting herself (or others) down in a humorous context, who is ultimately in control?

Throughout history, talented misfits have used their difference as a means of survival, foregrounding and capitalizing on the very stigma that threatens their existence. Excluded from the power center of society, these individuals have emphasized and relied upon their difference for a living. The artist, the fool, the social critic—individuals ranging from the unique Karen Finley to the acerbic Chris Rock—all stand aside from the center in order to critique it. Although they are not allowed within the ruled lines of society's pages, these "others" gain a certain freedom, a latitude that can only be experienced in the open space of margins. By "performing" their marginality, social outcasts call attention to their subordinate status; by commodifying this performance, they ensure that the dominant culture literally pays a price for this disparity.

Although many forms of popular culture entertainment involve the commodification of "performed marginality," the arena of stand-up comedy is of particular interest due to the elements of contradiction, interaction, and spontaneity inherent in this medium. Performing for and interacting with a live audience, comics participate in an immediate exchange—jokes for laughs and, more important, jokes for dollars. Audiences pay to laugh and to be laughed *at*. And comics wield rhetorical power in a context in which the marginal are not only accepted but valorized. Within the topsy-turvy world of stand-up comic performance, hierarchies are inverted, power relations are subverted, and a good time is had by all. Because it can avoid inflaming audiences by framing incisive—even incendiary—sociocultural critique as mere "entertainment," comedy is undeniably a unique and powerful form of communication.

Indeed, we need only look as far as the 2000 presidential election to see the impact and influence comedy has on the American public. As Sella (2000) reports, "a full 47 percent of Americans between the ages of 18 and 29 often gleaned information about the presidential campaign from late-night comedy shows" (74). Candidates themselves are acutely aware of the importance of stand-up (or sit-down) comedy. According to Chris Lehane, campaign press secretary for Al Gore, "We read the transcripts of those shows and watch them. . . . The monologues are evidence of when a certain story really breaks through. If it makes it onto Leno or Letterman, it *means* something" (Sella 2000, 74). Although any guest on a late-night comedy show risks embarrassment, even humiliation, Americans enjoy the intimate knowledge such an appearance may afford. As Sella explains, "There is no more efficient way to convey a potential leader's humor and modesty; it's a terrific way to humanize the Product" (75).[1]

Marks (2000) agrees, citing Hillary Clinton's appearance on Letterman's show as a response to Letterman's on-air claim that "The road to the Senate goes through this chair" (indicating the chair in which guests sit); Marks explains: "It is a measure of how important a sense of humor on camera has become to political discourse that candidates feel real pressure to perform" (32). As Letterman staff writer Gerry Mulligan observes, political candidates appear on late-night comedy shows because "You have to prove you're a good sport" (quoted in Marks 2000, 32). In the highly mediated court of public opinion, the ability to be funny—or at least to be able to "take a joke"—has become increasingly important. Why? Because comedy is an age-old proving ground that separates wits from fools with far-reaching rhetorical, political, and social implications.

Deborah Liebling, senior vice president of programming and development for the cable channel Comedy Central (seen in over 65 million households), suggests: "Comedy has always pushed the envelope or it's not really effective. . . . That is what comedy is—saying the things that are taboo" (quoted in King 2000). Because Americans are fans of controversy, contemporary comics consistently draw receptive audiences nationwide. Whether it is Leno and Letterman or Beavis and Butthead, coming out with Ellen or singing along with Rosie, comedy appears to hold unwavering appeal for the American public. Contemporary comics serve as both cultural barometers and cultural critics. By emphasizing and capitalizing on their marginality or "difference" from the mainstream, comics perform a unique and important social function dating back to the traditions of ancient fools—they hold up a mirror to the culture, showing us our (and their) frailties and foibles, eliciting the laughter of recognition.

My own experience as a professional comic affords me firsthand knowledge of the comedy industry. And industry it is—frequently dubbed the "rock & roll of the eighties" (Handelman 1988a), stand-up comedy is big business.[2] The "comedy boom," which began with the advent of cable television in 1975 (Borns 1987), afforded stand-up comics countless opportunities for performance. Still reaping the rewards of the 1980s/1990s boom, stand-up comics today receive extensive television exposure: the all-comedy Comedy Central cable channel features shows such as *Premium Blend,* and *Comedy Central Presents,* devoted exclusively to stand-up comedy, and network variety shows like *The Tonight Show with Jay Leno, The Late Show with David Letterman,* and *The Rosie O'Donnell Show* have regularly launched comedic careers.[3]

For those comics "not yet ready for prime time," however, the club scene offers numerous opportunities. In 1988, there were "more than 300 full-time comedy clubs in America, nearly a hundredfold increase from the early Seventies" (Strauss 1988, 90). In 1997, according to a 1997 Internet directory, there were as many as five hundred venues for stand-up comedy in forty-seven states.[4] As Louis Faranda, entertainment director for Caroline's, a major New York comedy club, noted at the time, "We're on an upswing bigtime. There's such a frenzy to find the next Jerry Seinfeld" (quoted in Crossen 1997). Quantity may adversely affect quality, however; as Bob Morton, former producer of *The Late Show with David Letterman* observed, because of the comedy boom, "the farm system has become the major leagues" (quoted in Weiss 1988, 60). Weiss agrees, noting that "Too many former rock-club owners have told too many guys who tell too many dick jokes they're a riot." It is precisely the preponderance of the "dick joke," defined as a "Line joke, or bit which is based on an explicit sexual or scatological reference" (Pulliam 1991, 164), that has supported the common assumption that stand-up comedy is an inherently "male" genre.[5] But what of the significant number of female practitioners? Are they simply male impersonators or are they performing a *different* type of humor?

The former producer of *The Tonight Show* (with Johnny Carson), Jim McCawley, believes that "there is an instinctive difference between men and women about what is funny" (quoted in Weiss 1988, 59). McCawley explains that to be successful, a comic must deliver twenty-five punch lines in six minutes. Although McCawley's observation is based on experience primarily with male comics, critics Linda Martin and Kerry Segrave (1986) note that Phyllis Diller earned the nickname "Killer Diller" because of her rapid-fire delivery—twelve punch lines per minute. Diller was, of course, emulating her idol, Bob Hope. Along with acceding to male-defined industry standards, female comics often make other concessions as well. For example, when producer Morton asked comic Diane Ford why female comics were willing to appear on an HBO special called *Women of the Night,* Ford replied, "I'll tell you why. . . . Someone gives you a break, you say, 'Thank you very much, Sir. I'd love to be on that show.'" When Morton asked if anyone questioned the title, Ford answered, "Sure. . . . I went up to everyone and said, 'What does this mean? . . . I couldn't make it as a prostitute, I have to do stand-up?' And you know what they said to me 'The smallest dressing room is yours'" (quoted in Weiss 1988, 60).

Because public comic performance historically has been dominated by males, female comics are often perceived as threatening by audiences, club owners, and even their male comic colleagues. Why is the humor created by women threatening? According to Judy Little in her classic 1983 text, *Comedy and the Woman Writer,* the humor of women is subversive; it is "renegade comedy" that "mocks the deepest possible norms, norms four thousand years old" (1). Indeed, marginal humor may empower the powerless, may invert and subvert the status quo and, in doing so, may make the dominant culture uncomfortable. Humor is inextricably linked to power. As Finney (1994) suggests, comedy "creates in-groups and out-groups by mocking aberrations from the norm or the norm itself" and consequently "acts as a form of social control" (6–7). A woman exercising control in any arena may meet resistance. Stand-up comedy provides a public context within which women can wield rhetorical power, can even insult men and get paid for it—provided they have the fortitude to withstand the often blatant biases of club owners. Sadly, one New York club owner speaks for many when he asserts, "Stand-up comedy is aggressive. It takes balls. Sure some women do it, but you kind of wonder about them" (cited in Horowitz 1997, 4). Another acknowledges hiring more male than female comics because "Stand-up comedy has a lot to do with control and power. And most men seem to exercise it more easily than women." As Horowitz explains, "Funny women have to achieve a delicate balance—projecting enough power to take control of the audience and enough vulnerability to be non-threatening" (13). Apparently, male comics do not have to be nonthreatening.

The strategies women have used for years to articulate their worldview through humor can teach us a great deal about humor, gender, and power, yet it is only relatively recently that scholarly research on women and humor has become legitimized. As Finney (1994) notes, during the last two decades, Judy Little, Nancy Walker, Regina Barreca, June Sochen, and others have fruitfully explored the cultural causes and consequences of humor produced by women. Much of the burgeoning literature in this area suggests that women create a distinct "women's humor" and "feminist humor" (at times these terms are used synonymously); however, definitional confusion and unsupported generalizations raise concerns about the usefulness of such a discrete and delimited category. It is precisely this confusion that I examine while scrutinizing both women's comedic performances and critical commentary on "women's humor."

Why study humor? Meredith (1971) asserts that: "One excellent test of the civilization of a country . . . I take to be the flourishing of the comic idea and comedy" (744). Pointing out the unique data offered by stand-up comedy in particular, Mintz (1987) maintains that "the student of a culture and society cannot find a more revealing index to its values, attitudes, dispositions, and concerns, than . . . the relatively undervalued genre of standup comedy," adding that it is "the most interesting of all the manifestations of humor in the popular culture" (85). Indeed, its interactive and improvisational nature makes stand-up comedy a unique forum in which cultural values are simultaneously affirmed and interrogated. In a sense, the stand-up comic functions as an ethnographer, a participant-observer who reports fieldwork findings. The ironic twist inherent in this brand of ethnography, however, is that the comic's audience is both the group observed and the group to whom findings are reported. According to Conquergood (1991), an ethnographer must be a "co-performer" in order to understand the embodied experience of people from disparate cultures. Through the process of interacting with an audience, a comic collects and presents "data," transforming "field notes" into an instant ethnographic performance.[6]

Koziski (1984) compares the comic to an anthropologist, explaining that both individuals see cultural patterns and then proceed to make the tacit explicit. Mintz (1987) notes that the stand-up comic functions as "our comic spokesperson, as a mediator, an 'articulator' of our culture, and as our contemporary anthropologist" (90). As Fisher and Fisher explain, a comic is "constantly taking mental notes," but "Instead of publishing his findings in a scientific journal he immediately acts them out in the broad metaphors of comedy" (cited in Olson 1988, 123). Like peer reviewers, audience members provide both data and evaluation, assuming an editorial role as their feedback constantly modifies the comic's creative output. The marginal comic, in particular, is "an inside actor with an outward glance" (Harman 1988, 127), uniquely positioned between two groups, able to comment to each about the other and, if successful, elicit laughter from both.

Marginal humor provides rich terrain for study; the performance of stand-up comedy is a unique arena in which to examine the multi-dimensional nature of this particular humor. Typically, humor—especially in its nonliterary forms—has been "denied legitimacy" in academia's hallowed halls (Boskin 1979, 4), rendered trivial and superficial (Fraiberg, 1994; Mintz 1988; Weisfeld, cited in Clay 1997), dismissed as decidedly "unscholarly" (Fraiberg 1994). Because, as Fraiberg (1994) points out, "The fit between what is considered funny and what is considered scholarly is at best an uncomfortable one" (317), humor created by women has not often been regarded as worthy of analysis. Fraiberg further notes that as subjects, feminism and women's studies have been deemed too political to warrant research. Consequently, the analysis of humor produced by women has long been doubly damned in academe. Although recent scholarship has made great strides in illustrating the merit of women's humorous discourse as a subject of scholarly inquiry, Mintz (1987) notes, "there is no developed study of the social and cultural functions of standup comedy" (87).

Yet humor enables us "to cope with the daily, hourly, inescapable difficulty of being" (Bentley 1971, 767). It is "ageless, universal and uniquely human" (Crossen 1997, A6). Humor delights, teaches, protects, and releases. It is efficient. It is portable. It is, most important, social. Why study humor? Because it is a cultural barometer, revelatory and liberating; it affords insights into power relations in contemporary American society. But why focus on humor created and/or performed by women? What is so compelling about their particular comedic performance of marginality?

Because humor created and performed by women is a public, societally sanctioned discussion of women's experience—an experience all too often relegated to the margins of society—it is fruitful for study by critics, feminist or otherwise.[7] Because stand-up comedy is a unique example of performed marginality, this genre is particularly relevant to the investigation of power relations in contemporary American culture. Kibler (1998) calls for such investigation, observing that research in this area must go further than the current focus on the way female comic spectacle undermines gender roles—that scholars should examine power and identity issues at a deeper level when discussing the subversive nature of women's humor.

Contemporary comics are the current practitioners of an age-old art; they carry on the oral tradition of ancient times through their jokes and stories. And stories, as Clair (1998) suggests (citing Aptheker's work), "represent a form of resistance that moves beyond the individual experience" (153).[8] Examining women's humorous performance as a potential site of resistance cloaked in the guise of entertainment can teach us about the power of telling one's own story in a culture that continues to marginalize women. Getting paid for performing their own marginality, strategically presenting themselves through potentially subversive discourse, female comics are important synec-doches of oppressed groups in our society. Ware (1992) asserts that "the position of women in a society indicates the level of civilization it has achieved" (14). Meredith (1971) believed that a culture's comedy was the barometer for its level of "civilization" (744). Perhaps a combina-tion of the two—the position of women as expressed through humor—provides a means of interrogating the power structure that undergirds the very notion of "civilization."

Examining the power relations inherent in female comics' per-formance of marginality offers insight into the dynamic nature of humor, gender, and power in American culture, revealing the interplay and interconnection among these constructs. As Hegde (1996) notes (after Hartsock), "in order to change the relations of domination that structure society and define subordination, usable theories are needed that begin from the experiences of the marginalized" (311). Exploring the way gender is rhetorically constructed and performed foregrounds its inherently discursive nature. Because, as Reeder (1996) explains, "gender tends to be accepted as pre-existing, natural order categories" (322), studying gender as a fluid, performed construct helps us under-stand the way it is produced, culturally negotiated, and reproduced. Additionally, examining women's strategic self-presentation in a comedic context shows us that "there is as much variance *within* groups as *between* groups if researchers would only take the time to look" (321).

Serving as art and entertainment, critique and commodity, a con-text in which the powerful may laugh at themselves and the power-less may (at least temporarily) prevail, stand-up comedy is a unique cultural performance. As Walker (1998), who has written extensively about women and humor, maintains: "humor is about risk and privi-lege; for groups exiled from the centers of power, comedy can signal the transformation of speechless outrage to persuasive, vocal, and joy-ous audacity. Humor works by bending or breaking the rules; it always has. But at this moment in our culture we are uncertain which rules are in ascendency, and we question whether or not any set of rules should exist when it comes to pleasure" (267).

Some female comics address power discrepancies directly—some even wear the feminist mantle with pride. Others offer a more dis-tanced cultural analysis, poking fun at ideological labels in general. Regardless of their particular political agendas, however, female comics have all been deeply influenced by the conditions feminism has produced. As Finney (1994) explains:

> Helping to create a common female consciousness, the twentieth-century feminist movement both induced women to discover the comic tradition which they had long possessed and encouraged them to become the subjects of comedy, its creators, rather than merely the objects of humor.... Performing, public, and powerful, the modern female stand-up comic epitomizes the strides made in the evolution of women's humor in recent decades. (4)

Clearly, female comics today have more opportunities to perform before live and television audiences than ever before. Although estimates vary, Walker (1991b), reported in 1991 that approximately one-third of professional stand-up comics in this country were female.[9] In 1989, I was one of 70 female members (or 17 percent) of the 404-member Professional Comedians Association. In 1997, of the 173 comics regularly featured at Los Angeles's acclaimed Comedy Store (breeding ground for talents such as Robin Williams and Roseanne), 33 (or 19 percent) were female, and in 1999, of the 181 comics listed in Yahoo's Internet directory, 21 (or 12 percent) were women. In 2001, several years post–comedy boom, there were, according to comic Shayne Michael (2001), only about sixty-seven functioning comedy clubs (excluding additional sites for those that are national chains) in the United States.[10] Despite fewer club venues and more intense competition for limited spots, however, female comics can still be seen frequently on cable and network television and in comedy clubs around the country. In fact, of the 63 stand-up comics featured in Comedy Central's programming during January and February 2001, 15 (or about 24 percent) were women.[11]

What are female comics saying and how are they saying it? Does their discourse constitute a genre separate from that of their male counterparts? And how does their performance of marginality onstage compare to that of other marginal comics? My approach to these and other questions is informed by a dual perspective—by my study of humor (specifically that created and/or performed by women), marginality, and feminist thought, and by my experience as a professional comic. Indeed, throughout this book, I wear two hats: that of a student/teacher of humor and that of a "recovering" comic with considerable experience in the trenches of this unique cultural form.

Is Walker (1988) correct in her assumption that women's relation to humor and American culture has changed over the last several decades? Are female comics talking about *different* topics today than they did twenty or thirty years ago, or are they talking about the same topics *differently*? Have messages changed, or have strategies of presentation changed? Both? Neither? And what does examining the performances of female comics tell us about ourselves and our society?

In order to examine the above issues, this book asks the question: How do contemporary American female comics perform their marginality onstage? Analysis of this performed marginality problematizes the existence of a genre called "female" and, more specifically, "feminist" stand-up comedy, and shows us that the performance of marginality may help us understand power relations in a broader cultural context. Throughout the book, I use numerous examples of female comic performance to challenge the assumptions critics have made about women, humor, and feminism. Ultimately, I argue that critical characterizations of "female" or "feminist" humor are, in fact, descriptions of all marginal humor—a humor that is itself part of a larger rhetoric of victimage.[12] Providing a framework within which to consider the implications of performed marginality, chapter 1 defines the terms of reference, discussing the relationship between humor and power and addressing the nature of marginal humor and of "women's" and "feminist" humor; chapters 2, 3, and 4 examine origins, traditions, and conventions of stand-up comedy; and chapter 5 and the conclusion consider the rhetorical and political implications of performing marginality.

HUMOR, POWER, AND MARGINALITY

Performance and Marginality

Before examining the way female comics rhetorically construct and perform their marginality onstage, we need to consider a framework for such analysis. This chapter provides an analytical context, focusing on definitions and discussion of key terms and concepts. Throughout this investigation, the terms "performance" and "marginality" are used extensively. Rhetorically laden, both words must be defined within the context of this analysis. With the rise of popular culture studies, the word performance has become problematic. When used indiscriminately, the term ceases to have real significance. As McNamara and Schechner (cited in Turner 1982) assert: "Performance is no longer easy to define or locate: the concept and structure has spread all over the place. It is ethnic and intercultural, historical and ahistorical, aesthetic and ritual, sociological and political. Performance is a mode of behavior, an approach to experience; it is play, sport, aesthetics, popular entertainments, experimental theatre, and more" (5). Although every human action can be considered a performance (Burke 1945; Goffman 1959), I am limiting the definition of the term in this study to include only those situations in which an audience is present.

Indeed, the distinctions between performance in everyday life and performance onstage are often arbitrary (Schechner 1977). Audience plays a crucial role in these distinctions, as Cage points out in his assertion that theater is actually attitude on the part of the spectator (cited in Schechner 1974). Stand-up comedy, more than most other performance genres, requires frequent audience participation (a feature

1

discussed in chapter 2 and considered at length in chapter 5). For the purposes of this investigation, *performance* refers to the actions of a female comic onstage at a comedy club or similar scenario before a live, usually paying, audience.

This particular type of cultural performance is compelling. It can be regarded as "social drama," an "empirical unit of social process" (Turner 1988, 92–93); it can be perceived as both efficacy and entertainment (Schechner 1974); it can be experienced as "a rehearsal for the revolution" (Boal 1985, 122). Performance is universal (Lee and Gura 1992; Long and HopKins 1982; Pelias 1992). Performance is revelatory to both performer and audience (Turner 1988). Performance "cannot escape reflection and reflexivity" (Turner 1982, 105). For reasons sociopolitical and psychological, cultural performance is fruitful for study.

Performance is also highly rhetorical, which is to say it is persuasive, advancing agendas and advocating positions.[1] Although not as overtly rhetorical as a political stump speech or a telemarketer's spiel, performance, particularly the performance of stand-up comedy, is inherently a rhetorical act. Because comic success is determined by audience laughter, comic performers are rhetorical strategists, attempting to elicit laughter and engage in cultural critique simultaneously. Describing the rhetorical aspect of performance as "efficacy" (one-half of his efficacy/entertainment dyad), Schechner (1974) discusses it as rooted in ritual, results-oriented, and focused on audience participation, ultimately asserting: "No performance is pure efficacy or pure entertainment" (468–70).[2]

Indeed, stand-up comedy is a unique hybrid of these components. The comic creates a fun(ny) discourse, actively solicits participation from the audience—laughter and occasionally backtalk—and, depending on the depth of the social critique advanced, is at times results-oriented. (Certainly the comic is always oriented toward the result of laughter.) It is precisely the entertaining nature of stand-up comedy that makes it efficacious—the rhetoric of social criticism that often lies just beneath humor's beguiling surface. Considering performance in general—and stand-up comedy in particular—as a dynamic of efficacy and entertainment is useful when examining the performed marginality of female stand-up comics. The performances of these women may be entertaining, but the marginality inherent in the performance allows it to be rhetorically efficacious all the while.

2

Discussing the rhetorical nature of performance within the context of social and aesthetic drama, Turner (1982) describes "liminoid" phenomena—marginal (often commodified) forms that may oppose prevailing social structures.[3] This construct is relevant to female comics performing marginality for money as it provides a way to describe the discourse that they co-construct with their audiences, one that, as Turner observes of all performative genres, "can be manipulated to support both conformative and subversive social and political positions." The genre of stand-up comedy affords female comics the freedom to engage in rhetorically charged social critique cloaked in the trappings of entertainment; in so doing, they are exemplifying the liminoid because, as Turner notes, by virtue of its liminoid nature, entertainment is "suffused with freedom" (116–20).

Performers have long been associated with both rhetorical power and marginal status. Bauman (1977) explains that performers are typically both admired and feared, "admired for their artistic skill and power . . . feared because of the potential they represent for subverting and transforming the status quo" and adds that this recognized potential is key to the "persistent association between performers and marginality" (45). Indeed, marginalized individuals are afforded a freedom unique to their insider/outsider position; in the context of stand-up comedy, women who perform their marginality may offer a potentially subversive critique of the hegemonic culture while simultaneously eliciting laughter and earning a living.

Although not used quite as ambiguously as "performance," the term "marginality" must also be defined within the context of this investigation. Since sociologist Everett Stonequist introduced the term in 1937, marginality has frequently been discussed as a sociological category (Githens and Prestage 1977; Harman 1988; Miller 1991; Mizruchi 1983).[4] Maintaining that "wherever there are cultural transitions and cultural conflicts, there are marginal personalities" (3), Stonequist notes that marginal individuals may assimilate into the dominant group, assimilate into the subordinate group, or accommodate (perhaps temporarily and incompletely) between the two groups. The more intimately and extensively the marginal individual's involvement with the dominant culture, Stonequist maintains, the more severe the devastation when he or she is rejected by that culture. According to Stonequist, marginality has its advantages as

3

well. Positioned as they are between at least two worlds, marginal individuals are afforded a unique perspective—a combination of "the knowledge and insight of the insider with the critical attitude of the outsider" (154–55).

Ortner (1996) calls the liminal space inhabited by the marginalized "borderlands." Originating in ethnic and minority studies, the term "borderlands" describes "the construction of complex, hybridized identities for those who must live within, yet are excluded from, the dominant cultural order" (181). In the borderlands, culture is fluid, dynamic, and constantly contested and (re)constructed. Borderlands or border crossings are not neutral, but spaces in which one individual is "Home" (not necessarily an advantage), and the other individual is "Other." Borderland politics are intimately concerned with issues of gender, race, class, material resources, political power and, inevitably, culture. In the borderlands, culture is "both the grounds of negotiation and its object: it sets the terms of the encounters, but it is also what is at stake" (82).

As long as human societies have existed, the marginal have made their presence known (Miller 1991; Mizruchi 1983). Lacking membership in the dominant culture due to gender, class, race, sexual orientation, or other characteristics, marginalized individuals have become "modern strangers" (Harman 1988) who seek a paradox— "to accomplish distance through membership and membership through distance" (153). The condition of marginality can be a double-edged sword. As Willie (1975) points out, "Marginal people who fall between the cracks may be alienated, but marginal people who rise above the cracks are synthesizers" (13).

Regardless of their image, however, marginalized people serve an essential societal function; without margins, the center cannot exist in daily discourse. It is precisely this discursive function that defines marginality for use in the present investigation. Assertions that "the marginal personality is a function of social conditions" (Stonequist 1937, 201) and that "Marginality is an essential component in healthy human society" (Willie 1975, 11) refer to marginality as an exclusively *sociological* condition. Examining marginality as a *rhetorically* constructed category that produces real social and psychological effects, however, facilitates discussion of power relations within American culture, specifically the ways in which marginality may serve as a subversion of the status quo.[5] As Yudice (1988) maintains: "In a sense, the postmodernist has taken the old 'myths of marginality' and turned them on their heads, endowing them with a 'positive,' 'subversive' sense. The 'laziness,' 'shiftlessness,' and 'cynicism' attributed to the 'marginal' by liberal sociologists and anthropologists of the fifties and sixties are transformed here into 'radical' and 'subversive' tactics of resistance and advantage" (216).

Indeed, marginality may ultimately serve as a powerful means of resistance to social, political, and economic inequities. As hooks (cited in Brooks and Jacobs, 1996) explains, "I make a definite distinction between that marginality which is imposed by oppressive structures and that marginality one chooses as a site of resistance—as location of radical openness and possibility" (291). Such a distinction between sociological and rhetorical marginality is key to understanding the potentially subversive nature of female comedic performance. Explaining that the hegemonic culture perpetuates itself by "assigning a group inferior status, then using that inferior status as proof of the group's inferiority" (520), Collins (1986) describes the marginal advantage: "When you have mastered the dominant discourse but are still able to stand apart from it (in the margin), you are in the best, most informed position to critique it" (529). In this way, the "stigma" usually associated with "marked" or marginal individuals (Jones et al. 1984) may be transformed rhetorically into a critical lens.

It is important to realize that although they are often closely allied, the terms "marginality" and "minority" are not synonymous. Minority is a quantitative concept dealing with sheer numbers, whereas marginality encompasses issues of power and control that are ideologically based. Jews outnumbered Nazis in concentration camps during the Holocaust, just as blacks do whites in South Africa and as women do men in the United States; all comprise a majority numerically, yet all are groups marginalized by the dominant or hegemonic culture. As Flora (1977) notes, "Such exploited majority groups are marginal to the distribution of power and wealth in a society, but absolutely necessary for its functioning" (77). In this sense, women may be considered a "marginalized majority" in the United States.

Considering marginality a rhetorically constructed category becomes problematic, as it raises the question—constructed by whom? If the marginal participate, at some level, in the creation of their label,

5

does the very construct then imply cooperation or at least consent? As Clair (1998) suggests, "we need to explore how these subordinated groups provide support for the oppressive system" (56) through their own discursive practices of within- and between-group privilege and abandonment.

Additionally, if the postmodern notion of a destabilized center is viable, and if the margins are constantly shifting, does the very concept of marginality become arbitrary? Clearly, the rhetorical construction of marginality must be explored in relation to issues of politics, power, and social control.

Unlike sociological marginality, which often stigmatizes, rhetorical marginality may actually empower. Individuals who are sociologically marginalized are usually distinguished by some immutable physical reality such as sex, race/ethnicity, age, size, or disfiguration/disability.[6] In a way, they cannot help but perform their marginality—they do not voice it, but rather it—nonverbally—voices them. Individuals who are solely rhetorically marginalized, on the other hand, may "pass" as members of the dominant culture.[7] Closeted gays and lesbians, for example, may avoid discrimination by "passing." Even when they are "out," however, many gays and lesbians are still only rhetorically marginalized, as there is no apparent physical feature that marginalizes them sociologically. By choosing to "perform" various "gendered" behaviors, gays and lesbians may construct a nonverbal marginality, but sexual orientation does not necessarily manifest itself in an overt sociological marginalization as biological sex or race/ethnicity does.

Indeed, Judith Butler and a growing number of other scholars argue that gender is a social construction separate from and not necessarily congruent with biological sex (Butler 1990; de Lauretis 1987; Dolan 1992; Forte 1990; Reeder 1996; Senelick 1992). Gender as a social construction offers an individual a broad spectrum of societally designated "feminine" and "masculine" characteristics from which to create a self-presentation. As I often explain to students, "Sex is what you're born with; gender is what you do with it."[8] Like gender, the condition of marginality in general may be socially constructed in that society plays a role in deciding which behaviors and characteristics are deemed marginal. It is the rhetorical construction of marginality and its performance at the individual level, however, that is the subject of this investigation.

Chaikin (1977) contends that "Each of us is the other to the others" (41); in a performance of marginality, this "otherness" is foregrounded. An example of performed marginality is the joke described in the introduction. When I performed the punchline "Hey, hey, hey— that's *stupid* bitch to you!" I was trebly marginalized: once by class/intellectual ability ("stupid"), again by sex ("bitch"), and finally by virtue of my profession as a performer, specifically, a stand-up comic (that is, a fool/artist/social critic). In this instance, I simultaneously constructed and performed my own marginality. As a comic, I was a protean, trickster figure, able to change my self-presentation at will (Abrahams 1968; Apte 1985; Jung 1959). I could change from stupid to smart, even from performer to audience member (once I left the stage); I could not, however, change the sociological marginality associated with my sex. In other words, I have no choice but to perform my sociological marginality—onstage and off. I am a woman, and that reality is obvious to anyone who sees me. My rhetorical marginality, however, is performed or not performed at will.

Returning to the joke in question, we need to consider the location of the margins in this particular context. By positioning myself apart from the dominant (that is, male) culture, I performed marginality by performing my "femaleness." (At other times, I performed ethnic marginality as well, by performing my Jewishness, another factor that separates me from the dominant culture but is not necessarily physically apparent.) In so doing, I "rhetoricalized" my sociological marginality. The audience knew I was female regardless of whether I called attention to this fact. By making my sociological marginality a rhetorical marginality as well, I sent a message that may or may not be read as subversive, depending on the audience member's particular frame of reference.

It is important to keep in mind that margins shift as the "center" shifts. I may be marginalized as a woman, subject to oppressive economic and social constraints, but a poor, Third World woman might perceive me—a white, mainstream, academic, liberal feminist—as part of the power center of a culture that oppresses her (Lorde 1983; Ware 1992). Indeed, marginality is rooted in the experience of the marginalized. And because experience is based in enactment, perhaps rhetorical marginality can be discussed in the same terms that Judith Butler (1990) uses to explore gender; perhaps, like gender, rhetorical marginality "is real only to the extent that it is performed" (278). Humor, specifically the performance of female stand-up comics, offers an arena in which to explore this possibility.

Humor, Power, and Social Control

According to Nilsen (1993), "Probably no academic field is emerging more rapidly than . . . humor studies" (ix). The umbrella of "humor studies," of course, encompasses the study of humor in a variety of disciplines, including anthropology, communication, education, history, linguistics, philosophy, psychology, sociology, and women's studies. Although numerous scholars have attempted to define and delimit the term, "humor" seems to resist hard and fast definitions. Because it is inherently subjective, because "funny" always means "funny to me," the best we can do is to say what we mean by "humor" in a particular context. For the purposes of this investigation, the term "humor" refers to material designed and performed to elicit laughter from an audience. (Although they are sometimes separately defined in humor research, the terms "humor" and "comedy" are used synonymously in this book.)

Throughout history, celebrated minds have speculated about humor. Graham, Papa, and Brooks (1992) note: "There are over 100 documented theories of humor . . . categorized into one of three broad theoretical perspectives: superiority theories, incongruity theories, and relief or arousal theories" (161). Beginning, of course, with Plato and Aristotle, but most fully developed by Hobbes and used to explain the social function of laughter by Bergson, the superiority theory, which predominated for over two thousand years, explains laughter as the result of feelings of superiority over others or over our own former position. The relief theory—best represented in the work of Freud—conceives of laughter as physiologically based, as an expenditure of excess psychic energy. Finally, the incongruity theory, developed by Kant and, most notably, by Schopenhauer, suggests that amusement is the result of the unexpected—of being surprised (Morreall 1987, 5–6). Because this investigation examines humor as it relates to issues of power and control, much of the analysis is informed by superiority theory, specifically as it illustrates the nature of the performed marginality discussed in chapter 5. Additionally, relief/arousal theory is extremely relevant to the consideration of audience throughout this study.

The relationship between humor and power has been widely discussed. Muggeridge notes that "By its nature humor is anarchistic . . . and implies when it does not state, criticism of existing institutions, beliefs, and functionaries" (cited in Dudden 1987, xvii). Mindess claims that "Humor . . . serves to liberate people from . . . constraints by rendering them meaningless or absurd" (cited in Nilsen 1993, 288). In this way, humor can be considered both a "lubricant" and an "abrasive" in social interaction (Martineau 1972, 106). Humor is also frequently seen as a form of social control. Pitchford asserts that humor is "a means of achieving consensus, a technique of social control, and a device for introducing competition and social conflict" (cited in Martineau 1972, 109), and Holland (1982) suggests that laughter can serve as a "social corrective" (17). Indeed, humor can empower the humorist; as Cohen (1999) notes, joking may sometimes be "a way of restoring to oneself enough power and control to speak the unspeakable" (45).

Regina Barreca (1991), whose work has focused on women and humor, maintains that "Making your own jokes is equivalent to taking control over your life—and usually that means taking control away from someone else" (110). Nilsen (1993) claims that "when a person tells a joke he is in a position of control; but when he hears a joke, it is the other person who is in control" (289). And Martin and Segrave (1986) note that "The nature of comedy as a weapon sets it apart from other forms of entertainment" (12). Clearly, humor is a complex and compelling form of communication. In the interest of examining female comics' performance of marginality, the present investigation explores the dynamic between humor and power along and among psychological, rhetorical, and economic axes.[9]

The Psychological Dimension of Humor

In his classic work on jokes, Freud associates joking with the expression of repressed aggression and desires. As Neve (1988) explains, according to Freud, "joking is a benign form of love-making" (42). Asserting that "the joke . . . is the contribution made to the comic

9

from the realm of the unconscious," Freud (1960, 208) suggests that adults laugh at "the comic" in order to rediscover the "lost laughter of childhood" (224). Freud's major contributions to the study of marginal humor are his distinction between "tendentious" (hostile or obscene) and "non-tendentious" (innocent) jokes and his related focus on the importance of audience (the latter is discussed at length in chapter 5). Tendentious jokes are especially relevant to marginal humor because they inevitably involve criticism of power and authority. In Freud's view, a successful tendentious joke involves three individuals: the teller, the butt, and the audience (Holland 1982, 49).[10] By laughing at hostile or obscene acts and images, Freud contends, we avoid feelings of shame and disgust; because we "exploit something ridiculous in our enemy," which we could not do in other contexts, tendentious jokes "evade restrictions and open sources of pleasure that have become inaccessible" (1960, 103).

Freud's influence is apparent in numerous theories of humor, particularly those that explore both the arousal and relief that tendentious jokes may provide. Commonly believed to serve a cathartic function, humor allows both performer and audience to experience a release—to be liberated through laughter. And yet, by its very nature, most humor can be construed as aggressive (Fry 1987, 60).[11] Indeed, as comic George Carlin explains: "Stand-up is a socially acceptable form of aggression. You get to name the targets, you get to fire the bullets . . . and the wonderful part is, after you've finished, you then say, 'Hey, can't you take a joke? This is humor, Sir! What's a matter with you?'" (cited in Borns 1987, 28). This act of aggression provides pleasure, as comic Jerry Seinfeld observes: "A really hard laugh is like sex—one of the ultimate diversions of existence. Laughing is that pure moment of pleasure, and it's free, and there's no waste product" (cited in Borns 1987, 269). In this sense, "Humor has both catharsis and arousal impact on its participants" (Fry 1987, 65).

Humor also produces cathexis, a release of libidinal energies (Berger 1987, 13). Stand-up comedy often deals with taboo topics such as sex and death. Audiences can go to a comedy club and not only hear these topics discussed but experience the release and relief of laughter in the face of (often repressed) anxiety. In this way, consumers of comedy encounter the Freudian "economy" of jokes. As Douglas (1975) notes: "At all times we are expending energy in monitoring our subconscious so as to ensure that our conscious perceptions come through a filtering control. The joke, because it breaks down the control, gives the monitoring system a holiday. Or, as Freud puts it, since monitoring costs effort, there is a saving in psychic expenditure" (294).

This "economy" serves what Holland (1982) calls "the benign but paradoxical social function of asserting our shared inhibitions by the very act of loosening them" (188).

Issues of identification are key to the psychological dimension of humor as well. Focusing on identification in his reader-response study of laughter, Holland (1982) develops his identity theory, illustrating the subjectivity inherent in our reactions to humor: "I am laughing because I confirm my identity through something outside myself. . . . Incongruity applies the same way to all cartoons. Superiority or arousal apply the same way to all laughers. The idea of confirming identity applies to all laughers at all cartoons, but in a different way for each" (173). Because no joke is funny to everyone and every joke is funny to someone, Holland contends, we can say that "amusement, like beauty, is in the eye of the beholder" (173). Identification is key to our enjoyment of humor, Holland argues, because "we laugh when we have recreated our identities through a stimulus suddenly and playfully" (174).

Clearly, in order for a person to laugh at a joke, she or he must first either identify or "dis-identify" with the teller or the target (who, in some cases, may be one and the same). When we hear a joke, we may laugh because we have found ourselves in a similar situation or we may laugh because the target (and/or teller) is so obviously unlike us. Even dis-identification requires identification, however; we cannot know who we are *not* until we first know who we *are*. Indeed, whether or not we identify and with which aspect of a joke we identify (teller or target or both) are both determinants of the extent to which we find a particular joke "funny." If, for example, we are members of a group being lampooned by a comic, we may simultaneously acknowledge our membership and dis-identify with the stereotypic features and foibles being presented. In this regard, humor can be alienating. As Rosenblatt (1991) maintains, "jokes are a way of putting people at a distance, and of keeping oneself at a distance from them. An act of aggression and self-protection all in one" (H5). Undeniably, a psychological lens offers a view of humor that helps to explain its functions and intrinsic appeal.

One reason to study humor is its revelatory nature; by examining what makes us laugh, we learn about ourselves and each other.

The Rhetorical Dimension of Humor

Of the three dimensions of humor discussed in this chapter, most salient to the present investigation is the rhetorical dimension. Chafe (1987) notes that "the humor state" may be an evolutionary defense in humans; because laughter can be infectious, inciting this state in others may disable them, ensuring our continued control of the situation. In this sense, humor is highly rhetorical. Chafe maintains that "To be in the humor state is in itself so enjoyable that it diverts attention and effort away from any decisive action a person might take" (21). In other words, humor is an important rhetorical tool; it arms speakers and disarms listeners, limiting options as it amuses, diverting while it deceives.

Unique to humor is its function as what might aptly be called "antirhetoric," that is, a rhetoric that always simultaneously promotes and disavows itself—renouncing its intent even as it amuses audiences and advances agendas. As mentioned by Carlin in the above discussion, regardless of the level of confrontation, even hostility, in a comic's performance, he or she can always say, "I'm just kidding" or "Can't you take a joke?" Although this disclaimer is sometimes a fairly thin veneer, it nevertheless functions as a rhetorical safety net. As Dets de Vries (1990) observes, "When something is said in jest it doesn't carry the same weight as it does in ordinary communication. Consequently, greater risks can be taken in getting a difficult message across" (760). The safety net may fail, however; political campaigns have been lost and won, careers created and destroyed, precisely because of the "weight" of a purported "jest" (Whitfield 1988). When an audience is not sure whether someone is speaking in jest, the discourse does carry the same weight as ordinary communication. And in the midst of an ongoing debate over so-called political correctness, certain rhetorically charged topics like abortion and rape are often perceived as "off-limits" and, consequently, will always be taken "seriously." As Cottom (1989) notes, "a joke . . . requires an audience, and not just any audience. It requires an audience that recognizes it as a joke" (14).

Humor is not kind. In his classic essay on laughter, Bergson contends: "Laughter is, above all, a corrective. Being intended to humiliate, it must make a painful impression on the person against whom it is directed. By laughter, society avenges itself for the liberties taken with it. It would fail in its object if it bore the stamp of sympathy or kindness" (cited in Korsmeyer 1981, 131). Indeed, Bergson's conception of laughter as a "momentary anaesthesia of the heart" continues to be a useful explanation of the way humor often functions in social interaction. As a social phenomenon directly linked to aggression, humor is inevitably tied to power relations among individuals and groups. In a public forum, humor often becomes overtly combative. Stand-up comedy is full of violent language: A comic tells jokes with "punchlines" and aspires to "kill" an audience or "die" trying. As Carlin noted years ago in his act, phrases like "knee-slapping," "busted a gut," "had me in stitches," and "bombing" all smack of violence. Likewise, the "put-downs," "barbs," and "squelches" comics use to suppress hecklers reveal the anger that frequently lurks just below the "humor" of many jokes.

Although comedy clubs are obviously venues in which aggressive humor flourishes, other public situations such as roasts, television talk shows, and the infamous Gridiron dinner in Washington provide sites for political humor to amuse and abuse simultaneously. Because of the social critique implicit in much contemporary humor, joketellers wield a unique power. Whether performing in a comedy club or out stumping for votes, humorists engage in a power play with real or imagined targets, entertaining audiences as they promote agendas.

More than any other type of performance, humor requires an audience. In private, an individual can be her or his own audience; in dyadic communication, one person may be the humorist and another the audience. But in public, the audience for humor serves a critical function. How do we know that humor exists in public discourse? People laugh. As Holland (1982) explains, "Only when some person laughs has the joke become a psychological event. And only when many people laugh does it become a social one" (187). In this way, laughter provides legitimation. Discussing the rhetoric of Freudian theory, Burke (1950) addresses this point: "In particular, we think of Freud's concern with the role of an audience, or 'third person' with whom the speaker establishes rapport, in their common enterprise directed against the butt of tendentious witticisms. Here is the purest rhetorical pattern: speaker and hearer as partners in partisan jokes made

13

at the expense of another" (38). In stand-up comic performance, the entire audience can serve as Freud's "third person," as the humorist enlists audience participation in scapegoating an individual or group who may or may not be present.

Humor is unique in many ways. Humor functions as a sort of judo rhetoric—like the martial art, humor uses an opponent against him- or herself; unlike judo, however, humor uses an opponent's weakness rather than his or her strength. Humor humanizes by humiliating—it targets and exploits the "butt" by lampooning flaws, whether they are physical characteristics or psychological/ideological foibles. When a stand-up comic attacks an individual or an institution, the target is exposed and vulnerable, power relations are subverted, and the marginal may temporarily transcend their social condition (Gilbert 1996). In this way, humor may serve a democratizing function (Coser 1960; Gilbert 1996; Whitfield 1988), playing a crucial role on the sociopolitical stage.[12] When issues of control, domination, and access to resources are foregrounded, performing marginality in an aesthetic/entertainment context (that is, stand-up comedy) becomes an important form of social criticism, a barometer of values and beliefs. As Whitfield asserts, humor is "an index . . . of popular will and opinion" (195) and, we might add, unpopular opinion as well.

Humor creates in-group/out-group distinctions and group solidarity. As Lorenz explains, laughter simultaneously "forms a bond" and "draws a line" (cited in Boskin 1979, 5). It is not surprising, then, that humor is accorded revered status in the political realm. As Schutz (1977a) explains, "The mock aggressiveness of political humor requires for its full satisfaction the humorous appreciation and vicarious participation of the audience in the 'kill' of the victim" (299). Discussing the power relations inherent in political humor, Schutz (1977b) contends that: "The basic structure of almost all political humor is the comic agon—a competition between two or more contestants in which one is perceived as the antagonist and the other, the ironist who retaliates humorously"(68).

In other words, humor functions in the political arena as a way to form and dissolve alliances via the one-up/one-down positioning intrinsic in a well-placed one-liner. Simply put, "If you can laugh at your enemy . . . you are in the position of power" (Barreca 1991, 56). Schutz (1977a) further maintains that political humor exposes defects, weaknesses, and contradictions—negative in its critique but positive for its palliative effect (as an "escape valve" for anxieties and aggression). Schutz contends that functioning as a "positive negativity," American political humor may actually serve the status quo, as "its very nay-saying maintains and strengthens politics" (14). Explaining that humor is a compromise that renders its target less threatening through laughter, Schutz (1977b) suggests that "To laugh at someone and with others in political humor is a step toward community" (69).

Discussing humor as inherently social, if not communal, Bergson (1956) notes that "Our laughter is always the laughter of a group" (64). Describing a "secret freemasonry" or complicity among laughers, Bergson assumes that members of a particular group laugh for the same reason. This assumption undergirds much contemporary scholarly work on humor—especially discussions of groups such as women and feminists. There is nothing about group membership, however, that necessarily guarantees that an individual will laugh for the same reason another group member laughs (this issue is considered in greater detail in chapter 5). Perhaps more important than why we laugh is that we laugh. The very act of many people laughing together—whatever the reason(s)—sends a message of cohesion and group identity (Coser 1960; Mitchell 1978; Nietz 1980). Rhetorically, regardless of the motivation of individual laughers, group laughter is generally interpreted as consensus.

Clearly, the audience plays a crucial role in stand-up comedy. As Carlin notes, during a comic's routine, audience members "vote all the way through, about every five seconds, on whether the work of art is going the way they'd like. And if it isn't, the comic gets the message immediately and can change it" (cited in Borns 1987, 284). Through the politics of laughter, the audience serves as ultimate arbiter of humor and power in public discourse. As consumers, audience members literally pay a price to be amused (and sometimes abused). Although the rhetorical dimension of humor affords insight into the social and political negotiation of power in comic performance, it is the economic dimension that addresses the issue of commodification.

The Economic Dimension of Humor

When a woman performs her marginality in the public setting of a comedy club or even on a cable television special, she is earning

15

money. Quite simply, her marginality is commodified through her public performance, ensuring an exchange between performer and audience. Audiences pay money to be entertained; comics get paid to be entertaining. The bottom line is that regardless of whether female stand-up comics are considered artists, entertainers, social critics, or all three, they are selling a marketable item—humor. Audiences exchange dollars for laughs and, in so doing, empower the performer economically. Of course, as consumers, audience members must have access to economic resources in order to afford the cover charge and two-drink minimum standard in most comedy clubs. Who is in control of this situation? Where does the power reside? Stephen Greenblatt (1989) explains:

> the work of art is the product of a negotiation between a creator or class of creators, equipped with a complex, communally shared repertoire of conventions, and the institutions and practices of society. In order to achieve the negotiation, artists need to create a currency that is valid for a meaningful, mutually profitable exchange. It is important to emphasize that the process involves not simply appropriation but exchange, since the existence of art always implies a return, a return normally measured in pleasure and interest. (12)

For Greenblatt, all art is a process of negotiation and exchange; as both art and entertainment, therefore, stand-up comedy in comedy clubs is clearly a commodification of contemporary cultural values. The audience pays to laugh but, more important, the audience also pays to be laughed at, attesting to the subversive potential of commodified comedy.

A woman onstage authorized through humor to perform her marginality as a social critique is not only rhetorically powerful but, in a sense, economically powerful as well. At times, she is getting paid to subvert the status quo by making members of the dominant culture laugh at themselves (even if this entails laughing at her first). If we consider the performance of marginality by female stand-up comics to be strategic self-presentation employed in order to appeal to those in control of economic resources, then the social critique at the heart of much stand-up comedy can be seen as a type of rhetorical lobbying. Female comics use a variety of techniques (examined at length in chapter 4) to lull the audience (many of whom are members of the dominant culture) into a sense of complacency through

16

laughter; once disarmed, audience members continue to pay—attention to and dollars for—this "commodity."

When a stand-up comic performs for a paying audience, money is exchanged for laughter, social criticism is embedded in the material eliciting the laughter, the comic/social critic gets paid, the comedy club makes money, an economic symbiosis has been achieved. Perhaps it is not surprising that a comic's jokes are called "material," for, within the commodification of cultural performance, jokes are exactly that—the material of capitalist currency. The economic dimension of humor illuminates the various exchanges—aesthetic, monetary, sociopolitical—that occur in the context of stand-up comic performance. In order to explore in detail the relationship between humor and power within female comic performance, however, we must first consider marginal humor.

Marginal Humor

Humor and humorists are commonly associated with marginality; most notable in this regard are professional comics, the contemporary analogues of fools (Klapp 1962; McMullen 1970; Welsford 1935).[13] Marginality may, in fact, be crucial to this profession; as Zijderveld (1982) suggests when discussing the decline of professional "wise fools" in the eighteenth century, "the court jester institutionalized and professionalized to such an extent that he lost his marginality—which is an essential ingredient to folly—and grew into just another courtier" (123). From the physically deformed fools of the ancient world (Welsford 1935, 74) to the Jewish, African American, and female comics of today, marginality has been key to the comic persona. Indeed, performing and capitalizing on their marginalized status is integral to the potentially subversive discourse these comics generate. Drawing on their shared history of oppression, marginal comics serve as licensed social critics, using rhetorical strategies such as self-deprecation to critique and sometimes subvert the status quo.

Perhaps it is not surprising that many of those who tell jokes for a living tend to be society's "misfits," the people most adversely affected by established power relations. As Douglas maintains, humor confronts and changes existing power/control dynamics, and for this reason, all jokes are potentially subversive. Yet contradictions are inherent in humor as well; jokes may function as both "rites" and "anti-rites"—

17

in other words, "as public affirmation of shared cultural beliefs and as a reexamination of these beliefs" (Douglas, cited in Mintz 1987, 87). In this way, "Humor and laughter often dramatize the violation of a norm and at the same time reaffirm the norm" (Coser 1960, 88).

Indeed, comics are in the business of both violating and affirming cultural norms. A comic's marginality and performance context grants him or her the authority to subvert the status quo; in this way, deviance from social norms and dominant cultural traits serves as a license for social criticism. As Mintz (1987) explains, "The key to understanding the role of standup comedy in the process of cultural affirmation and subversion is a recognition of the comedian's traditional license for deviant behavior and expression" (88). Noting that typically a comedian is perceived by audiences as somehow "defective," piteous, and marginal, Mintz suggests that audience laughter reflects not only a feeling of superiority to the comic, but a sense of relief that we do not possess such weaknesses. As what he terms a "negative exemplar," Mintz contends that the comic functions as a "shaman" who leads the public "in a celebration of a community of shared culture, of homogenous understanding and expectation" (89).

Marginal comics themselves share certain cultural values. As Boskin (1979) asserts, "American humor of the twentieth century is the humor of the urban, alienated minority groups whose experience has largely been that of outsiders" (49). Members of marginalized groups, Boskin contends, share a humor of oppression; for example, humor directed against African Americans and women tends to depict them as unintentionally funny. Marginalized individuals have recourse, however; discussing the tradition of Jewish humor, Dorinson and Boskin (1988) observe that "after centuries of massacres and indignities, emancipation created another comedic possibility: the humor of marginality" (167).[14] This marginalized status, according to Cohen (1999), enables American Jewish humorists to possess "the stance of an outsider, and the soul of a critical student" (68). Laughing at absurdity, Cohen believes, is characteristic of American humor in general.

What, exactly, constitutes "American humor"? Although defining and delimiting the genre is beyond the scope of this study, it is important to note the influence of marginal traditions. For example, practitioners and critics alike agree that Jewish humor has played a major role in shaping the comedy we now perceive as simply "American." As Porges (cited in Kaplan 2001) observes, "When you analyze it, Jewish humor in America is distinct for one simple reason: it's urban. And urban imediately means smart-ass" (3). This urban sensibility helped bring Jewish humor into the mainstream until it became synonymous with "American humor."[15] Certainly, it is difficult to discern a dividing line between contemporary Jewish and "American" humor; the pervasive influence of Jewish and other marginal traditions continues to be evident in present-day comedy in the United States.

Marginal traditions of humor are inevitably linked to power dynamics, and laughter can be liberating, even empowering. Levine (1977) notes that "The need to laugh . . . often exists most urgently in those who exert the least power over their immediate environment" (300). And Janus (1981) explains that humor "is especially needed and adopted by those who have no other 'recognizable' form of power" (167).[16] As Rabbi Joseph Telushkin maintains, "In the past, when we felt politically powerless, humor was a tool" (cited in Kaplan 2001, 6). Perhaps marginal voices provide part of the honest and "realistic" spirit of American humor described by Bier (1984), a "commentary on the general repressiveness against which American humor is set" (103). These marginal voices in humor commonly feature the use of self-deprecation. This particular comedic strategy has been investigated as it is used by women (Barreca 1991; Boskin 1979; Fraiberg 1994; Horowitz 1997; Little 1983; Walker 1987, 1988, 1991a, 1991b), minorities (Apte 1987; Boskin 1979; Boskin and Dorinson 1987; Gruner 1997; Levine 1977; Mintz 1988), and "fools" in venues ranging from royal courts (Klapp 1962) to comedy clubs (Mintz 1987) and modern organizations (Dets de Vries 1990).

In recent years, however, there has been a decrease in the use of self-deprecation in ethnic humor—a trend that may be attributed to the shift from America's emphasis on assimilation to cultural pluralism (Apte 1987). Because various ethnic groups no longer feel the need to internalize WASP values and have become increasingly sensitive to the damaging effect negative stereotyping has on their public image, only group members have license to joke about the group—outsiders do not. What begins as appeasement of the dominant culture ("See, I'm laughing at myself—please don't hurt me") may be liberatory, but risks becoming self-flagellation if it continues for too long (Apte

1987). Thus, the "laughter through tears" characteristic of traditional Jewish humor (Davies 1990, 96) features a "triumphant outcry . . . the cry of freedom" (Grotjahn 1987, 98). Today, this cry has become a warning to the dominant culture: "Only we can make fun of ourselves. If you do, we won't like it and we don't care if you think that we do not have a sense of humor. We think that we do, since we can and do laugh at ourselves! When you laugh at us, however, we think your motives are ulterior and we think you are bigots, racists, and highly prejudiced, and we will not tolerate it!" (Apte 1987, 37).[17] By challenging humor derogatory to them and creating humor in which the dominant group is the butt, marginal factions of society may be making an essential move from being "muted" to being "voiced" (Kramarae 1981, 59).[18]

Ironically, one way marginal individuals gain a voice is by being self-effacing, even self-disparaging. Because of its revered status in our culture, having a sense of humor has become a "core value" in American society, and "Engaging in mild self-deprecating humor is generally perceived as a clear indication of having a sense of humor" (Apte 1987, 28–30). Perhaps this is the reason that women and minorities frequently put themselves down; in order to show the dominant culture that they have a sense of humor, disenfranchised groups must be the butt of their own jokes. In stand-up comedy, performers from these groups must be "buffoons" before they can be "wise fools" (Klapp 1962, 89).[19] Indeed, the dynamic between victim and victor in stand-up comedy is a complex and powerful one.

Another strategy of marginal humor is subversion. Like self-deprecation, strategic subversion through humor has been studied primarily as it is used by women (Barreca 1991; Walker 1988, 1991a, 1991b) and minorities (Boskin and Dorinson 1987; Dorinson and Boskin 1988; Levine 1977). Indeed, both strategies are features of marginal humor, although there is some disagreement about the potential for self-deprecation to be interpreted as subversive (this issue is explored in detail in chapter 5). It is clear, however, that these two strategies may dovetail within a single joke. My "stupid bitch" joke is a good example of this. By insulting myself, I achieved several goals: (1) I showed the audience the ludicrousness of the situation; (2) I illustrated the abuse women face on the street daily; (3) I bested the fictive abuser through humor, thereby winning the "last laugh" and maintaining the ultimate power position; and (4) I exploded the myth that women are weak, defenseless, or inferior in any way by having assuaged the male ego while simultaneously showing that anyone capable of such a retort is clearly anything but stupid. Indeed, as Barreca's (1991) summation of Walker indicates, women's humor is not always perceived as subversive because what appears to be submission to stereotypes is often a "thinly veiled indictment of society" (185). Clearly, self-deprecation and subversion can be conflated in a carefully constructed joke.

One way that marginal comics create a subversive discourse is by co-opting hegemonic humor. As Hopkins (1990) contends, "The ruling class's humor isn't the same when its victims become its mouthpiece, magically transforming offensive material into a brash form of social commentary" (1). This explains the "turnabout is fair play" nature of much marginal humor. Comic Carol Leifer's classic mockery, "I don't have any kids . . . at least none that I know about!" is a perfect example of Hopkins's assertion. Audiences laugh appreciatively at this line; clearly, they are amused—but not overtly threatened. Perhaps women and minorities must seem nonthreatening as fools did in order to become licensed social critics. Perhaps speaking the truth with impunity is, as Zijderveld (1982) suggests, a privilege accorded only to those with no real power to subvert the dominant group. Making the "Master" laugh is one thing; unseating him from a position of power is quite another.

The license and licensing of social critics are integral to an understanding of the way comedy works in public. Members of a group are permitted to tease and even insult that group; once a member steps outside, however, he or she may only publicly criticize his or her own group—unless, of course, he or she is a licensed social critic, a professional fool like David Letterman. A contemporary analogue to the medieval court jester, Letterman is allowed to attack any group because he is, after all, a fool. Although he does not speak from an ethnic or sex-based position of marginality, he constructs and performs a rhetorical marginality, presenting an offbeat persona (continually calling attention to his "goofy" appearance and referring to himself as a "dweeb") who delights in testing the rigid parameters of network television. Even so, he is no match for the establishment.[20] Letterman is irreverent, but he is not dangerous.

21

He is influential, however. Strauss (1988) notes that, according to an advertiser in the *New York Times,* comics are "the intellectual spokesmen for their generation" (90), and Handelman (1988) asserts that "most of America takes its world view from two late-night-talk-show hosts—two middle Americans who have more freedom and more air time to discuss the day's events than network anchors do."[21] Technology allows "fools" like Letterman to perform for and influence millions of people every night. As discussed in the introduction, many young Americans learn about current events—political and otherwise—solely through their viewing of Letterman and other late-night entertainment.

Through the years, some of the most popular segments of Letterman's show have been his "stupid pet tricks," "stupid human tricks," and the sardonic "top ten" lists. It is not the guests or features that keep audiences tuned in, however—it is Letterman himself. What makes the pet or human tricks funny is Letterman's wry commentary. He is a parody of a host hosting a parody of a show, unmasking celebrities by deliberately undermining their public personas, occasionally berating the audience, and "breaking frame" at every opportunity to mock the medium of television itself. Although he is undoubtedly one of the most "powerful" comic figures in this country, David Letterman poses no real threat to the status quo. He is truly a wise fool—able to reflect society back to itself without fear of retribution.

Indeed, as they have throughout history, professional fools in contemporary society can critique the dominant culture, speaking the truth with impunity (Klapp 1962; Mintz 1987; Welsford 1935). Marginalized individuals are granted a unique authority when they are paid to make the public laugh; comics onstage are, in effect, licensed social critics. The comic critiques society and is critiqued by its members in the process. In a sense, the comic functions as a heckler of the status quo; the audience is thus in a position to out-heckle the heckler. In this way, comics and audiences establish a perverse symbiosis—the audience (many of whom are members of society's power "center") literally pays for abuse. By laughing at a comic's jokes—especially those ridiculing the establishment—audience members laugh at the roles that they (perhaps unwittingly) construct and perform. The U.S. Constitution allows all citizens the right to speak out against oppression in public. An individual who performs his or her marginality in order to elicit laughter and a paycheck and simultaneously creates a potentially subversive discourse, however, wields a power exclusive to the office of professional fool.

Perhaps no humor is more overtly subversive than the virulently antiestablishment humor of the baby boom generation. Caustically lampooning every "ism" they find, practitioners of "Boomer humor" have often been accused of "Going Too Far" (Hendra 1987). Although this trend of outraged social criticism masked as comedy exists today in the acts of controversial figures like Judy Tenuta, most contemporary stand-up comics play it safe, preferring to perform the "entrepreneurial comedy" that will land them the coveted Letterman (or Leno) spot (449). Clearly, there are no comics working today whose social critiques rival those of the king of comic outrage, Lenny Bruce (which is at least partly attributable to the difference between the cultural climate of the 1960s and that of the new millennium). Additionally, audiences can distinguish between real outrage and an act designed to shock; the latter is not often tolerated, as Hendra points out: "The minute Going Too Far becomes a self-conscious, planned course of behavior, you forfeit your satirical license" (22).

Going Too Far can also get a performer censored. From Solon, censured for rousing the masses in ancient Greece (Sonkowsky 1983, 7) to Carlin, censured for obscenity by the FCC, from Plato's suggested ban of poets to MTV's actual ban of Andrew "Dice" Clay, from fools getting whipped to comics getting "blipped," censorship is the fate of performers who are too outspoken, too outrageous, or too out of step with society in any way. Perhaps most contemporary stand-up comics are relatively well behaved, but there will always be those who push the envelope, asking, "Just how far is *too* far?" Along with being licensed social critics, comics show us what fools have always shown the world:

> traditional fools were not merely the ideologues of their societies. . . . Theirs was a critical function, but their criticism was of a metaphysical, rather than socio-political nature. These fools . . . offered a glimpse into the vortex of human existence by erecting an awe-inspiring, looking-glass reality which showed to their contemporaries who they could become, should they abandon the values, norms and meanings of their tradition. (Zijderveld 1982, 161)

The above discussion raises many important questions: Who gets licensed as a social critic, by whom, and for how long? When does a social critic's license get revoked, and under what conditions? Who *never* gets licensed and why? These issues are complex and provocative—undoubtedly linked to the very nature of humor and the structure of society. The performed marginality of female stand-up comics provides a template for exploration of these and other questions.

As licensed social critics, comics have always been "defective" in some way; whether physically deformed and kept as favored "pets" in the courts of old or simply as members of a disenfranchised group in contemporary culture, the more marginal the performer, the greater the comic "capital" available to him or her. Within the context of contemporary stand-up comedy, the cumulative nature of performed marginality is apparent—that is, the more marginal the performer, the greater the potential for comic commodification of these features. Whereas Rita Rudner can perform her marginality as a woman and Mario Joyner can perform his marginality as an African American, Ellen Cleghorne can perform her marginality as both a woman and as an African American. She does, in fact, and uses this combination as the basis of much of her material. In a 1991 appearance on cable television, for example, Cleghorne used the following:

> I was on *Oprah* . . . every time I'd tell people I was gonna be on Oprah, the first thing they'd ask me was . . . "What's the topic?" . . . I'm a woman, I'm a comic—what else could the topic be? "Women who have sex with their dogs—next on the *Oprah Winfrey Show.*" Did the show, got to ride first class on the airline. . . . Every time people would pass me by, it'd be like, "Honey, look—it's a black girl in first class—betcha she on her way to the *Oprah Winfrey Show*—betcha she had sex with a dog."

Lampooning sexual and racial stereotypes, Cleghorne constructs and performs her marginality as a "black girl"—one who appears conspicuously out of place in first class and whose sexual appetite is discerned as deviant.

More subtle than Cleghorne's construction of self, however, is her construction of the "other," the dominant culture. From her vocal inflection and gestures, it is apparent that the speaker who says, "Honey, look—it's a black girl in first class" is female; it is also apparent that she is white. Her facial expression is one of shock, and her hand cupped to the ear of her imaginary husband suggests the hushed and "taboo" nature of such an occurrence. By portraying a white woman (and her silent but complicitous husband) as racist and racially sexist, Cleghorne

24

creates a subversive message. She simultaneously performs the hegemonic discourse and mocks it, thereby exposing its particular biases.

African American women like Cleghorne are not only doubly marginalized but, as bell hooks (1984) points out, they have no institutionalized "other" to discriminate against or exploit. Unlike white women and African American men, who may function as either oppressor or oppressed (African American men may oppress women in general; white women may oppress African Americans and other minorities), African American women are marginalized by both race and sex. Rather than considering it a disadvantage, hooks advocates using this unique position, reminding us that, "It is essential . . . that black women recognize the special vantage point our marginality gives us and make use of this perspective to criticize the dominant racist, classist, sexist hegemony as well as to envision and create a counter-hegemony" (15).

Cleghorne does precisely that. In fact, the above example of Cleghorne's humor functions in much the same way as my "stupid bitch" joke; in both cases, the comic performs her marginality in order to make audiences laugh—ultimately, at social constructions that they (even unknowingly) help to create. In order to advocate change, the marginal person must first acknowledge present conditions. And in order to make fun of the powerful, the powerless person must disarm them. As licensed social critics, marginal comics employ a variety of rhetorical strategies to accomplish this task and, in so doing, create a subversive humor unique to their insider/outsider status.

"Women's Humor"?

Clearly, female comics produce a discourse that can subvert patriarchal norms, performing a marginality that transcends race and class, but is there an identifiable genre of "women's humor"? As Unterbrink (1987) points out, "It seems incongruous that women's observations about dating, sex, marriage and motherhood are labelled 'women's humor' while the material men have performed for well over a century about dating, sex, marriage, and fatherhood has never been labelled 'men's humor'" (3). Nevertheless, numerous critics discuss a genre called "women's humor," generally referring to humorous writing and/or performance created by women. Further, critics discuss a genre of "feminist humor," sometimes conflating it with "women's humor," sometimes distinguishing the two. Because of the confusing and at times indiscriminate use of these terms, the genres of "women's humor" and "feminist humor" are more often assumed than defined (this issue is examined further in chapters 2 and 5). Definitional confusion about the genre itself is an impediment to any serious study of the humor created by women; consequently, the assumptions that women's humor or even feminist humor are, in fact, distinct genres should be questioned.

Even this questioning is difficult however, because historically women's humor, like all manifestations of women's experience and accomplishments, has been marginalized. Scholars of women's humor commonly believe that, as in other areas such as literature, women have traditionally been excluded from the "canon" of great humor. As inhabitants of the private rather than public sphere, with little if any true political power, women humorists, like all women, have often been denied access to the "old boys' club." In the arena of comedy, as in many other professions, women have long been considered supporting rather than leading players. Whether it is outright discrimination or the more subtle and usual denial of opportunity based on male privilege, female humorists have been kept "in their place." They have been considered what Barecca (1988) calls "the unofficial discussing the insignificant" (6).

Additionally, women have often been accused of not having a sense of humor when they do not laugh at jokes that denigrate them.[22] This situation poses quite a paradox; as Merrill (1988) asserts, when jokes that objectify, victimize, and vilify women are told, for a woman "to be amused, she must discount and devalue her own experience" (279). In order to prove that they have a sense of humor, women have frequently found themselves laughing at jokes that demean them. If we consider the release of laughter roughly the intellectual equivalent of orgasm, then perhaps women have been "faking it" for years, laughing to please men at the very moment of perceived "violation" (Barreca 1991; Gilbert 1989). In this way, women may have participated in their own oppression through their ostensibly "accepting" laughter. Unlike the self-deprecation common to all marginal humor in which the joketeller/target may become empowered by a joke's subversive potential, "put-down humor," in which the target remains passive, does not empower that person in any way.

Even today, misconceptions about humor by women abound. Throughout history, women have been labelled "unfunny" by a perverse syllogistic reasoning: Only men are funny; girls aren't men; therefore, girls aren't funny (Merrill 1988, 279). As Kramarae asserts, "male beliefs about gender differences in humor, or at least their statements about women's lack of a sense of humor, appear to be one of the firmest, more constant of the 'accusations' made by men about women's speech behavior" (cited in White 1988, 53). In humor, just as in all aspects of human behavior, sex roles are usually clearly delineated: Men are the initiators of humor; women are the reactors. The distinction begins in childhood. As Beatts (1975) explains, when she was growing up: "If you were a boy, having a sense of humor meant . . . pouring salt on the head of the girl who sat in front of you so it would look as though she had dandruff. If you were a girl, having a sense of humor meant laughing when someone poured salt on your head" (140). White (1988) agrees, noting that "women who are perceived to have a good sense of humor are not those who produce humor but those who display appreciation for the male sense of humor. . . . In essence, women are socialized to provide an audience for male risibility" (76).

Excluded from the canon, charged with being humorless if they do not laugh to accommodate sexist jokes, women as the creators of humor have only relatively recently been the subject of sustained scholarly analysis. Walker (1988) contends that the paradox of women's humor is the "invisibility of the tradition, not merely to the dominant culture, but to women themselves" (122) due to "their close involvement with members of the dominant group" (138). As Barreca (1988) notes, "It is the inability of the critical tradition to deal with comedy by women rather than the inability of women to produce comedy that accounts for the absence of critical material on the subject" (20). In fact, scholarly research on "women's humor" is a small but burgeoning area. Typically, however, this work has focused on humorous writing by women.

Until the 1970s, only two anthologies of American women's humor existed (published in 1885 and 1934). In 1983, Judy Little published her groundbreaking volume, *Comedy and the Woman Writer,* advancing the first scholarly analysis focused exclusively on women's humorous writing. Like many critics before and since, Little characterizes women's humor as one that subverts patriarchal norms; she delves deeper than others, however, in pointing out just why this subversion is so problematic for audiences conditioned by these norms. Explaining that expectations of sex-appropriate behavior are deeply entrenched as "primary socializations" taught to us in early childhood when we believe in only one reality, Little notes that although all comedy may mock norms, women writers mock "norms which have been considered stable values for millennia" (2). The norms under attack are so basic, Little argues, that we do not even recognize them as norms—they are the implicit, usually lifelong assumptions we make about the way men and women should behave. These assumptions are fairly fixed, as Little notes: "Human beings in the twentieth century may worry about the relativity of time, space, morals, and the habits of small particles, and they may well fear their own capacity for self-destruction, but their expectations with regard to the basic identity and behavior of each sex are still remarkably constant" (10).

Little's cogent analysis offers a reason that the humor produced by women has often been regarded with fear and suspicion. As she explains, women comic writers attack the primary norms traditionally attacked only during liminal (festive, carnival) occasions, but unlike the circumscribed nature of carnival's topsy-turvy world, in women's comedic writing, "the comic context is a liminal one in which inversions are not turned upright again . . . not resolved into an orderly close that would reaffirm . . . the traditional, most intimately learned, norms of primary socialization" (21). If the humor created by women sends dominant cultural values into a tailspin, it is small wonder that such humor may be perceived as threatening. As Toth (1984) notes, "since women's humor characteristically criticizes and subverts patriarchal norms, it is not always amusing to the other sex—which may account for its absence from many humor anthologies" (212).

Certainly, there exists a wealth of material that could have been included in such collections. As Dresner (1988) maintains, as early as the seventeenth century, American women were producing written humor that articulated distinctly "feminist" concerns. Sheppard (1986) notes that in the nineteenth century Kate Sanborn published *The Wit of Women* in an effort to prove the existence of such a phenomenon. And Toth (1984) points out that suffragists such as Sojourner Truth and Anna Howard Shaw caustically critiqued patriarchal norms, delighting their female audiences with witty social commentary.

As women became vocal social critics, so too did they become humorists. Walker (1988) suggests that women's cultural identification with subordination, coupled with their "apartness" from the dominant culture, has resulted in the "double text" women writers have frequently employed, simultaneously describing and critiquing women's position in society.[23] The work of Dorothy Parker, and later the many post–World War II "domestic" writers, reflects the marginality that enables these women to critique the dominant culture and laugh at its mores. As Walker (1991b) explains: "there is a vast difference between laughing at a joke of which a woman is the butt and deliberately creating a humorous piece in which a woman is an inept housekeeper, a dumb blonde, or a gossip: the former may be a conditioned response to the humor of the dominant culture, while the latter is frequently a subversive attack on the status quo" (62).

In the context of stand-up comedy, this "double text" is evident in the self-deprecatory jokes still used by some female comics. Putting herself down as a way to gain audience identification and acceptance may still be one of the most effective rhetorical strategies available to a woman performing humor. Although creating identification with an audience is necessary for any humorist, it may be particularly important for women; scholars of women's humor and feminist humor believe that women identifying with each other through humor are taking the first step toward the solidarity feminists have so often sought. The desire for solidarity is often frustrated, however, because, as Walker (1991b) points out, "unlike other oppressed groups, women do not constitute a group in the usual sense" (57). Similarly, Ware (1992) notes, "political unity between women across race and class is potentially one of the greatest forces for change in the world, but there is nothing about being a woman which necessarily guarantees that unity" (254). Some semblance of connection, if not unity, may be achieved, however, through the humor women create. Critics maintain that by laughing at the commonalities of experience that transcend race and class, women find community; they engage in what Barecca (1991) calls "Laughter in the kitchen," sharing humor generated from and relevant to their daily lives.

Indeed, the humor of women, like that of all marginalized groups, may serve as a means of facilitating in-group cohesion. Throughout this investigation, humor created by women is examined to gain insight not only into women's experience but into that of other marginalized groups, for marginal humor—whether its creator is marginalized by gender, race, or any other characteristic—has unique features. One aspect of shared humor among marginalized groups is its tendency to unmask the unabashed hypocrisy of the dominant culture. As Walker (1988) asserts: "a dominant theme in women's humor is how it feels to be a member of a subordinate group in a culture that prides itself on equality, what it is like to try to meet standards for behavior that are based on stereotypes rather than human beings" (x).

Although this feature applies to all marginal humor, aside from a passing comparison between humor created by women and by minorities, neither Walker nor other critics attempt to tease out further implications. Clearly, these connections should be explored. Additionally, when defining any rhetorical genre, critics must not only delineate its features but provide evidence to support their claims.

Many scholars of women's humor, however, do neither. For instance, critics claim that women's humor is often characterized by subtlety, ridicule of circumstance rather than character (Merrill 1988) and the use of stories instead of jokes (Walker 1988), but these assertions are rarely supported by specific examples. Rather, assumptions are made based on essentially the same logic undergirding comic Jay Leno's classic observation that the major difference between the sexes is that men find the Three Stooges funny and women do not.

Scholars who make a distinction between "women's" humor and "feminist" humor generally cite the women's movement of the 1960s as the single greatest influence on the creation of "feminist" humor.[24] According to Dresner (1988), this was a humor that "reinforced the validity of women's perceptions about their oppression and subordinate status, undermined the bases of male chauvinism, and supported the legitimacy of women's demands for political, social, and economic equality" (149).

Walker (1988) maintains that women's humor and feminist humor are not synonymous, that feminist humor is always either "a subtle challenge" to stereotype or circumstance or a blatant confrontation of "the sources of discrimination" (13), and that "Both subtle and overt feminist humor have existed in American women's writing for at least 150 years" (153). Comparing these two types of humor to the two types of political activism that formed the women's movement of the 1960s,

Walker likens the "subtle challenge" humor to the "reform oriented" women's rights advocates who sought to change the system from within; the confrontational humor, she argues, can be compared to the women's liberationists who proposed a "radical transformation" of the system (146–47). Scholars have characterized feminist humor in various ways: Walker (1991b) describes it as exhibiting "a consciousness of common oppression" (69).[25] Modleski (1991) calls it "scathing and often exhilarating" (57); White (1988) claims that it "allows for identification and self-differentiation by its users, . . . exposes cultural inequities, . . . serves a bonding function, . . . stresses the shared experiences . . . of women, . . . and . . . positively values women and their experience" (87); Barreca (1991) asserts that "Feminist humor is serious, and it is about changing the world" (185).

The above definitions share obvious commonalities. Additionally, most scholars who use the term feminist humor describe it as both angry and affirming. Merrill (1988) maintains: "Comedy is both an aggressive and intellectual response to human nature and experience. A cognizance of women's right to be both aggressive and intellectual is a relatively new historical phenomenon. What is even more recent, and radical though, about feminist humor is that it addresses itself to women and to the multiplicity of experiences and values women may embody" (278).

Barreca (1991) explains that "Aggression in humor can be directed at you, it can be deflected by you, or it can be directed by you" (72) and notes that by using feminist humor, women are directing aggression, realizing that "If you can't talk back to the boss, you'll never be the boss" (125). Although there is some agreement among scholars on basic principles (for example, women's humor is not typically abusive; feminist humor is always, at some level, subversive), the genres of women's humor and feminist humor need to be interrogated further if critics (academic or otherwise) are ever to use these terms in a way that promotes rather than impedes dialogue—a central feminist concern.

Women in Stand-Up Comedy

Very little scholarship has focused on women's humor or feminist humor specifically as they relate to stand-up comedy, and virtually none of the work in this area attempts to distinguish either women's or feminist humor from other types of marginal humor. My own act used to include the following joke: "Do you know that it now takes as long to cure a yeast infection as it did for God to create the world? Kind of puts things in perspective, doesn't it?" Undeniably, it was the women in the audience who laughed the loudest. Does that make the joke an example of women's humor? I consider myself a feminist—does that mean I necessarily performed feminist humor? Women have been performing comedy in this country since the late nineteenth century. To some, the very fact that women got up onstage alone and took up time and space makes this a "feminist" act. To others, only humor in which patriarchal norms are overtly attacked qualifies as "feminist." Typically, critics contrast "feminist" humor with "sexist" humor, never acknowledging that some types of "feminist" humor—indeed, some types of feminism—are sexist toward men.[26]

Martin and Segrave (1986) maintain that between 1860 and 1920, against a background of "growing feminist consciousness . . . female comedians of national repute emerged" (33), but that soon afterward, "The images of woman as dumb, man chaser, and physically unattractive, even when they weren't, would dominate the nature of female comedy for three decades, with no loosening up until the end of the 1950s, and no real change until the late 1960s" (100).

Although they chronicle female comic performance in detail, Martin and Segrave limit their definition of feminist humor to material that is generally perceived as an overt attack, or at least threatening. In fact, women have historically assumed a variety of comedic postures onstage; any notion of feminist humor must be considered in light of these female comic types.[27]

Walker (1988) maintains that "Humor's inherent posture of superiority—even aggression—is in conflict with traditional notions of female submissiveness and passivity" (14). It is precisely this function of humor—as aggression and social control—that causes problems for many female comics. Although more women than ever before are performing stand-up comedy, audiences are still more accustomed to seeing men in a position of power; hence, when watching a female comic, they may experience a type of ideological resistance spawned from centuries of cultural conditioning. As Kibler (1998) notes: "Recent feminist accounts of women's comic performances hold that these performances are open to liberating feminist laughter and/or misogynist interpretations: comic women who violate gender codes call attention to the artificiality of femininity but are also open to attack for their deviation from the norm" (61–62). Similarly, in the 1991 documentary *Wisecracks,* comic Robin Tyler observes, "Women aren't supposed to dominate one man, let alone a whole audience!" Regardless of content or style, a comic onstage is, rhetorically, in a position of control. And for female comics, audience resistance to this "authority" is a potential obstacle.

Onstage or off, women often face an unresolvable dilemma: Demonstrating a sense of humor may be the equivalent of divesting oneself of womanhood, yet laughing indiscriminately at their own expense trivializes women's entire self-concept. The realization of this double bind, critics argue, is the essence of and inspiration for a distinctly feminist humor. Barreca (1991) asserts that "nearly all women's humor is in some way feminist humor (with the exception of those early, self-deprecating 'I'm so ugly . . .' jokes associated with the very earliest comedians)" (182). In fact, those early jokes can be seen as strong feminist statements still in use today. As Walker (1991b) notes, "self-deprecating humor may be evidence of strength rather than weakness" (62).[28]

In the arena of stand-up comedy, women must meet a paradoxical challenge: They must "measure up to conventional male-identified standards while simultaneously attempting to call them into question" (Pershing 1991, 203). Like other marginalized performers, the female comic simultaneously affirms and subverts the status quo; unlike performers marginalized by race or other characteristics, however, the female comic performs for an audience usually at least half comprised of members of her marginalized group. She is, after all, part of the marginalized majority. As noted earlier, however, marginal status can actually yield advantages. For example, doubly marginalized individuals may have a special insight into both dominant and marginalized cultures. Sochen (1991) points out that African American and Jewish female comics have a "double advantage" because "as women and as members of a discriminated-against minority, they understand the strengths and foibles of their oppressors. . . . As outsiders looking in, women—black and Jewish women particularly—became sensitive commentators on American life. As survivors, they laughed rather than cried at their observations" (14–15).

Claiming that a shared experience of alienation and marginalization lies at the heart of much women's humor, Pershing (1991) explains that women identify with women's experience and that stand-up comedy based on that experience fosters a sense of community. Comic Kate Clinton maintains that this type of humor is "stand-with" rather than "stand-up"—a comedy of activism and social action (cited in Pershing 1991, 224–25). Ironically, the very women who create this type of humor are often reticent to label it "feminist." As comic Carol Montgomery notes, although a significant number of female stand-up comics are feminists by definition, most prefer to say simply that their humor is generated from a "female perspective," lest they be branded political and, therefore, unfunny (Klein 1984). Additionally, female comics worry about scaring off potential audiences, in the United States and beyond. As Alison Field, a member of the British female comedy trio Sensible Footwear (a group that lives and performs in Canada) explains: "I think we consider ourselves feminists. We don't necessarily always use it in our publicity, depending on who it's going to alienate before we've even started" (cited in Hengen 1998, 254).

There is a consensus among female comics that men—whether audience members or other comics—are intimidated by a woman in a controlling position onstage. Perhaps this accounts for the degrading introductions male MCs often give female comics. I remember being introduced as a "female comic" (just in case, I assume, my sex was not apparent) and a "lovely lady." These labels are irritating, though not nearly as egregious as others. Montgomery, for example recalls being introduced as "A lovely lady with big tits," and Emily Levine remembers her moment in the spotlight as "a woman who fucked her way to the top" (cited in Martin and Segrave 1986, 8). These introductions not only predispose the audience, they unnerve the performer. Yet the same men who perpetrate this practice frequently introduce male comics as "A very funny guy," or "A good friend of mine," using club credentials rather than sexual barbs.

Why? What is so frightening about a woman telling jokes? This is not a new query. As Levy (1997) points out, historically, men have feared witty women; viewed as dangerous, clever women have typically been portrayed by male writers as shrews, witches, and bitches. Beatts (1975) speculates: "I don't know what they're [men] worried about. Maybe knowing that humor is the best of weapons, they're

34

reluctant to put it into our hands. Maybe they think we'll be funnier than they are. Maybe they're afraid we'll put salt on their heads" (186).

Indeed, the aggressiveness inherent in humor can cause it to be interpreted as a challenge. Barecca (1991) explains, "women's comedy is more dangerous than men's, because it challenges authority by refusing to take it seriously" (14). Although many male comics attack the status quo, the potential challenge that female comics may pose bears the unique rhetorical power of a marginality that transcends race and class.[29]

Despite the odds against them, women are performing their marginality comedically now more than ever, having finally become a recognized force in the comedy industry. Cable television specials, along with Comedy Central and network television variety shows, have provided female comics with much-needed mainstream exposure. Other television shows and movies have also served as vehicles, launching the careers of comedy superstars Roseanne and Whoopi Goldberg. Most notably, on network television, the popular situation comedies *Ellen* (Ellen DeGeneres) and *Grace under Fire* (Brett Butler), along with Rosie O'Donnell's highly acclaimed daytime variety show, have all featured former stand-up comics who parlayed their stage abilities into screen success.

The club scene, too, has changed. As the demand for live comedy in small towns as well as big cities has increased, doors have opened for female comics. Although they have more opportunities to perform, however, female comics are still faced with a double duty—to educate as well as entertain their audiences.[30] As comic Joy Behar explains in *Wisecracks* (1991), female comics do not compete with each other but work to condition audiences. The very fact that female comics are often ghettoized, featured on network or cable television shows with such names as *Girls Night Out, Women of the Night,* and *Ladies of Laughter,* indicates an attempt to acculturate audiences, to introduce them to "something completely different." During the late 1980s in New York City, I performed regularly on "Women's Comedy Night" at two different clubs. Audiences were essentially being told, "This is what to expect." Neither of these clubs offered "Men's Comedy Night," because, of course, every night was Men's Comedy Night.[31]

Although to date no statistical study of demographics among professional American stand-up comics has been done, several sources provide data for women's involvement in the industry. Because the *Tonight*

Show during Johnny Carson's tenure was widely regarded as a national comedy stable, I consulted *TV Guide* listings for the month of October (the month the show began) between 1962 and 1990. Of the 497 days that guests were listed during this time period, seventy-two male comics made a total of 241 appearances while twelve female comics made a total of 33 appearances (these numbers include comics like David Brenner, Jay Leno, and Joan Rivers in their role as guest host).[32]

In 1987, Betsy Borns profiled forty-three comics for the book *Comic Lives*—twelve female; in 1991, Hank Gallo profiled forty comics for the book *Comedy Explosion*—ten female. In 1988, Ronald Smith published *Comedy on Record: The Complete Critical Discography,* "a listing of virtually every comedy album released in America" (3). Beginning with comedy albums from the late 1950s (with a few ten-inch albums from the early 1950s—the first twelve-inch LP was released in 1958), Smith provides 560 entries (including comedy teams, actors who sing funny songs, groups like National Lampoon, and various artists, commentators, and individuals who perform material that may be construed as comic), 64 of which are for solo female comedy albums.[33] Of the 41 comedy collections listed, 27 contain women (though usually only one), including an album entitled *Kings of Comedy* (containing performances by Moms Mabley and Joan Rivers).

Smith rates each album, assigning a value of one to three stars. A three-star rating is accorded an album by Richard Pryor containing the following material: "White women'll suck your dick right away. Black women you have to beg 'em for months . . . you fuck white women, if they don't come they say, 'That's all right . . . I'll use the vibrator.' Black woman'll talk about your ass: 'That it? You gotta grind this pussy. Nigger, fuck me! Shit!'" (509). Smith gives only one star, however, to Robin Tyler's album, maintaining that "much of Tyler's material is simply too baiting, broad, and bitchy. . . . The album has some minor interest showing just how humorless the drive for equal rights could get" (643–44). And noting that Christine Nelson performed "parody songs from the female point of view," Smith adds, "Unfortunately, back in 1963, the female view was dreary" (467).

Although Pryor's graphic sexual material receives top rating, Rusty Warren, a "bawdy" 1960s performer, does not fare nearly as well. Assigning each of her eleven albums only one or one and one-half stars, Smith asserts that "Even in the leering, obsessed, inept and brainless 50's it's hard to imagine an audience desperate enough, uptight enough, and drunk enough to laugh at Rusty Warren and her irritating, brassy rantings and ravings. . . . The best part of Warren's records are the album covers. The Julie London of sex comedy records, her album covers . . . could be extremely attractive, especially compared to Belle Barth's" (664–65).

Although the number of female comics performing professionally in this country continues to increase, Smith's perspective is representative still of a substantial portion of comedy club audiences—those who laugh most at "dick jokes," preferably told by a male comic.[34]

What do female comics think of the inequities they face? Gail Singer's 1991 independent film, *Wisecracks,* a documentary of North American female stand-up comics, combines excerpts of live performances with interviews, exploring women's humor and feminist humor from the perspectives of the comics themselves. Comics' beliefs include Maxine Lapiduss's suggestion that dick jokes condition audiences to expect and laugh at distinctly "male" rhythms, Ellen DeGeneres's statement that women have to "apologize" for being funny, and Robin Tyler's assertion that men don't generally listen to women but *must* listen to one with a microphone. A review of *Wisecracks* from the Cannes Film Festival (*Los Angeles Daily Variety* 1991) notes that the film "seriously bogs down when dry backstage interviews dwell on feminist rhetoric such as 'we live in a sexist society and comedy has traditionally been a man's domain,' but . . . picks right back up after that."

In another review, entitled "Female Humor Stands Up," arts critic Michael MacCambridge (1992) observes that "Because stand-up comedy has traditionally been a male domain, female comics have walked into the bright light with another strike against them, their gender," but later contends that "among the ones who succeed, it's almost always insightful, intelligent material—rather than gender or appearance—that makes them successful." MacCambridge further maintains that "Paula Poundstone and Ellen DeGeneres stand out as two who most effectively mine the traditional Carlin-Cosby-Seinfeld vein of observational comedy." Concluding that *Wisecracks* "drags at times" because "Singer can't resist some overly pedantic segments in which she attempts to connect female comedy with feminism (the relation only works in the loosest sense)," MacCambridge nevertheless notes that "there are a few moments where the concerns of the gender and the context of stand-up comedy fuse perfectly," citing comic Emily Levine's material: "Every time I go to the mechanic, they always look at me like I'm stupid. And they say, 'It's a gasket, honey . . . ' Like I don't know what a gasket is—a gasket is $150. But a 'gasket, honey' is $200" (11).

Many of the critics whose views are discussed earlier in this chapter would undoubtedly take MacCambridge to task for the assumption that the above joke is related to gender but not feminism. By exploding the myth that a woman is ignorant and inept in the "male" world of auto repair, Levine affirms not only women's competence but their knowledge of an attempted patriarchal ruse; in this way, she pokes fun at a sacrosanct "male" institution, using a type (the patronizing auto mechanic) to debunk a type (the naive female car owner). Is this joke "feminist"? Is it "female"? Or is it simply a joke told by a woman (and hence from a female perspective)?

Hopkins (1990) explains, "Power doesn't just reside in not being the target of a comic's jokes. Real power is being the one who's telling them" (1). Clearly, female comics—like all comics—are in a rhetorically powerful position onstage, speaking into a microphone before a live audience (and sometimes a much wider audience reached through cable or network television). Yet the comedy created and performed by women is often interpreted—by academic and popular critics alike—as "soft," or at least as distinct from traditional "male" humor— distinctly less abusive and threatening. This belief is evident in Thompson's comment that "we never think of the class clown as a woman" and Wilson's observation that "Women's humor seems to be very much about connecting" (both cited in Kolbert 1993, 27–28). This essentialist notion of a "kinder, gentler" humor produced by women reinscribes traditional sexual stereotypes and grossly oversimplifies both the content and style of contemporary male and female stand-up comics.[35] Ironically, it is often the critics most adamantly opposed to labels who wish to apply the label "women's humor" or "feminist humor" to the performances of female comics.

As this chapter suggests, the vocabulary itself is extremely problematic. Certainly, this is not surprising in light of the continuing debate over the meaning of the word "feminism." What is feminism? This investigation does not presume to answer the question, only to ask it. Indeed, a number of self-designated feminists—from moderate academics to radical activists—have been interrogating feminism for years. The only idea with which all feminists seem to agree is that feminism is not monolithic. Some scholars view this fact as liberatory and, in an attempt to remain true to the multivocality they see as the heart of the women's movement, have even chosen to use the plural, "feminisms" (Warhol and Price Herndl 1991). Others, however, are not as optimistic. For example, hooks (1984) asserts: "A central problem within feminist discourse has been our inability to either arrive at a consensus of opinion about what feminism is or accept definition(s) that could serve as points of unification" (17).

Black (1976) explains: "Groups of people become distinctive as groups sometimes by their habitual patterns of commitment—not by the beliefs they hold, but by the manner in which they hold them and give them expression" (85). In other words, a *rhetorical* group does not necessarily constitute a *political* group. It is precisely because many women (and some men) do not want to be allied with feminist rhetoric (particularly the radical strains that have received such negative press) that they resist the label.[36]

Equally problematic is the fact that numerous definitions of feminism abound—some action-oriented like hooks's (1984) assertion, "Feminism is the struggle to end sexist oppression" (26), others more ideological such as Barreca's (1991) statement that feminism means "learning to laugh at what we find funny instead of just following along with the laugh track" (176). Still others do not purport to have a definition of feminism at all—do not, in fact, mention the word— but merely offer a philosophy of life: "Offer your experience as your truth" (Oliveros, cited in Le Guin 1989, 150).

Many contemporary feminist scholars focus on the extent to which gender roles have become naturalized and normalized (Butler 1990; Reeder 1996; Sullivan and Turner 1996).[37] This process is dangerous because, as Gould explains, "appeals to reason or to the nature of the universe have been used throughout history to enshrine existing hierarchies as proper and inevitable" (cited in Sullivan and Turner 1996, 29). Indeed, accepting gender roles and their accompanying benefits and disadvantages as the "natural" design of the universe is a powerful means of maintaining the status quo, the very system of oppression that many female comics challenge through humor.[38]

Although the link between feminism (or any ideology) and "fun" is paradoxical to many, it is precisely this connection that undergirds any notion of a distinctly "feminist" humor.[39] Clearly, feminism is a word and an ideology fraught with conflict. Attempting to discern *a* feminist humor is no more possible than attempting to define a unitary feminism. In order to explore the existence of a genre called "women's humor" and even more specifically, "feminist humor," a conditional definition must be used. For the purposes of this investigation, therefore, feminism is considered to be sexual egalitarianism— an idea that promotes humanism and pluralism, seeking to eradicate the privileging of one sex over the other.

Barreca (1988) maintains: "Feminist criticism has generally avoided the discussion of comedy, perhaps in order to be accepted by conservative critics who found feminist theory comic in and of itself" (4). And yet, as scholars have recently begun to point out, female comic performance provides a unique and compelling template upon which to explore the relationship between gender and power in contemporary culture. As Walker (1988) explains: "The overtly feminist and the androgynous humor of recent years have a tradition of their own that parallels closely the ebb and flow of the women's movement; their flowering now, in what has been called a 'post-feminist' era, suggests that in some fundamental ways the relation of women to humor—and thus to American culture—may have been altered" (182). Perhaps realizing that rather than being totally separate from it, humor (just as any discourse) created by women is as much a part of the women's movement as Friedan's *The Feminine Mystique* and Faludi's *Backlash*—Diller and Cleghorne as integral as Steinem and hooks—is a necessary precursor to asking questions regarding the existence of women's humor and feminist humor.

THE QUESTION
OF GENRE

As discussed in chapter 1, the terms "women's humor" and "feminist humor" are used indiscriminately—sometimes synonymously—and rarely defined. Rather, within discussions of women's and/or feminist humor, genres are simply assumed and specific generic constraints and features never considered. The problem of classification is apparent to some scholars. As Stillion and White (1987) note, "the number of women succeeding as stand-up comics has grown considerably in recent years, though it is not clear whether or not to classify them as feminist humorists. . . . Unlike traditional male comics, their humor does not put women down, but with some exceptions . . . female comics may not be feminist comics because of their need to contend with audience reactions to violating certain sex-role stereotypes" (219–20). Although they often do not delineate specific generic features, many scholars maintain that historically, comedy has been defined and dominated by men and is, therefore, a "male" or "masculine" genre (Auslander 1993; Barreca 1988; Horowitz 1997). These same scholars and others suggest that there is a distinct genre of "female" and even more specifically, "feminist" humor generated and performed by women.

The purpose of this investigation is not to provide definitive answers about nomenclature or ideology. Rather, this study explores the way female comics, as members of a marginalized group, "perform" their marginality onstage in an attempt to discern the existence of a genre called "female" and/or "feminist" stand-up comedy and the power relations such performance necessarily entails. In order to provide a framework for analysis, this chapter discusses the nature of genre and generic criticism, provides a detailed description of the genre of stand-up comedy, and problematizes the notion of a subgenre of "female," specifically "feminist," stand-up comedy.

Genre and Generic Criticism

As human creatures, we are constantly categorizing data collected throughout our daily experience. Constructing a genre is one such means of categorization. But what is a genre? Rhetorical critics and theorists have offered a number of definitions: "a construct of the critic which guides investigations" as well as a construct in the minds of the audience and a feature of the rhetorical discourse (Borman 1976, 173); "groups of discourses which share substantive, stylistic, and situational characteristics" (Campbell and Jamieson 1976, 20); "an aspect of cultural rationality" (Miller 1984, 165); and finally, "a tool of critical explanation" (Rosmarin 1985, 49). Explaining that genre is "itself a suasive instrument" (41), Rosmarin suggests that "genre is not . . . a class, but rather, a classifying statement. It is therefore itself a text" (46). Although Rosmarin is referring specifically to literary genres, the notion of genre as text and "metatext" applies to all genres (in fact, all criticism). Rosmarin's definition of genre as "writing about writing" (46) certainly applies to "writing about speaking" and "speaking about speaking" as well. Generic criticism creates a unique relationship among critic, text, and audience. As Campbell and Jamieson point out, "Generic analysis reveals both the conventions and affinities that a work shares with others; it uncovers the unique elements in the rhetorical act, the particular means by which a genre is individuated in a given case" (18).

In short, generic criticism explores both similarities and differences. By revealing the ways in which a particular text resembles other texts, the critic simultaneously describes features unique to that text. Ultimately, however, "in a genre, the significant rhetorical similarities outweigh the significant rhetorical differences" (Campbell and Jamieson 1976, 23). Generic criticism is at the heart of all criticism. Because "Inherent in each classification are two comparative standards—the comparison of like to like, the comparison of like to unlike" (26), similitude necessarily implies difference and vice versa. As Rosmarin (1985) asserts, "an eye for resemblance is always also an eye for difference" (25). Rosmarin further notes that "most criticism, even that which professes its disinterest in the generic and the suppositional alike, reveals that it is already both" (28).

What, then, distinguishes generic criticism from other types? (Note that even in the question, various genres of criticism are assumed.) Campbell and Jamieson (1976) suggest: "A genre is a group of acts unified by a constellation of forms that recurs in each of its members. These forms, in isolation, appear in other discourses. What is distinctive about the acts in a genre is the recurrence of the forms together in constellation" (20). Generic criticism, therefore, focuses on the unified recurrence of particular forms within specific action. For example, within the genre of stand-up comedy, a performer is alone onstage before an audience. And although this particular form also occurs within the genre of one-person shows and performance art, it is the recurrence of the combination of the solo performer with other forms (for example, monologue, humorous material, time limit, interactive nature) that distinguishes stand-up comedy from other performance genres.

Another feature of generic criticism is its use of hierarchical division and subdivision. According to Simons (1976): "If one genre is to be distinguished meaningfully from another, it follows that there must be a larger class of rhetorical practices into which both genres can be put, and that this class itself might constitute a genre distinguishable from another at its own higher level of abstraction" (37). Simons is suggesting that critics who assume the existence of a genre called "women's humor" or one called "feminist stand-up comedy" also assume the existence of a "larger class of rhetorical practices" that includes "men's humor" and "antifeminist stand-up comedy."

As previously mentioned, however, scholars often assume the existence of a genre without ever attempting to define or delineate its features and constraints. Campbell and Jamieson (1976) address this problem, explaining: "In a number of cases, critics have assumed, a priori, that a genre already exists and is known and defined . . . an essential and preliminary procedure defining the generic characteristics has been omitted. Generic critics need to recognize explicitly the assumptions they are making and the procedures required to establish their claims" (23). Observing that most genres are established deductively from a touchstone or model, Campbell and Jamieson explain that it is the confusion between deductive and inductive approaches that often creates difficulties in critical analysis. Indeed, critics not only confuse inductive with deductive generic analysis, they frequently seem to confuse form with content. When discussing "put-down" humor, for example, critics sometimes draw a distinction between the way comics use put downs and the object of a particular put-down, hence the erroneous binary labelled "sexist" vs. "feminist" humor.

Still, mistakes are part of any endeavor, scholarly or otherwise. As Rosmarin (1985) notes, "the inevitability of making mistakes is not the bane of criticism but, rather, its enabling condition. It makes classification possible, and classification enables criticism to begin" (22). Generic criticism, Rosmarin contends, is both a rhetorical and pragmatic enterprise, and "in the purpose and act of criticism . . . we fully realize the power of genre" (49). Finally, Miller (1984) maintains that "what we learn when we learn a genre is not just a pattern of forms or even a method of achieving our own ends. We learn, more importantly, what ends we may have" (165). In this way, generic criticism affords insights not only into the text under analysis but into the entire critical process as well. The limited scholarly discussion of stand-up comedy usually either assumes that the genre has been adequately defined or provides a sketchy description of some of its features. The following section seeks to fill this gap in the existing literature.

Stand-Up Comedy as Genre

The Evolution of Stand-Up Comedy

As mentioned in chapter 1, stand-up comics are the contemporary analogues of fools—marginalized individuals who perform social critique with impunity. The tradition of professional fools, which dates back to ancient Greek and Egyptian civilizations and flowered in the persona of the medieval court jester, ultimately spawned the contemporary stand-up comic. Although other comic figures such as that of the primal protean trickster of world literature and oral traditions (Abrahams 1968; Apte 1985; Jung 1959; Sheppard 1983), the hapless schlemiel of Yiddish folklore and Jewish humor (Wisse 1971), and the clown of physical comedy (Swortzell 1978; Welsford 1935) clearly influenced the development of contemporary comics, it is primarily the persona of the "wise" or "sage" fool that provides the template upon which future comic generations were built.

When we think of the fool, it is usually in the traditional medieval garb of eared cap and bells. But the fool was not born in this apparel; the court fool or jester dates back to the second century A.D. when buffoons and "parasites" crashed royal feasts in Greece. Although some buffoons were mere scamps in search of a free meal, others were actually professional laughmakers, exploitative rogues who played comic tricks on people and rushed to the nearest court to tell their tales (Welsford 1935), not unlike comics who play "road" clubs across the country today. Even the word *comedian* has its root in the Greek *komoidos,* a sort of MC who presided over the *komos* festival[1] (Wilde 1968, 8). Aristotle discussed buffoons, and the rhapsodes recited lines about Thersites, an early fool who appears in *The Iliad* (and later in Shakespeare's *Troilus and Cressida*) (Goldsmith 1955, 72).

After the fall of Rome, the buffoon disappeared but regained prominence in Italy during the late Middle Ages and the Renaissance. With the transformation from buffoon to fool came increased prestige, as medieval fools acquired kings and even a pope for patrons. Meanwhile, the "mythical" fool had appeared in Arabic, German, and English literature. "Natural" fools, often the physically deformed or dwarfs, were kept at court as lucky mascots (a tradition that Welsford traces back to fifth dynasty Egypt as well as ancient Rome); "festival" fools were used as scapegoats (Welsford 1935, 74). Author of the classic work on fools, *The Fool: His Social and Literary History,* Enid Welsford points out that the court fool was sometimes a close relation of the court poet, "himself, a descendant of the inspired seer" (79). Although medieval court jesters were often "wits," highly regarded and handsomely paid, "natural" fools, usually of low origin, were treated as pets, occasionally exchanged among Italian aristocrats. In the sixteenth and seventeenth centuries, "wise" or "sage" fools flourished and profited. As Welsford notes, the "profession of folly seems to have been sufficiently profitable to attract persons of superior education" (165). The eighteenth century, however, saw the decline of the English fool (though "fool societies" thrived in France and Germany) and the continuation of another tradition—that of the clown (it should be noted that some scholars use the terms "fool" and "clown" interchangeably).

Originating, of course, in ancient Greece, clowns became indistinguishable from jugglers, minstrels, and the like during the Dark Ages and did not reemerge as professional actors until the Middle Ages.

From the commedia dell'arte's Harlequin and Pulcinella and France's Pierrot to the legendary antics of Joseph Grimaldi in the nineteenth century, clowns provoked, delighted and touched audiences on the world's stage (Welsford 1935, 323–24). The eighteenth century also produced a prototype for the vaudeville houses of nineteenth-century America: Introduced by a funny MC, "penny gaff" comedy sketches in England gave way to the British music hall and ultimately influenced burlesque and early American minstrel shows (Franklin 1979). Benjamin Keith popularized the word "vaudeville" in America in the mid-1880s. Female performers, who had been onstage since the 1860s as chorus line members, were becoming part of male/female comedy duos by 1870. This development attracted female patronage—an occurrence called the "most important moment in the development of the theatre" (Martin and Segrave 1986, 29).

Vaudeville and Broadway follies introduced such memorable names as Jolson, Cantor, Fields, Crabtree, Dressler, and Brice as well as teams like Harrigan and Hart. Silent film stars Lloyd, Keaton, and Chaplin became America's clowns. After the collapse of Wall Street and the death of vaudeville, the "Borscht Belt" chain of Catskill resorts became a stable for such talents as Adams, Kaye, Buttons, and Berle. Known as "toomlers" (from "tumult makers" designated to "stir up" guests), these performers paved the way for generations of (specifically Jewish) comics to come. By the end of the 1930s, burlesque shows were replaced by nightclub comedy; bohemian sectors like Greenwich Village opened what were to become legendary coffeehouses—the prototype of contemporary comedy clubs. Thus began the tradition we know today as stand-up comedy (Franklin 1979, 13–19).

Undoubtedly, the art of contemporary stand-up comedy is an amalgam of various traditions. The most important and readily apparent, however, is that of the wise or sage fool. As previously mentioned, the wise fool enjoyed high status both as medieval court jester and resident Renaissance wit. Far from being merely a simple stooge or butt of others' ridicule, the wise fool was an extremely powerful critic whose words often carried enormous weight. Like contemporary comics "playing" a crowd, wise fools typically used comedy as a leveler, bringing "the mighty" down to the fool's level. Commonly associated (as they still are) with fertility, satire, and making merry, wise fools were versatile entertainers, childlike in their love of play and able to be both wit and stooge, depending on situational demands (McMullen 1970). The wise fool's position is neatly summed up as follows: "as satirist the fool forces society to make a critical re-appraisal of itself, but as entertainer he relieves the tension accompanying this uncomfortable experience through laughter" (19).

Throughout an impressive career, the wise fool has fulfilled a variety of functions. Among them was the exceedingly popular mock sermon, a favorite with audiences who appreciated the relationship between folly and religion (Villanueva 1982). Breaking distinctions between wisdom and folly, the fool served as an "educator who drew out the latent folly of his audience" (Welsford 1935, 27–28). As the "Lord of Misrule" (a tradition that originated in pagan Rome), fools were literally given not only "free rein" but "free reign" within circumscribed activities. As Welsford explains, during the twelfth-century "feast of fools," the clergy's "emphasis on the idea of temporary misrule and tolerated folly must have helped to develop the medieval idea of the fool as licensed critic of society" (204). Indeed, it was precisely the intellectualization of folly that made the fool's license a privilege (218). As Shakespeare's Viola says of Feste in *As You Like It*, "This fellow's wise enough to play the fool" (quoted in Welsford, 254).

Indeed, the wise fool is more accurately described as a "foolmaker" (Klapp 1962, 89) because of the social critique beneath even the most blatant self-disparagement. Even the famous costume so amusing to the upper echelon of court society was a parody of that very society—a mockery of the garrishness and frivolity of court fashion (Goldsmith 1955, 5). As a marginalized figure, the wise fool subverted the status quo through wry commentary on societal values and mores. It was, in fact, the loss of marginal status that accounted for the wise fool's decline in the eighteenth century (Zijderveld 1982). The wise fool is alive and well, however, in the persona of numerous contemporary stand-up comics. As Klapp (1962) observes, institutionalized clowning is well developed in all major cultures (69). And Swortzell (1978) notes that "the clown's role as commentator and social critic persists today" (8–9). The trick, it seems, is for professional fools to be institutionalized to an extent (enough to be licensed social critics whose performances are officially sanctioned) but not so much as to negate their marginal status.

Throughout history, wise fools—both male and female—have thrived in domestic, political, and academic spheres (a medieval German fool was even appointed professor of poetry at the University of Wittenberg), providing entertainment and education to all. In the late 1920s, the traditional "clown" became a "comedian" (Swortzell 1978). As licensed social critics, comedians retained vestiges of their jester past. Scholars have long acknowledged this link; for instance, Will Rogers's popularity with U.S. presidents "prompted one critic to imagine Rogers as a modern court jester, an honored guest at the White House whose persistent satirical attacks helped popularize the President's New Deal policies" (147). The Marx Brothers have been viewed similarly as: "during the Depression these court jesters, attacking the Establishment in all its weaknesses, spoke to and for the frustrated, embattled American, reminding him that his survival depended on independence of mind, defiant enterprise, and above all, irreverence of spirit" (194).

Considered by many the "driving force behind the shift from schpritz to reality" (Borns 1987, 238), Lenny Bruce is generally viewed as a catalyst in the genre of stand-up comedy. More than any other performer, Bruce is responsible for resurrecting the wise fool persona and establishing the sociopolitical humor often performed by comics today. Before Bruce's emergence in the 1950s, audiences focused on a comic's *act*. After Bruce, the rhetorical focus of stand-up comedy shifted from act to *performer*. Aggressively antiestablishment, Bruce's persona appeared consistent onstage and off. He was acerbic, angry, and unique. Quite simply, no one else could perform Lenny Bruce's act. Although few comics working today risk the strident, controversial persona of Lenny Bruce (the notable exceptions are comics like Andrew "Dice" Clay and Judy Tenuta, neither of whom has ever been incarcerated for their work), most comics, whether or not they are conscious of his legacy, are able to do what they do because of Bruce.[2]

In the late 1950s and early 1960s, other distinct comic personalities emerged—Phyllis Diller, Dick Gregory, Robert Klein, and Joan Rivers, to name a few. Both male and female contemporary stand-up comics such as Jerry Seinfeld and Roseanne acknowledge the influence of earlier talents like Diller and Klein.

Whether or not they are aware of the historical tradition of the fool, most comics working in America today retain vestiges of the wise fool in their daily lives. Like their foolish predecessors, comics still "sleep among the spaniels" (Armin, cited in Zijderveld, 1982, 186).[3] Unless they attain headliner stature, the pay is incredibly low—they *lose* money playing or attempting to play showcase clubs in major cities; they invariably must hold day jobs; and conditions on the road are fairly squalid, often consisting of fast food and lodging in the notorious "comedy condos" owned by many clubs. Finally, their audience serves as absolute monarch—for it is the nightly crowds that determine comics' survival. More likely than the court fool to attack institutions, the contemporary comic is still a *reflector* rather than a *reformer* (Midwinter 1979, 15). Although they are able to reach a much wider audience due to electronic media, the vast majority of largely unknown stand-up comics today depend on the same thing that fools did for success and survival—audience laughter.

Certainly, the clown, fool, and trickster all have contemporary analogues—sometimes within the persona of a single comic (for example, Bruce or Roseanne). From the "clowns" of physical comedy or slapstick like Lucille Ball, Dick Van Dyke and, more recently, Carol Burnett, Chevy Chase, Steve Martin, and Jim Carey, to "trickster" comic personalities like Clay and Tenuta who revel in internal chaos, to "something less sinister and more socially comfortable" (Gifford 1979, 35), the "fool" performances of talents such as Elayne Boosler, Carol Leifer, Jerry Seinfeld, and others presenting ironic commentary on external realities, contemporary comics are walking manifestations of their long and varied history. As noted earlier, contemporary stand-up comics are often a fusion of several traditions. They are able to play multiple roles and "deceive" with jokes, yet they illuminate truths through satirical attacks. They are champions of postmodern angst, yet they play the buffoon, mock themselves, and deftly show us our imperfections. Above all, they retain many of the characteristics of the wise fool: "He had the gayety of the jongleur, the candor of the ancient poets and philosophers, and the ironical perception of a Socrates. He sometimes combined a shrewd, proverbial wit with the more than earthly wisdom of the Erasmian fool" (Goldsmith 1955, vii).

Some major players in the current comic arena acknowledge this legacy. For example, Ben Karlin, head writer for *The Daily Show,* notes: "You almost have to be left-of-center to be a comedy writer. . . . I've never met anybody who wasn't. I mean go back to the jester. Obviously, in this society, the conservative political mind-set is king" (cited in Sella 2000, 78). Ironically, for all of their subversive effect, some comics themselves may be seen as performing a "conservative" function. As Letterman staff writer Gerry Mulligan suggests, "Historically, if you think about it, comedians' behavior has been conservative ... they point out anything that isn't normal. They say, 'Look at that guy's lime-green pants!' They make fun of silly new dances" (cited in Sella 2000, 80). Whether perceived as conservative or subversive, the discourse of contemporary comics is a current incarnation of an ancient form. After discussing the historical development of the stand-up comic persona, we can now consider the development of the form itself.

The Lyceum Contribution

Although vaudeville is generally considered the origin of contemporary stand-up comedy (Borns 1987; Franklin 1979; Martin and Segrave 1986), McManus (1976) offers an additional perspective: the lyceum.[4] In his discussion of nineteenth-century platform humorists Charles Brown ("Artemus Ward"), David Locke ("Petroleum V. Nasby"), and Henry Shaw ("Josh Billings"), McManus suggests that these showmen "changed the lyceum, completing its shift from education to entertainment" (151). McManus points out that the original lyceum lectures on technology expanded to include a variety of topics, becoming "a major social and cultural institution in the northern states, especially New England" (141), but that it was the introduction of platform humorists that forever changed the face of the lyceum stage. Maintaining that it was the nineteenth-century "literary comedians" like Brown, Locke, and Shaw who "developed an original American art form, solo concert comedy" (135), McManus explains that prior to these performances on the lyceum circuit (1861), "No single [American] performer had developed and then become exclusively identified with a unique, comic persona" (139–40).

It was by combining the burlesque traditions of the American theater with the lyceum platform, McManus asserts, that performers developed the "in one" persona—unique by virtue of being both non-stereotypical and non-reproducible—that would become a standard in American "concert comedy" (151). Although the platform humorists he discusses performed personas that were quite obviously "characters," McManus contends that they were characters unique to these particular performers. In this way, platform humorists can be seen as influences on later generations of "character" comics, like "Bobcat" Goldthwait, the late Sam Kinison, and Judy Tenuta, whose "petite flower, giver-goddess" stage persona is unique and very different from her offstage self. The difference between an "in one" persona and that of Lenny Bruce is the link between performer and performance; audiences perceived Bruce to be the same person onstage and off. Indeed, it was this congruence between "real" and "stage" selves that made Bruce a comic catalyst. Although McManus notes that within the "in one" tradition, "The persona of the performer and personality of the creating artist are inextricably connected" (152), the difference between practitioners of the "in one" comic tradition and comic descendants of Bruce is one of seamlessness (or perhaps, "seemlessness," for the onstage persona literally seems less different from the offstage persona—that is, more autobiographical—than do those in other comic traditions).

When I was performing stand-up comedy in New York in the mid-1980s, I was told several times by Comedy Club owners that I had too happy a childhood to be a stand-up comic. What they meant was that I was not foregrounding the trendy, angst-driven humor that characterized the acts of so many of my comedic colleagues. In essence, I was being told that I was not performing enough autobiography. And yet, even amid the topical musings and witty one-liners, I was engaged in autobiographical performance. Like any comic, I was performing a version of myself that suited the audience and the occasion. What was it that made club owners perceive the performance of personal pain and anger as more "authentic" than the performance of humorous anecdotes about family members?

Performing autobiography is, in one sense, something we all do every day. When creating a staged, public autobiographical performance, however, we select bits and pieces of ourselves to share with an audience. In the genre of stand-up comedy, performers present a pastiche of observations and characters both real and imagined. At bottom, however, is the autobiographical self—a multifaceted, protean entity that encompasses both onstage and offstage personae. And unlike other autobiographical performance, stand-up comics simultaneously perform self and culture, offering an often acerbic social critique sanctioned as entertainment because it is articulated in a comedic context. Part autobiography, part education, part entertainment—

lyceum performances clearly share some characteristics with contemporary stand-up comedy. McManus suggests that features of "concert comedy" such as funny stories, political satire, and one-liners originated in lyceum performance—however, it is important to remember that McManus refers exclusively to American traditions. As discussed at length earlier in this chapter, the genre of stand-up comedy clearly has roots dating back much farther than nineteenth-century America.

The Origins of the Comedy Club

Martin and Segrave (1986) link the development of American comedy to that of mass entertainment from roughly 1830 to 1860. Because of the transportation revolution brought about by the advent of train travel, Martin and Segrave maintain, entertainment could reach a wide audience. The audiences for the earliest variety shows were men in towns all over the country without much money to spend; consequently, entertainment at this time had to be inexpensive and portable. Traveling comedy variety shows were ideally suited to this purpose. After 1865, these variety shows were "cleaned up" and the audience broadened to include women (29).

As discussed earlier, after the decline of vaudeville, burlesque, and Broadway follies, solo comic performance ultimately found an audience in the intimate environs of the coffeehouse. The first venue devoted entirely to stand-up comedy was Pip's Comedy Club in Brooklyn, which opened its doors in 1962 and eventually spawned comic talents like Robert Klein and David Brenner.[5] In 1963, Budd and Silver Friedman opened the now-famous Improvisation (or Improv) in Manhattan. In 1972, The Comedy Store opened in Los Angeles. In 1975 and 1976, two other major clubs—Catch a Rising Star and The Comic Strip—opened in Manhattan. And in 1975, after his divorce from Silver, Budd Friedman opened The Comedy Store's main competition, the L.A. Improv (Borns 1987). According to Gallo (1991): "in the '70s there were only a handful of notable showcase clubs on either coast and just a few more in the middle of the country. But by 1983 . . . there were some 50 to 75 full-time, bona fide comedy clubs in the nation—a number that grew to 200 by 1985 and increased to more than 300 by the end of the decade" (1).

Indeed, as the "rock-n-roll of the 80s," comedy burgeoned. Not only did clubs proliferate nationwide, but cable TV launched a series of specials featuring established comics like Elayne Boosler, Billy Crystal, Carol Leifer, and Robin Williams on HBO and Showtime. Soon cable offered programs like MTV's *Half-Hour Comedy Hour* and VH-1's *Stand-Up Spotlight* featuring "new" comics as well as programs featuring showcase clubs like A&E's *Live at the Improv* and *Caroline's Comedy Hour.* In 1989, HBO premiered the Comedy Channel; in 1990, MTV followed suit with HA! The TV Comedy Network. Finally, in 1991, the two merged into Comedy Central, a channel that continues to feature numerous stand-up specials, clips, and information about comics' tours along with talk shows and other programs hosted by stand-up comics (Gallo 1991, 2).

When, exactly, did the "comedy boom" begin? Budd Friedman "dates the start . . . to '82, and like everyone else—*Saturday Night Live, Late Night,* HBO—he takes credit for it" (Weiss 1988, 59). Borns (1987) explains that the "single greatest impact upon stand-up comedy" has been television. Observing that "this phenomenon . . . must be examined in two parts—B.C. (Before Cable) and A.D. (Anno Davido) [Latin for "Year of David Letterman"]" (45), Borns notes that before cable, comics' televised performances were no longer than five minutes, but that "Then, in the mid 70s, came cable, and with it, the need for low-cost, easy-to-produce entertainment. Stand-up comedy fit the bill; it came fully assembled, with writer, star and supporting cast included" (45). From 1975, Borns explains, comics began to appear on HBO specials, and thus began the national exposure that ultimately helped make stand-up a household word. As veteran comic Tom Parks notes: "In 1974 and 1975, it was the Improv and Catch in New York and the Comedy Store in L.A. and that was it; there were no comedy clubs. If you were in Birmingham, Alabama, and said, 'stand-up comedy,' people would think, 'Bob Hope' . . . that was all they knew. It took cable to expose America to comedy as an art form—and they sure went for it" (quoted in Borns 1987, 47).

One thing is certain: Stand-up comedy today is big business. Showcase clubs like the Improv and Catch a Rising Star now have successful franchises in several major cities.[6] These clubs charge patrons a cover and two-drink minimum, showcase both new and veteran comics—usually ten to fifteen a night, each usually performing a set of twelve to twenty minutes—and pay them only cab fare. The road clubs, on the other hand, can be found in virtually every sizable town across the country; these clubs—whether part of a chain like Zanies, Punchline, or Funny Bone or a single club like Charlie Goodnight's—feature an "opener" or MC (often a local comic) who performs for about fifteen minutes, an experienced, out-of-town "middle" or "feature" act who performs for approximately thirty minutes, and a known headliner (preferably with national TV appearances to his or her credit) who performs for about an hour.

Many comic celebrities began their careers in the road club proving ground. For example, in 1985, when I was performing five-minute sets at one of the premier road clubs in the Southeast, Charlie Goodnight's in Raleigh, North Carolina, I was fortunate to work on a night when Rosie O'Donnell was headlining. This was well before she became established in her career (she had won the grand prize on the show *Star Search,* hosted by Ed McMahon—an accomplishment that launched her headline status in the comic community), yet she offered some excellent advice that served me well: "Never ask the audience a question if you don't already know the answer." Ultimately, I became an opening act at Charlie Goodnight's—an opportunity that allowed me to meet comics Cathy Ladman, Judy Tenuta, and others, all of whom were extremely helpful in providing guidance to a fledgling career.[7]

Both showcase and road clubs often provide shows every night of the week, with road clubs featuring up to three shows on Saturday nights. Clubs have very little overhead, generally charge a cover of fifteen to twenty dollars and a two-drink minimum and, in the case of road clubs, often provide lodging for comics in a club-owned condo. As noted earlier by Borns, comics are cheap labor. They require only a stage and a microphone and work for relatively low pay. Because in the last several years the "comedy boom" has become the "comedy glut" as aspiring comics compete for spots in clubs and on cable and network TV, comics will undoubtedly continue to perform, regardless of wages. All over the country, audiences are laughing. And club owners are laughing all the way to the bank.[8]

Generic Features and Constraints of Stand-Up Comedy

Like all genres, stand-up comedy possesses a number of distinguishing features. First and foremost, stand-up is a solo art. The comic works "without a net," relying only on her- or himself to "cover" mistakes.

The comic performs (ostensibly) original material in monologue form. Despite the form, however, comic Jerry Seinfeld maintains:

> Comedy is a dialogue, not a monologue—that's what makes an act click. The laughter becomes the audience's part, and the comedian responds; it's give and take. When the comic ad-libs or deals with a heckler, it gets explosive response because it's like, "Hey, this is happening now! This isn't just some pre-planned act." So whatever lends itself to that feeling is what makes comedy work—that live feeling. That's why comics ask, "Where are you from?" It brings a present moment to the show. (cited in Borns 1987, 16)

Seinfeld mentions several other generic features of stand-up comedy—specifically, its element of spontaneity and its dependence on audience interaction (the two are, of course, inseparable).

Because of these features, stand-up comedy is a self-correcting genre. If a joke is not "working," a comic can revise or delete it onstage. As Borns (1987) explains: "Comics today are actually able to do their writing onstage. They can concentrate more on details, like word combinations, inflection and placement by hearing an audience's initial reaction to a joke, studying it and repeating the process night after night until it gets its maximum reaction" (244). Indeed, stand-up comedy is unique in that a "rehearsal" may become a performance onstage, before a live audience, as each new audience's response helps the comic create humor.

Comics must be highly adaptive. They must be able to deviate from their "set" material in order to comment on audience participation or lack thereof, as well as any interruption occurring in the room (because clubs serve drinks, it is not uncommon to hear the clatter of a tray falling to the ground followed by a standard comic response, "Oh—you can just put that anywhere."). Some comics even capitalize on interruptions; Paula Poundstone, for example, delivers a running commentary on audience members' bathroom breaks as an integral part of her act. Indeed, audience interruption is itself a feature of stand-up comedy. Audience response is a barometer for the comic. Audience members' playful participation is the sign of a "healthy" act. It is precisely when comics are not getting a response that they become nervous and may even resort to questions of the "Is this an audience or an oil painting?" variety. Of course, no response at all may be preferable to a hostile heckler. Often inebriated, this type of "participant" is loud, threatening, and relentless. At times, such a person will be forcefully ejected from the club, but often only after doing considerable—sometimes irreparable—damage to a comic's act.

Generally, however, heckling is done in a spirit of fun. And heckling is a feature unique to the genre of stand-up comedy, in that it is expected and even at times encouraged. As Borns (1987) notes: "If you're not satisfied with the proceedings of a movie or play, you can either keep quiet and smile—or leave. If you're not happy with a stand-up comic's act, you can always yell, 'Hey, what the hell are you talking about?' and, most likely, you'll get an answer" (25).

The trick for the comic is, of course, to get the last laugh. Although the comic has the microphone with all the rhetorical and technical power it wields, once a heckler "steals the show" by rallying the rest of the audience to his or her cause, it is virtually impossible for a comic to regain control.[9]

Another feature of stand-up comedy is its brevity. As mentioned earlier, it is only as a headliner or the star of a cable special that a comic performs an hour of material. Comics essentially have a comedic wardrobe of sets varying in length from five to sixty minutes. On any given night, a comic can open the comedy closet, select an eight-, twelve-, or twenty-minute set, and perform. Time limits are essential for logistical purposes—showcase clubs have a certain number of acts to get through every night, and television, especially network, functions within rigid temporal parameters. To ensure that a comic will "get off" (the stage) within a set time limit, comedy clubs use a red light visible only to the comic as a signal that time is up. If the light is ignored, it will be flashed so that the comic cannot miss the signal. If all else fails, the MC will generally intervene. Comics who exceed time limits are scorned by club management and other comics alike.[10]

The technical, physical features of stand-up comedy are simple. The comic generally performs on a small, bare stage (many showcase clubs use a faux brick wall as background) with a microphone that may be used either in or out of its stand. The comic is usually quite close to the audience, typically within ten to fifteen feet of the first row (depending, of course, on the size of the particular venue). This lack of "aesthetic distance" is one of the features that makes stand-up a highly risky art; the comic is alone onstage, quite literally vulnerable to all manner of attack.

Although comics' acts vary considerably (even throughout a single career—for example, George Carlin), certain features of comic material are standard. Some comics tell stories. Some comics tell jokes. Some comics use props (they are literally called "prop comics"). Some do impersonations. Some sing funny songs. But the "pure" stand-up comic relies mainly on original thought and audience response, period. Perhaps the only characteristic common to all comics' acts is the use of punchlines. As Chris Albrecht, an executive at HBO, explains, "There's a certain rhythm comics use (da-dum-da-dum . . . boom!), and because they've heard it so often, audiences know they're supposed to laugh at that rhythm—so they do" (cited in Borns 1987, 42).[11] Indeed, timing is essential to stand-up comedy. As Holland (1982) observes when discussing "play" and "timing" as necessary conditions for laughter, "A tragedy is just a comedy slowed down" (32).

Several of these features of stand-up comedy also serve as constraints within the genre. Technical and formal constraints include the solo nature of the act, proximity to the audience, original, memorized material, ability to adapt spontaneously to audience response and interruptions throughout the act, and set time limits. Comics also typically perform at night—sometimes quite late. Both comic and audience may be tired, and the audience is usually drinking alcohol to boot. Comics must be able to adapt the pace and intensity of their acts accordingly.[12] The biggest constraint of all, however, is that the comic must be funny. By whatever means necessary—finely crafted material, an engaging stage persona, adroit handling of audience participation, spontaneously generated humor—in order to be successful, a comic must be deemed funny by the audience. John Limon (2000) offers three theorems of stand-up comedy relevant to any discussion of generic features/constraints: "If you think something is funny, then it is. A joke is funny if and only if you laugh at it. And the only end of standup is to make people laugh." Limon further explains: "What those theorems make clear is that an audience has a definitive role in regard to a standup act that no other audience at an art performance has" (5).[13]

Stand-up comedy has content or political constraints as well. Every culture and every audience has its sacred cows. The comic must be able to gauge just how far is too far to push the envelope on any given night. Some comics consider any topic fair game. As veteran George Carlin notes, "I have no emotional attachment to the culture; it frees me to

57

hold everything up to ridicule" (cited in Campbell 1999). Comics are often expected to be offensive. They frequently perform material that may be considered racist, sexist, homophobic, ageist, sizeist—potentially every "ist" that exists. As Schutz observes, "whatever the esthetic and moral judgement of them, ethnic jokes, comic insults, and dirty jokes are the popular humor of America" (cited in Gruner 1997, 76).

Indeed, comics' frequent use of stereotypes ensures that they will offend or at least generate controversy. Are stereotypes always oppressive, or might they serve as a means of transgression—a way to call attention to the ludicrous and unfair nature of many dominant cultural practices? Gruner (1997) asserts that "if one truly despised a particular ethnic group, ridicule would be the least deadly weapon available to operationalize that hatred. . . . Stereotype is merely a very handy kind of shorthand to provide the essential framework for understanding the content of a joke" (99).

Spencer, on the other hand, argues that in some cases (such as the notorious Jewish American Princess or "JAP" jokes), "Humor . . . serves as the primary mechanism for labeling, stereotyping, and communicating prejudice" (cited in Gruner 1997, 103). Still, Cohen (1999) asks us to consider the possibility that "mean jokes" might be beneficial, that "Perhaps they help us to bear unbearable affronts like crude racism and stubborn prejudice by letting us laugh while we take a breather" (84). Do comics' use of stereotypes expose prejudice or merely perpetuate it? This issue continues to be debated among scholars and audience members alike (and is considered in greater detail in chapter 5).

Regardless of her or his own ideological predisposition, however, in order to succeed, a comic must know which topics are "off limits" in general as well as with each new audience. The audience expects the comic to violate expectations. In this sense, the violation of expectations may itself be considered a generic constraint (and, of course, if violation is expected, it is not actually violation but simply fulfillment of expectation).

Finally, hecklers provide a major generic constraint for stand-up comedy. Just as audiences expect comics to violate expectations, comics expect audiences to interrupt (and just as with the comic's expected "violation," in this sense, the interruption itself—because it is expected or at least anticipated—may be considered not so much an interruption as part of the act). Schechner asserts that "persuading spectators to participate gives a performance status of ritual by transforming them into a community, and is thus a political act demanding or representing and so indeed automatically achieving radical changes in the social order" (cited in Innes 1981, 182). Within the genre of stand-up comedy, the ritual of heckling and squelching functions as a rhetorical gambit—a constraint that, if deftly utilized, enables the comic to preside over the temporary social order of the club community.[14]

Considered as a constellation, the various generic constraints discussed above all function to make stand-up comedy a unique and risk-filled genre of popular culture art/entertainment. In order to explore power relations within this genre, it is useful to examine the similarities between stand-up comedy and "carnival."

Stand-Up Comedy as Carnival

Both carnival and stand-up comedy are associated with sexuality and sensual pleasure. In fact, in their frenetic rhythms, explosion of sweat, sound, and ultimate gratification, both can be metaphorically represented as cultural orgasm. Barreca (1988) maintains that as a genre, comedy has traditionally been concerned with "celebration of fertility and regeneration; comedy as the vulgar and exaggerated presentation of the familiar . . . as catharsis of desire and frustration . . . as social safety valve . . . as carnival . . . as unconscious, psychological reaction to personal and social instabilities . . . as happy ending, joyous celebration, and reestablishment of order" (8). Indeed, comedy has long been inextricably linked to carnival and the temporary chaos that context entails.

Discussing and building on Bakhtin's notion of carnival, Stallybrass and White (1986) explain that in carnival, social norms are subverted, that, in Bakhtin's words, "carnival celebrates temporary liberation from the prevailing truth of the established order; it marks the suspension of all hierarchical rank, privileges, norms and prohibitions" (7). During carnival, Stallybrass and White contend, "Symbolic polarities of high and low, official and popular, grotesque and classical are mutually constructed and deformed" (16). It is precisely this topsy-turvy context that is recreated in contemporary comedy clubs. In a comedy club, the marginal (grotesque, real, and sensual) subverts the hegemonic (classical idealized forms), creating a new order from disorder. It is not surprising that comics often discuss sensual, even scatological experience, allowing the audience to participate vicariously. Just as the revelers in carnival, the marginal comic subverts the status quo by lampooning and hybridizing or mixing binary opposites such as "high" and "low" culture.

The three symbolic processes discussed by Stallybrass and White—demonization, inversion, and hybridization—can all be seen in the context of contemporary American stand-up comedy. Roseanne (1987), for example, uses all three in her act when she claims that men read maps better than women "because only the male mind could conceive of one inch equaling a hundred miles." Insulting men (demonization) and speaking from the rhetorically powerful position of being onstage with a microphone (inversion), Roseanne hybridizes the standard male "dick joke" with her own acerbic critique. And, as Auslander (1993) illustrates, Roseanne's 1987 HBO special can itself be seen as an example of hybridization as resistance to patriarchal norms. Resistance to these (primary) norms can be dangerous because, according to Little (1983), "Such norms are the order that we expect to return to after the festive disorder" (10). Describing the comedy of women as "liminal," Little explains that it is potentially threatening to the social order. She further notes that "Liminality is the most ambiguous, the most potentially anarchic phase of ritual" but that "it is also the most creative" (6).

The comedy club, like carnival (or, in Stallybrass and White's discussion, the fair or marketplace as well) is a "site of pleasure . . . local, festive, communal, unconnected to the 'real' world" and, like carnival, commercial as "a practical agency in the progress of capital" (Stallybrass and White 1986, 30). Finally, like carnival, the comedy club is officially sanctioned disorder. As Stallybrass and White note, kings and queens were actually crowned during carnival. Today, presidents are inaugurated while comics lampoon them in clubs. In this way, citizens now, as during carnival, are "allowed" to have fun while the status quo is perpetuated and social control is maintained by the "official culture" (13). Hence, no truly political subversion occurs. As Little (1983) maintains, "ritualistic or festive suspension of usual roles and rules is, on most occasions, an ultimate affirmation of the ordered world" (14). Certainly, contemporary comedy clubs function as "practical agencies in the progress of capital." Dollars are exchanged for laughs and everyone walks away happy. Stallybrass and White observe that "carnival was the repeated, periodic celebration of the grotesque body—fattening food, intoxicating drink, sexual promiscuity, altered ego-identity" (189). Similarly, Borns (1987) notes: "The comedy club, as it exists today . . . is an establishment dedicated to the making of money, the creation of art, the furthering of alcohol consumption and the performing of both humorous insights and filthy smut—often by the same person" (1). Clearly, carnival is alive and well in the contemporary comedy club.

The "inappropriate" behavior of stand-up comics is a breach of social norms. Of course, the norms must first be established in order to be subverted. As Bakhtin's model of carnival suggests, the high/low binary is essential to culture—one cannot exist without the other (Stallybrass and White 1986, 16). Boal (1985) explains that, at its origins, "'Theater' was the people singing freely in the open air; the theatrical performance was created by and for the people. . . . It was a celebration in which all could participate freely. Then came the aristocracy and established divisions; some persons will go to the stage and only they will be able to act; the rest will remain seated, receptive, passive—these will be the spectators, the masses, the people" (ix–x).

Carnival turns this notion upside down as "the people" perform and lampoon the dominant culture in the process. In contemporary comedy clubs, the spectators can participate directly in the performance at any juncture. Additionally, although the comic is clearly in the rhetorically powerful position, today more than ever before the comic is most likely "of the people," rather than part of the hegemonic culture.

Ultimately, just as during carnival, in a comedy club, "active reinforcement" occurs as categories opposite to those normally enforced are staged (Stallybrass and White 1986, 189). Audiences can enjoy—even participate in—discussion of taboo topics, engage in excessive drinking, smoking, and eating of "forbidden" foods, and all the while, perhaps unwittingly, help to ensure that the social order is maintained—that, in fact, the hegemonic coffers are filled. How does the performance of marginality contribute to maintaining the status quo? How might female comics in particular be complicit in this process? To answer these questions, we must ask whether there exists a distinct subgenre of "female," specifically "feminist" stand-up comedy.

Female/Feminist Stand-Up Comedy: A Possibility?

Before examining the "evidence" for "female" and/or "feminist" stand-up comedy, we must question the assumption upon which this "evidence" is based—the belief that men and women speak different languages. Since Robin Lakoff's landmark (1975) work on male and female speaking styles, *Language and Woman's Place,* a growing number of studies on the sociolinguistic nature of gender suggest that men and women speak different dialects if not completely different languages (not to mention come from two different planets!), and that the major distinction between male and female speech behavior is the powerlessness of women's speech—a feature for which women are thought to be responsible. Robert Hopper (1992) points out that this "genderlect hypothesis" can be problematic because in subscribing to it, "Most of us . . . have confused stereotypes with evidence" (3). Hopper further explains that research on courtroom language has shown that powerless speech is not exclusive to women but characteristic of inexperienced, unemployed, or low-status speakers of either gender (in the context of courtroom behavior). The resulting "powerless speech hypothesis," Hopper maintains, locates the cause of women's powerless speech in "sexist social practices" rather than assigning the responsibility for "powerless" speech to the female speakers themselves (4).

Enumerating the "tangle of methodical difficulties" that plagues studies in this area—from excessive use of self-report to problems in measuring both independent and dependent variables of "powerless speech"—Hopper asserts: "A decade into this research we have achieved contradictory results and small effects" (5–6). After considering and testing the role of addressee in conversation, Hopper concludes that although powerless speech hypotheses merit further consideration, these issues must be distinguished from genderlect hypotheses because "There is virtually no evidence connecting the two" (14). Indeed, many contemporary communication scholars share Hopper's belief that research on the relationship between gender and communication is fraught with disagreement (Adler et al. 1998; Pearson, West, and Turner 1995; Stewart et al. 1996). Additionally, it is important to realize that whether research on gender and language has been quantitatively oriented, measuring speech particles (Hopper 1992) or has used a critical/interpretive approach (Gilligan 1982; Kramarae 1981)—whether it is found in scholarly journals or on the *New York Times* bestseller list (Gray 1992; Tannen 1990)—the work on female vs. male communication has focused on a *conversational* context.

"Women's Humor" and "Feminist Humor"

Scholarly discussion of gender differences in humor has focused on quantitative assessment of humor preferences (Brodzinsky, Barnett, and Aiello 1981; Butland and Ivy 1990; Cantor 1976; Chapman and Gadfield 1976; Love and Lambert 1989; Moore, Griffiths, and Payne 1987; Mundorf et al. 1988; Pearson, Miller, and Senter 1983; Zillman and Stocking 1976), naturally occurring instances of humor in conversation (Barreca 1991; Jenkins 1986; Kramarae 1981), and humorous writing by women (Dresner 1991a; Gagnier 1991; Levy 1997; Little 1991, 1983; Toth 1984; Walker 1991a, 1988). Very little research discusses gender differences specific to the genre of stand-up comedy; the limited studies in this area (for example, Barreca 1991; Walker 1988) seem to base assumptions on data from other contexts such as those mentioned above. A notable exception is Horowitz's 1997 book, *Queens of Comedy,* which explores women's comic performance, focusing on the work of Lucille Ball, Phyllis Diller, Carol Burnett, and Joan Rivers. Horowitz's extensive interviews with these and other comics along with her historical overview of female comic performance add much to the literature in this area, yet Horowitz herself offers no theoretical synthesis regarding gender and humor. This is hardly surprising when even investigations of gender differences in humor in a conversational context frequently offer conclusions that appear derived more from intuition than empirical data.

Discussing joking among women in a conversational context, for example, Jenkins (1986) asserts that "humor among women is different from humor among men and is consistent with women's predominant conversational style which is cooperative, inclusive, supportive, integrated, spontaneous, and self-healing" (135). Jenkins further contends: "For men the goal of conversation is to show yourself off to your best advantage. For women the goal is to achieve greater intimacy. . . . Men in their groups seem to be saying, 'I'm great. I'm great too. Gee, we're a great bunch of guys.' In contrast, women seem to be saying, 'Did this ever happen to you? Yeah. Oh, good, I'm not crazy'" (137). Claiming that women's sharing of and laughing at common gaffes is only negative in "the competitive atmosphere of men," Jenkins notes that women's ability to be "less than ideal selves" with each other facilitates bonding.

Jenkins's assumptions, though compelling, are unsupported. Maintaining that men's humor is more formulaic and performative and women's more context-bound, Jenkins asserts that feminists avoid using humor against (other) women.[15] Ultimately, Jenkins suggests that in both content and form, women and men's humor overlaps, and that "it is how they practice these forms that characteristically differs" (147). It is important to realize that Jenkins's arguments refer to humor in a conversational context. Indeed, like most discussions of male vs. female or feminist humor, scholarship on female vs. feminist humor is based on either women's humorous writing or conversational discourse. Clearly, the genre of stand-up comedy is highly particularized; any examination of female stand-up comics, therefore, must necessarily consider the features and constraints of this genre.

As mentioned earlier in this chapter, studies purporting to examine "women's humor" or even more specifically, "feminist humor" rarely delineate features or constraints of these putative genres. Often the label "women's humor" simply seems to mean "humor created by women." Discussing the historical male "accusation" of women's lack of sense of humor, Kramarae (1981) finds a male bias in discussion of women and humor and suggests that "it would be useful if researchers involved in the study of female/male interactions consider those interactions as the surface reflections of differing world views" (57). In other words, Kramarae argues that humor is not a function of some immutable biological reality but rather a socially constructed phenomenon. Noting that humor is culture-specific, Kramarae maintains that, as a "muted group" that must acknowledge and adhere to the worldview and conventions of the dominant group, women "have not developed as much a sense of group humor as men since the language and the models of joking available to them do not reflect their world models" (58).[16]

Clearly, gender, race/ethnicity, class, and sexual orientation are but a few of the factors that shape an individual's frame of reference. Hence, a woman might perceive a joke differently than might a man, just as a Jew might perceive a joke differently than might a gentile, and any member of a marginal group might perceive a joke differently than members of a dominant group. Does this mean that women have created a unique genre of humor? Does point of view constitute genre? Arguably, humor created by women—whether in speech or writing—differs from humor created by men. Through its mockery of social conventions, its laughter at patriarchal norms, women's humor can be seen as subversive (Barreca 1991; Finney 1994; Fraiberg 1994; Gagnier 1991; Horowitz 1997; Levy 1997; Little 1983; Walker 1991a, 1988). But this transgressive strategy is by no means unique to women; rather, it is characteristic of the humor of all marginal groups.

Horowitz (1997) describes male comedic style as aggressive and profane and female comedic style as humanistic. Comic Susie Essman (cited in Kaplan 2002a) maintains: "There's always been a certain mean streak in comedy, and women weren't always comfortable with their own aggression and meanness"; however, as Kaplan suggests, feminism empowered women to express this aggression through humor (3). Indeed, as is evident in the acts of contemporary comics such as Roseanne, Judy Tenuta, and others, generalizations about the "warm, fuzzy" nature of women's humor are often unfounded. Barreca (1991) argues that women's humor is engendered by the "laughter in the kitchen" in which women participate when creating and sharing humor among themselves. Maintaining that this experience is unique to women, Barreca paints a rosy picture of support, nurturing, and intimacy and predicts that "When we take the laughter out of the kitchen, we'll find that, like all the other good things that kitchen has yielded up over the years, it's nourishing and healthy—and that there's enough to go around" (121).

Barreca's rich and evocative metaphor can be easily applied to the in-group humor of other marginal groups (gays and lesbians, for example, who undoubtedly experience "laughter in the closet" within their own speech communities). So, too, can Gagnier's (1991) notion that "women's humor tends toward anarchy rather than the status quo" (934), because, in fact, so does the humor of *any* group exclusive of the status quo. The question is not whether women's humor is different from men's humor, but whether women's humor (and ultimately feminist humor) can be conceived as a definable and unique genre. Scholars have noted the link between women's humor and that of minority groups (Dresner 1991b; Walker 1991b), but to date, no discussion of a genre called "marginal humor" subsuming both categories has been offered. Rather, scholars have pointed out the difference between women and minority groups; because of frequent and sustained contact with the dominant culture, they suggest, women do not feel connected to other women as a group and so do not have the same consciousness of common oppression as do minorities (Sheppard 1991; Walker 1991b).

Unlike the categories called "Jewish humor" and "black humor," in which members of the group are often both creator and butt, however, the category of women's humor is usually discussed by critics as one that subverts by (directly or indirectly) calling cultural values into question. (In fact, humor created and/or performed by women in which they are the butt is generally viewed as antifeminist, even antifemale by critics—a phenomenon discussed at length in chapter 5.) Often cited in examinations of women's humor is McGhee's 1977 assertion: "Because of the power associated with the successful use of humor, humor initiation has become associated with other traditionally masculine characteristics, such as aggression, dominance, and assertiveness. For a female to develop into a clown or joker, then, she must violate the behavioral pattern normally reserved for women" (cited in Sheppard 1991, 41). It is precisely the labeling of behavioral characteristics as intrinsically "male" or "female" that confounds so many discussions of feminist humor (or anything "feminist," for that matter).

As psychologist Alice Sheppard (1991) asks, "Is the central locus of humor to be found in behavior, thought processes, or social interactions? Should its essence be posited as process, structure, or symbolic interaction?" (48) The answer to this question is key to determining the existence of a distinctly female or feminist humor. Offering a taxonomy of five types of women's humor (role-consistent, role-reversal, role-dilemma, role-transgressive, and role-transformative), Sheppard explains that whereas role-transgressive humor may be a case of women "simply redefining male social territory as their own," role-transformative humor is that which "most obviously and directly seeks to attack [traditional] gender roles" (47). It is only to illustrate this last type of humor that Sheppard uses the example of female stand-up comics.

These various perspectives on the nature of women's humor are confusing. Even more confusing is the assumed genre of feminist humor because, as discussed in chapter 1, the phrase combines two words that are used in a variety of—sometimes contradictory—ways both separately and together. Additionally, as Finney (1994) points out, the phrase "women's humor" has frequently been substituted for "feminist humor" by theorists who consider the ideological implications of the word "feminist" too risky. The result is an inaccurate label if the critics truly mean "feminist humor" (which may be created by humorists of both genders). Many definitions of feminist humor include the notion of strength and hope. Others are based on challenge and confrontation. Gindele (1994), for example, maintains that "Feminist comedy, aiming to liberate, stages the collapse of patriarchal desire to enable female and social desire" (140). Finney notes that "It has frequently been argued by theorists of women's comedy that men, as those traditionally in power, use humor to vent dissatisfaction but ultimately to preserve things as they are, whereas women use humor to shake things up" (9). And McWhirter (1994) suggests that even "women's laughter is inherently subversive, compatible with and perhaps even essential to feminist political struggle" (189).

All of the above scholars describe a humor that seeks not to insult or offend a specific male, but rather to unmoor the entire system of patriarchal oppression. Critics have called for women to produce their own "fighting humor" (Weisstein 1973, 90), to be "rebellious and self-affirming" (Merrill 1988, 271). Are *these* the defining features of feminist humor? And, even more problematic, what constitutes the so-called genre of feminist stand-up comedy? The existing scholarship on female/feminist stand-up comics is generally limited to case studies (Dresner 1991b; Horowitz 1997; Pershing 1991; Sochen 1991; Williams 1991) or brief mention in a larger discussion of feminist humor (Finney 1994; Merrill 1988; Walker 1991b) or stand-up comedy (Olson 1988). The paucity of research in this area is complicated—as is any genre called "feminist"—by its very label. Fraiberg (1994) calls for more research in this area, noting that "Stand-up becomes a matter of agency when cultural critics begin to account for what the laughs mean, where they are coming from, and who is included" (329).

By some standards, any woman who gets up to speak at any time is performing a "feminist" act. By this definition, all female stand-up comics are feminist. But what of those who target themselves or other women as the butts of their jokes? Are they still performing a feminist act? And most important, if stand-up comedy is, indeed, a male-defined and male-dominated genre and women performing in that genre must observe the same constraints as their male counterparts, does this force female comics to perform "male" behaviors, or does the problem lie in the labels—male, masculine, female, and feminine—so readily applied to all cultural phenomena? Is aggression inherently male? Inherently feminist? Both? Or is it simply a characteristic of stand-up comedy? Exploring these questions necessitates a closer look at what critics and comics alike mean by "male-defined."

Stand-Up Comedy as a "Male-Defined" Genre

Both critics and practitioners maintain that stand-up comedy is a male-defined genre (Auslander 1993; Pershing 1991; Weiss 1988), or, put a bit more crudely by Hoffman, "the quintessential old-boy network" (cited in Martin and Segrave 1986, 313). The current zeitgeist has been called postmodern, postfeminist, postcolonial . . . but certainly, it cannot be called "postdickjoke," as the "dick joke" is often used as a metaphor for the male-defined nature of stand-up comedy. Perhaps the most blatant representation of traditionally conceived "masculinity" in stand-up comedy, dick jokes range from scatological references to literal "crotch grabbing"—almost invariably guaranteeing an "easy" laugh. Indeed, it is the dick joke, above all, to which comics and critics alike refer when labeling stand-up a male-defined genre. Why do dick jokes remain popular? Because whether directly or indirectly, they are obscene—classic examples of the "tendentious humor" Freud described. Comics use what "works," and dick jokes are guaranteed to amuse audiences of both genders in a surprising variety of contexts. Simply put, dick jokes get the quickest and biggest laughs, and in stand-up comedy, size does matter.[17] As Freud (1960) observed, "A non-tendentious joke scarcely ever achieves the sudden burst of laughter which makes tendentious ones so irresistible" (95). Influenced by Freud and other relief-arousal theorists, some critics believe that dick jokes provide catharsis for the audience. As Weiss (1988) observes, "Civilization is overpressurized, clanking and groaning, ready to burst, and comedy comes in wearing coveralls to open the bleeder valve and let off the pressure with dick jokes" (118). Weiss additionally recounts attending a ceremony at which Milton Berle received a Lifetime Achievement Award and told approximately ninety dick jokes for an acceptance speech.

One example of a male comic's dick joke is the experience of comic Margaret Smith. Discussing the difficulty of following a male comic who objectifies women, Smith remembers: "At one gig in Chattanooga, the guy before me ended by saying, 'I like to fuck women with no legs, 'cause I put 'em on the end of my dick and spin 'em.' The audience cheered. 'Put 'em on the end of my dick and spin 'em.'

'Ladies and gentlemen, please welcome Margaret Smith!'" (quoted in Strauss 94)

We can only imagine Smith's feelings of anxiety and humiliation as she reached for the microphone, the "tool" of her profession. The microphone, itself, is often compared to a penis, perceived by some to be "a steel phallus women can't wield" (Weiss 1988, 60). The microphone is also frequently cited as a source of power; as Auslander (1993) notes, "When discussing the dynamic of their work both male and female comedians stress the importance of control over the audience, of mastery of the performance context, in which the microphone plays a significant role" (318).

In an attempt to encourage a break from the male-defined genre of dick jokes in 1978, Mitzi Shore opened the Belly Room at The Comedy Store in L.A.—a space smaller than the club's main room that featured only female comics and launched talents like Whoopi Goldberg and Sandra Bernhard (Handelman 1988b). Designed to facilitate an environment of intimacy and support, the Belly Room began to include male comics—at their insistence—in 1979 (Martin and Segrave 1986, 318). Some comics and critics reject "women's comedy" nights hosted by many clubs, claiming that this is a way of ghettoizing female comics. A number of female comics, however, welcome the opportunity to perform exclusively with other women. As comic Lotus Weinstock explains, performing with male comics requires conforming to "male" rhythms, as a female comic must "put out, put out, get to the punch quicker.... If you come on after four men, forget it. The audience has to get out of that yang aggressive thing. The only time gender doesn't get in the way is when confidence speaks louder than gender, and the only way to do that is to work at it" (quoted in Martin and Segrave 1986, 316). Are the rhythms of stand-up comedy inherently "male?" What implications does this have for female stand-up comics? By the phrases "put out" and "yang thing," Weinstock suggests that male comics deliver a sort of rhetorical "wham—bam—thank you, ma'am" to the audience, whereas female comics care more about rhetorical foreplay.

The crucial questions here are: When female comics perform traditional stand-up rhythms, are they becoming rhetorically male by speaking as men, or are they simply assuming a rhetorically powerful position onstage? *Must power and aggression in stand-up comedy be considered male constructs?* Is it possible to define power within the genre of stand-up comedy as audience perception of performer control of the rhetorical situation—that is, as a nongendered phenomenon? Hollywood comedy writer Emily Levine asserts: "What an audience responds to most is a performer who is in charge. They prefer you at your strongest, male and female" (cited in Dolan 1989).

Is stand-up comedy inherently male? The rhythms, the power of a monologue (for, despite audience interaction, a comic's act is still at bottom a monologue) and a microphone, the aggressive, even abusive material—are these elements necessarily "masculine" or simply features of a powerful discourse? Auslander (1993) contends:

> Women comics who choose to remain within the conventional form and performance contexts of stand-up comedy are essentially appropriating a cultural form traditionally associated with, and still dominated by, male practitioners. Undoubtedly, they are offering themselves to "the oppressors' forbidding or disapproving gaze" and run all the risks attendant on doing so. But those risks may be worth running if they give women greater access to the cultural arena to engage the male public sphere. (320)

Clearly, the notion of female or feminist stand-up comedy is extremely complex. To some, the descriptor "feminist stand-up comic" is an oxymoron, synonymous with "feminist misogynist." To others, it is a liberatory role, long overdue. Schuler (1990) maintains that feminist performance "often deliberately attempts to disregard and/or subvert hegemonic theatrical conventions" (138). Inge (1985) claims that "While masculine humor satirizes those who violate social norms . . . feminine humor tends to attack the norms themselves" (5). Little (1983) suggests that "feminist comedy . . . will very likely draw upon liminal imagery. It will mock assumptions . . . it will challenge a worldview" (178).

Discussing feminist cultural criticism of women's stand-up comedy, Fraiberg (1994) explains that women enjoy both performing and watching stand-up comedy for its subversive nature—because it is "humor that gets away with something" (328). The title of Fraiberg's essay, "Between the Laughter: Bridging Feminist Studies through Women's Stand-Up Comedy," is itself telling, indicating a willingness to use the term "feminist" synonymously with "women" when labeling an academic discipline, but not when referring to the comedy produced by feminist women used as examples throughout. As Finney (1994) notes, Fraiberg's essay focuses on the way female comics "mediate the gaps between the theoretical positions of academic feminism and the experiences of women who attend their performances" by using humor "to call critical attention to status quo mechanisms of power and subordination"(9). Finney adds: "For female stand-up comics like these, entertainment is the sugar that coats pills often otherwise difficult for audiences to swallow." In other words, audiences might be receptive to "female" humor, but are generally resistant to any overtly "feminist" discourse.

How do we know that female or feminist humor exists? What does it look like? What does it sound like? Gloria Kaufman, coeditor of the oft-cited 1980 volume, *Pulling Our Own Strings: Feminist Humor and Satire,* distinguishes between the two, claiming that "female humor, while it may recognize cultural inequities, does not seek to change them," whereas feminist humor does; feminist humor is one of hope, whereas female humor is one of hopelessness; and "female humor often parallels male humor inasmuch as both perpetuate harmful myths and stereotypes of and about women" (cited in White 1988, 79). Never do these abstractions seem to concretize into a discussion of specific generic features and constraints. White contends that "feminist humor is specific to feminist culture and is an artifact of that culture" (80) without bothering to explain exactly what constitutes this apparently monolithic "feminist culture." In 1973, a reviewer for *Ms.* asked, "doesn't feminism necessarily imply a new comedy, a comedy built not on masculine put-downs, but on some common and ironic self-vision that brings the audience along?" (cited in Martin and Segrave 1986, 421) Today, scholars continue to ask this question—a question complicated by competing conceptions of words like "feminism" and "comedy."

Subverting conventions, attacking norms, and calling standards into question are all strategies seen in *any* type of marginal humor. What, then, do female comics *say* and *do* onstage that distinguishes them from other marginal comics? Does their performance of marginality contain unique characteristics that distinguish it as a definable genre, separate from the performance of male comics? And, if so, does it qualify as or is it distinct from "feminist" stand-up comedy? In order to explore the above questions, we must first ask: What do contemporary American female comics speak about onstage? Chapter 3 provides an answer.

FEMALE COMICS: TALKING THE TALK

In order to explore the way contemporary American female comics perform their marginality onstage, we must ask: What do they speak about? How do they speak? This chapter provides an answer to the first question by identifying eleven categories of topics women comics address. The categories were generated through analyzing video and audio recordings (and several written excerpts) of female comics from the 1980s to the present. (Earlier historical examples are discussed in chapter 4, which focuses on several traditions within female comic performance.)

The eleven topical categories apparent in the performances of contemporary American female comics are: sex, relationships, weight/body image, fashion, religion/ethnicity/region, family, gynecology, domestic activities, politics, popular culture phenomena, and random observations. In order to determine the content of female comic performance currently seen on cable and network television (as well as in comedy clubs), this chapter describes the eleven topical categories, providing several examples of each. In the case of topics that fall into more than one category (for example, when discussing her Jewish mother, Cathy Ladman is focusing on a topic that fits both the "family" and "religion/ethnicity" category), I have selected the category that appears most relevant to the example.

Sex

This category includes sexual acts and activities (with special attention to orgasms), gender differences in sexual behavior and desire, depictions of sex and sexuality in popular culture media, age concerns (that is, too young or too old), body parts, masturbation, birth control, pregnancy, and childbirth. This category, together with the following category, relationships, constitutes most of the material performed by contemporary female comics in this country. The taboo nature of sex and sexuality make this provocative material particularly popular with audiences. For example, Carol Henry (1990) remembers, "I grew up sheltered . . . my mom saying, 'Sex is a dirty, disgusting thing you save for someone you love.'" Karen Haber (1990a) asks the audience if they have ever had "sex so good . . . it's like shopping." She then discusses the repercussions of women telling the truth in bed: "the end of life as we know it . . . get off of me—no, you're not hurting me, you're just annoying me . . . you thought you could hurt me with *that?*" And Ellen Cleghorne (1991) asks, "How many ladies like to cuddle after sex? . . . How many of y'all just like to get up, take a shower, get your money, and go home?" Specific sexual acts also account for a good deal of material. Carol Leifer (1992) tells men: "Making love to a woman is like buying real estate—location, location, location!" Abby Stein (1991) contends, "A Jewish guy's idea of oral sex is talking about himself." Diane Ford (1992) claims that she likes to "sit around, drink beer, fart, and watch football." When her husband says, "That's not very ladylike," she replies, "Neither is a blow job, and you don't complain about *that.*"

Televised sports are not for everyone, however; Caroline Rhea (1991) maintains: "It's so much easier to fake an orgasm than it is to pretend you like watching football." Diana Jordan (1993) says that she and her fiancé have a "Milly Vanilly relationship . . . he fakes commitment—I fake the orgasm." And Karen Haber (1990b) admits that she knows she is in love because "I've faked it for him the way I've never faked it for any man in my life." Offering a slightly different perspective, Diane Nichols (1990) explains: "The only thing worse than a guy who doesn't care if you have an orgasm is a guy who's gonna give you one if it's the *last* thing he does. . . . After *ten* hours—who cares, Top Gun? Bring that plane in for a *landing!*" Finally, setting the record straight, Wanda Sykes (2001) asserts:

> Guys always wonder, why do we fake it? To get you the hell *off* of us! We *know* it's not gonna happen. I tell a guy in a minute, *boy*—if he does somethin' right, I tell him, "Hey—that was *good*—jot that *down*—no, write that down—make a *blueprint*—that was *good*—you stick with that, alright? Wait,

no, no—don't get *fancy* on me—take some new route that you don't know anything *about,* because you're gonna get *lost,* and just like a *man,* you ain't gonna stop and ask for *directions.* You gonna keep *goin'* till you run out of *gas*—leave *me* stranded in the middle of *nowhere*—gotta get *myself* home.

Age differences between partners are frequently addressed. After referring to an audience member as a "strapping young buck," Susie Essman (1988) asserts that "younger guys . . . no idea what they're doing, but they can do it all night." And Marsha Warfield (1987) notes, "Some people say older men have more endurance, but let's think about this for a minute—who wants to fuck an old man for a long time?" Comics themselves acknowledge the aging process; as Laura Kightlinger (2001) admits: "The only thing I care about doing is just staying at home and lying in bed with my boyfriend and just watching—another couple— because I just feel . . . I've earned a reputation as an actress now in bed, that I don't have to do my own stunts."

Birth control is another common source of material for female comics. Elayne Boosler (1984) confides that after diaphragm insertion, "I don't want to make love, I want a certificate of achievement!" Roseanne (1987) claims that she and her husband practice "a new method of birth control . . . every night before bed, we spend an hour with our kids." Finally, Anita Wise (1991) advocates male birth control: "contraceptive beer . . . something we women could be sure you were taking." Body parts also provide a frequent topic. As Anita Wise (1992) explains, "Some men think that the bigger a woman's breasts are, the less intelligent she is. . . . I think it's the opposite—the larger a woman's breasts, the less intelligent the men become." Janine Digiulio (1993) notes, "I recently heard about a society where it is still a ritual when a woman turns of age, the men there will cut off her clitoris," and adds, "We should be thankful that this will never happen in our country because the men here don't know where the clitoris is!"

Occasionally, female comics tell "dick jokes." Roseanne (1992) reminisces about the atmosphere of the 1960s: "If we were all holding hands, no one could push the button—and if we all had a great big dick in our mouths, no one could speak ill of another . . . let's start by holding hands." The issue of penis size is often the focus of this type of sexual material. Lizz Winstead (1990) discusses "male menopause," stating, "Every time I see a guy around forty in a Corvette, I just want to scream out, 'Sorry about your penis!'" Elayne

Boosler (1988) assures men, "If it's attached to *you* and it reaches *us,* it's long enough." And Louise Dumbrowski (1993) asks the audience, "Do you think size matters?" and continues, "I do—I think small men are better—'cause they're *angrier!*"

Sexual communication and miscommunication are often mentioned in female comics' acts as well. After describing a man bragging that he knows a woman is satisfied because she stops moving, Ellen Cleghorne (1991) counters, "That doesn't mean she's satisfied—that means she's *dead!* She's probably layin' there thinking, 'Maybe if I lay real still, he'll get offa me—maybe he'll call 911 and I'll get a ride home.'" And Caroline Rhea (2001) confides:

> Latin men are incredibly noisy in bed—I had no idea that there even *were* that many saints. . . . Ya know what else Latin men do? They say, "Mommy" during sex. . . . I said, "Honey, what is this 'Ay, Mommy' thing?" And he said, [in Puerto Rican accent] "Sweethear,' when I say, 'Ay, Mommy,' I wan' you to say, 'Ay, Poppy.'" . . . Yeah, that's Spanish for "Daddy"—yeah, that's what I want to scream out during sex—the next thing you know, I'll be saying, "You never loved me, I'm in therapy because of you—ayyayyyaiiii!"

Masturbation is also frequently discussed, usually indirectly. Leah Krinsky (1993) says that she drives "a 1983 Corolla . . . I can feel every little bump on the road—so I'm not getting it fixed . . . thank you for understanding." And Stephanie Hodge (1991) tells men, "The only thing you've got that I need I can buy and put batteries in!"

Relationships

This category focuses primarily on gender differences in relational behavior and the difficulties these differences entail. Also included in the category are topics such as the stages of relationships (for example, flirting, dating, breaking up) and marriage/divorce. Karen Haber (1985) says that she wants to call a guy before a date and ask, "Hey— are you an asshole? [pauses] That's okay, 'cause I date assholes." Carol Siskind (1992) describes her reaction to a man not calling for two weeks: "Two weeks? Do you know what that is in *girl years?*" Finally, Judy Tenuta (1987) asks, "How many of you ever started dating someone because you were too lazy to commit suicide?"

Meeting men is another common topic. Kathleen Madigan (1992) says she has heard that the laundromat is a good place to meet guys and adds, "like I want to be forty and dating a guy who can't afford his own dryer." Margaret Smith (1992) describes a guy in a bar asking, "Hey, cupcake, can I buy you a drink?" and her response, "No, but I'll take the three bucks." And Rita Rudner (1987) notes, "When I meet a guy, the first question I ask myself is, 'Is this the man I want my children to spend their weekends with?'" Caroline Rhea (2001) discusses a novel way to meet a potential mate:

> Don't you love passing construction workers and having them say just *disgusting* things to you just for the hell of it? . . . Ya know, it wouldn't even *bother* me that much if they could show me one marriage that has come from that *kind* of introduction! . . . "Mommy, how did you and Daddy meet?" "Well dear, I was walking along the street one day, and *your* father screamed the most *disgusting things* at me—oh, something about wanting to eat his lunch off my *ass*—hungry?"

Many female comics discuss the reasons for not being in relationships. Leah Krinsky (1993) reveals that she has "no one in my life—apparently, I lack the low self-esteem necessary to make those compromises." Margaret Smith (1992) admits, "I can't get a relationship to last longer than it takes to tape their albums." And Joy Behar (1992) explains, "I want a man in my life but not in my house—just come in, attach the VCR, and get out." Some female comics talk about being attracted to the "wrong" men. Pam Stone (1992) asserts, "Women are always attracted to wild, he-man behavior, and yet that's the first thing we complain about. . . . I'm sure a month after dating Tarzan, Jane was going, 'Well—I didn't know when we first started goin' out you didn't have a *car*.'" And Suzy Soro (1993) claims that women don't like "nice guys," speculating: "At the Last Supper, Jesus would have gotten on my nerves. . . . 'You're a carpenter? Wow—that's fascinating . . . what's that? You have no money and you live with your mother? Yo, Judas—wait up!'"

Female comics are also occasionally critical of women's behavior toward men. Diane Nichols (1990) explains, "God had to give the Ten Commandments to a man—if he'd given 'em to a woman, she would have gone, 'Well, I know that's what he *said,* but I really don't think that's what he *meant.* . . .'" Pointing out that men get annoyed with women's constant attempts to analyze them, Wanda Sykes (2001) notes, "when a man is quiet for a few minutes, we automatically *ask* him, 'What are you *thinking?* Come on, now—what are you *thinking?*'

And they all say the *same* thing, 'Nothin'.' *Believe them!* They can do that for *hours.*" Suzy Lowks (1990) tells men to think of women "as a telephone—we like to be held close, we like to be listened to—and if you push the wrong button—you're *disconnected!* . . . But there's one on every corner and it only takes a *quarter,* so there you go!"

Another common topic is fantasy vs. reality in relationships. Karen Haber (1990b) wishes for a "whorehouse" for women so that:

> we can get it the way we really want it—we pay our money, and guys pretend they like talking to us and care about our lives! Then they hold us real tight and say, "Oooh—you're *so thin,*" and even if they've never seen us before, they have to go, "Have you lost weight?" And then we have sex, and right before that ultimate moment, they'll have to shout, "I can't believe how great your shoes match your *dress!*"

Cathy Ladman (1992a) discusses the reality of romance as she describes buying a Barbie doll for her niece and finding "Gift-Giving Ken." She says, "I really don't think this is gonna prepare her for adult relationships. How about Date-Breaking Ken? I-Still-Live-With-My-Mother Ken? Oh-You-Don't-Mind-If-My-Friend-Bob-Joins-Us Ken?" Female comics also give men advice about how to attract women. Carol Siskind (1993) explains that men's tattoos should say, "'I'm looking for a committed relationship,' 'I love to express my feelings,' 'I will always leave the toilet seat down.'" And Carol Leifer (1992) asks, "How does *Playgirl* stay in business? Women don't buy it because to see a naked guy, all ya gotta do is *ask* him. . . . If you want to get me excited, put a picture of a guy in an Armani suit calling me *back!*"

The topic of marriage/divorce provides a wealth of material for female comics. Carol Leifer (1993a) claims, "I had a mixed marriage—I'm human, he was a Klingon." Wendy Liebman (1992a) says that she had "a very messy divorce because there was a child involved—my ex-husband." Roseanne (1987) cautions women, "You may marry the man of your dreams, ladies, but fifteen years later, you're married to a recliner that burps." And Suzy Soro (1992) claims, "I've never been married—I *have* had a similar experience—I was hit by a car and left by the side of the road for dead." The effect of anticipating marriage is also frequently discussed. Cathy Ladman (1992b) recollects wistfully, "I couldn't wait until that wonderful day when my boyfriend would turn to me and say, 'Oh, *alright.*'" Rita Rudner (1991) says, "I broke up with my boyfriend because he wanted to get married. I didn't want

78

him to." And Sue Kolinsky (1992) complains that at thirty-five, getting family pressure to marry is like looking at someone who is seventy and saying, "When are you gonna break your hip? All your friends broke *their* hips."

Occasionally, female comics discuss friendships; although this material includes mixed-sex friendships, often the focus is on "girlfriend" humor. For example, Wanda Sykes (2001) claims that "Women . . . don't look out for each other," explaining that "my girlfriends wouldn't tell me this guy was ugly. . . . my friend would go, 'Oh, girl, he's *nice*—those were *nice pants* he had on . . . he *shopped* for those— you can't *find them* anywhere—he's *nice.*'"

Weight/Body Image

Included in this category are the topics of dieting, eating in general (with particular attention given to the difference between private and public—especially date-related—eating), working out, descriptions of body parts, and plastic surgery or other cosmetic procedures. The subject of food in relation to overeating and dieting is frequently discussed. Linda Smith (1993) says that she eats her pasta "al dente," admitting, "I don't like it that way—I just can't wait." Discussing the fact that women don't eat on dates, Elayne Boosler (1984) concludes that women gain weight living with men, saying, "You starved your whole life to get one, you got one, you're gonna *eat* now!" And Suzy Lowks (1990) tells her audience, "This morning I thought, 'I'm doin' it all today'—so I took thirty-seven Dexitrim—I'm really excited about it—I've lost ten pounds since three o'clock."

Comics who are noticeably heavy often perform fat jokes. A prime example is Roseanne (1987). Complaining that "People are rude to the fat," she responds to a fictitious salesgirl, "Hey—I eat the same amount of food that you eat—I just don't *puke* when I'm done!" Monica Piper (1990), describes "a conference at my gym for bulimics and anorexics—the bulimics *ate* the anorexics! . . . They were back ten minutes later." Body parts, specifically breasts, buttocks, and thighs, are often subjects for material as well. Cassie Chappell (1991) notes that instead of a G-string bathing suit, "right now I'm hovering at LMNOP." Joy Behar (1989) claims that it was better to be a woman when Reubens was painting, asking, "What do you mean, no dessert?

I've got a sitting with Caravaggio in the morning, and if he doesn't see some cellulite, I'm history!" And Caroline Rhea (2001) exults, "I love Latin men because *they* love cellulite, and I'm their queen!"[1]

Female comics also comment on the physical appearance of other women. Jann Karam (1991) notes that in department stores, "when women are too old and ugly to work in cosmetics, they go to fragrance . . . then gift wrap—then credit." Lamenting the unfair cultural expectations for female attractiveness, Wanda Sykes (2001) explains: "A guy can be ugly and it's not a handicap. . . . A guy can be ugly and just go on with his ugly life and have a good time. Even in entertainment, he can play any *role* he wants—he could be a *doctor, lawyer,* special *agent.* If you a ugly woman in show business, you pretty much playin' an *ugly woman.* That's your *role.* They say, 'Your character is *ugly.* And you just show up on the show, and we talk about your ugly ass. That's about it.'"

Female comics frequently comment on various methods women use to enhance their physical appearance. For example, discussing cosmetic surgery, Nora Lynch (1993) issues the following clue to men: "If a woman is prone and a significant part of her breast does not fall into her armpit—they're not hers!" Finally, noting, "The higher the hair, the dumber the girl," Pam Stone (1992) describes her friend Tiffany "from Laguna" in a valley girl voice: "First I'm gonna get liposuction on my thighs and then a boob job and then a nose job and cheek implants, and then I'll be perfect." Stone responds, "Not until you get a brain tuck."

One of the most popular topics in this category is working out. Diana Jordan (1993) says that she has been "pumpin' iron—*becoming* that man I wanted to marry." Jann Karam (1990) claims that guys at her health club are "freaked out" by the sight of a woman working out. She recalls them asking, "Where did you learn to do all those exercises?" and adds: "like I'm gonna go, 'I don't know—my boyfriend was a weight lifter and I look at pictures in magazines, but I could never learn on my own—I'm a girl, I'm too stupid—I don't even know how I got here . . . will you buy me something?'"

Finally, Carol Leifer (1990) confesses that she did try "that Jane Fonda tape—*Barbarella.*" She speculates about pioneer women [in a heavy New York dialect]: "Ya know, Marge, I find that hoeing is so good for the upper arms. . . . So I'm plowing, the oxen break free—

drag me through the mud on my face . . . but the next day, my skin had such a glow."

Fashion

This category includes shopping, gender differences in clothing styles and preferences, and commentary on specific outfits or articles of clothing (either something owned by the comic or worn at the time of the performance). For instance, Cathy Ladman (1993a) admits to being a "shopaholic" who buys "stuff I don't need . . . a jock strap to hang garlic." And Rita Rudner (1991) says that she shops "for consolation" after a breakup, confiding, "Sometimes if I see a really great outfit, I'll break up with someone on purpose. Once I saw a great outfit and I wasn't dating anyone, so I went up and hugged a stranger and slapped him and bought it." Some comics speak about fashion sabotage. Pam Stone (1992) for example, maintains that women compete with each other and lie to eliminate the competition. Portraying an ostensible friend, she says, "Pam—you know what would look really good with those culottes? Clogs! Black knee socks and clogs—that would look *so* good!" She suggests the reason for Sinead O'Connor's baldness: "one of her friends probably said, 'Sinead—you're so *pretty*— shave your head!'"

Religion/Ethnicity/Region

Comprising a substantial amount of contemporary female comics' material, this category features discussion of religious background and attendant rituals (with most of the focus on Judaism and Catholicism), influences on current behavior, dissatisfaction with marginalized status and characteristics/characterizations of people of various religions, ethnicities, and regions. Brett Butler (1993) says, "I married a New Yorker—my husband's Jewish—don't think his parents aren't tickled to death with my butt . . . look who's comin' to Hannukah—yee ha!" Butler then imitates her in-laws in a New York dialect: "A divorced older southern gentile comedienne who bleaches her hair—why didn't you just shoot us in our sleep?" Cathy Ladman (1993a) describes her mother as such a Jewish mother that she was "sent home from jury duty—she insisted *she* was guilty." Karen Haber (1990a) tells of being captain of her cheerleading team in high school. "We were six whining Jewish girls . . . cheer was, 'Tsk—when are you gonna *sco-ore?*'" And Ladman (1992a) comments on the three wise men bringing frankincense and myrrh to the baby Jesus: "Myrrh? To a *baby shower?* I'm sure Mary was very polite. She probably said, 'Myrrh—how lovely . . . one can never have too much *myrrh.*' . . . Years later, Mary and Joseph would be having a party. 'Who's coming?' 'The Wisemens.' 'Ach—I hate the Wisemens—they always bring bad gifts . . . I hope they follow the wrong star and get lost. . . . Bad mood? Sure I'm in a bad mood—I haven't had sex—*ever!*'"

Discussing Catholicism, Linda Smith (1992) imagines a yuppie priest sending the wine back in church, saying, "You call *this* Jesus?" A number of comics perform jokes about the pope. Judy Tenuta (1987) boasts, "I'm dating the pope—actually, I'm just using him to get to God." Robin Tyler (1993) notes: "The pope runs all over the world condemning homosexuality, dressed in high drag" and adds, "even if you don't believe in the *Bible,* you still gotta respect the woman who typed all of that." Kathleen Madigan (1990) observes that "Baptists quote from the *Bible* because they know Catholics have never opened one . . . we just took everyone's word for it—it got such great *reviews.*" Issues of race and ethnicity are also discussed—primarily by members of the group in question. For example, Ellen Cleghorne (1990), an African American comic, asks why it is that "When white women are naked, that's *pornography,*" but "when black women are naked, that's *anthropology.*" Margaret Cho (1992), a Korean American comic, describes a recent audition experience: "'Could you be a little more—oh, I don't know—*Chinese?*' 'Well, actually, I'm Korean.' 'Whatever.'" Liz Torres says that she was recently named Puerto Rican Woman of the Year: "They didn't bother to give me an award. They just spray-painted my name on the Empire State Building" (Martin and Segrave 1986, 415). Finally, Caroline Rhea (2001) discusses cultural differences, remembering, "I went out with this . . . Puerto Rican doctor—the P.R. D.R.—he took me *salsa* dancing. I thought I was doing really well and then I overheard this evil woman in the corner going, 'Oh—look at the *deaf* girl trying!'"

Regional jokes are quite popular among female comics as well. Casey Fraser (1993), the self-proclaimed youngest professional stand-up comic, asserts that at fourteen, growing up in Greenwich Village, "I don't know my Bill of Rights, but I know my Miranda rights." Brett Butler (1992a) notes that she is "So southern, I'm related to myself." Describing her ex-husband (1993), Butler recalls: "'redneck' is too simplistic and pejorative . . . I was married to a subliterate, terracotta-toothed imbecile with violent tendencies—wait—other words are comin' to mind— I was married to a simian, knuckle-draggin', cousin-lovin', dog-sellin', trailer-dwellin', brainless amoeba on the booger farm in the Bayou. . . . I know that sounds really hateful, but I assure you—he doesn't understand hyphenated references." And Roseanne describes Santa Fe: "a très chic, aerobicizing, sushi-eatin', hot-tubbin' type of town, n'est-ce pas?" She adds a description of Tulsa, calling it "a Willie Nelson, cinder blocks, beans and weenies town—colorful—brown and yellow. . . . Tulsa Barbie— comes with black roots, varicose veins, and a bowling bag."

Family

Perhaps one of the most universal topics in the performances of contemporary female comics is family. The material in this category focuses primarily on parents. Other family members discussed include children, siblings, aunts, uncles, and grandparents. Cathy Ladman (1993a) tells of a recent nightmare: "I dreamt my parents came to visit me . . . that's it." Karen Haber (1990a) says that her dad used to hand her dates a shotgun and say, "Use it if you have to." Kathleen Madigan (1990) muses, "Dad just turned fifty—same age as Mick Jagger . . . so hard to imagine him out on tour—draggin' that recliner from town to town." And, with relief, Margaret Smith (1993) notes, "saw my mom today—it's okay—she didn't see *me* or anything."

Parenting is also frequently discussed. Wendy Kamenoff (1992) maintains that "Raising a child properly is the hardest job in the world . . . which is ironic because it's the easiest job to get—all you need is a surface, really." Carrie Snow (1991) asks, "How can I have children? I have white couches." Laura Kightlinger (2001) discusses her apprehension about parenting, noting that, "As a mom . . . I'd hate to hear, 'Mom, who do you love the most?' because then . . . I'd have to say, 'You *know*—I never wanted children.'" Roseanne (1987), on the other hand, asserts that having been married for fifteen years with three kids "shows that I breed well in captivity." Finally, Wendy Liebman (2001) tells her audience: "I took last year off to have a baby—and that didn't happen. I did get a tattoo—it's over my ovary—it's an expiration date.... [If she had children] I'd be so overprotective—I would never let the kids outside—my body.... I'm feeling very maternal—I started going out with a guy who has a five-year-old mentality."

Siblings and other relatives are often the subject of female comics' material as well. Judy Tenuta (1987) tells an audience member that he reminds her of "my brother Bosco—like you but with a human head." Finally, Kathleen Madigan (1992) recalls her father saying that her uncle "smoked six packs a day, drank a quart of vodka, and was hit by a truck," and contends, "but Dad, he was drunk, running out in the road lookin' for his lighter."

Gynecology

This category includes visits to the gynecologist, premenstrual syndrome, menstruation, feminine hygiene products, and mammograms. Menstrual cycles are frequently discussed. Cathy Ladman (1992b) complains, "I'm premenstrual, I'm postmenstrual, I'm midmenstrual— I have five good minutes every month—I'm usually asleep [wakes up] ... Oh—was I nice?" Roseanne (1987) says that when her husband tells her, "Maybe you're ovulating," her response is "Yeah—you better stand back because it's a full moon and you're lookin' at high tide!" Discussion of gynecological exams comprises much of the material in this category. Joy Behar (1992) asks her audience, "Is there a gynecologist here? Because I want to ask him to come up here, lay on the cold floor, put your knees to your nose and relax."

Louise Dumbrowski (1993) notes: "I made the mistake of going to a nurse practitioner ... really earthy ... halfway through the exam, she pulls out a mirror. I said, 'What's that for?' She said, 'Don't you want to look at your cervix?' I said, 'Nooo. My cervix is like God to me—I don't have to see it to believe it exists.'"

Finally, Leah Krinsky (1991) recalls:

> the doctor tells me to get undressed, and then he leaves the room ... he said, "We have to do this out of respect for the patient's dignity." I said, "Look, Bub, in five minutes, I'm gonna be butt-naked on that table with knees in the air—at that point, my dignity's pretty much shot for the day. Now, I'm payin' a lot of money for this examination, Doc—I want you to stay put and watch me strip. While you're at it, turn off the lights and get me drunk like the other guys do, huh?"

84

Feminine hygiene products are also frequently discussed by female comics. Wendy Liebman (1992b) says, "These aren't shoulder pads, they're maxi pads. I feel fashionable—and fresh." And Elayne Boosler (1984) discusses "breathable panty shields," asking, "do you want something breathing down *your* jeans that doesn't pay rent?" Finally, Kate Clinton (1990) notes that in order for Dustin Hoffman to portray a woman accurately in the movie *Tootsie,* he "needed to feel what it's like to sneeze and blow your tampon out a quarter of an inch."

Female comics occasionally discuss mammograms in their acts. Margaret Smith (1992) suggests, "You shouldn't be called Ma'am until you get your first mammogram." Monica Piper (1990) remembers that during her mammogram, the intent seemed to be to "squish the boobies flat . . . sunnyside up." And Kate Clinton (1990) says that during her experience, the "nurse is a beautiful platinum blonde—reaches out and grabs me—no, 'You wanna go out to dinner?'—*nothing!*"

Domestic Activities

Included in this category is material about cooking, cleaning, shortcuts in completing domestic tasks, and assessments of gender differences in the areas of cleaning and organizing. Suzy Soro (1992) asserts, "I don't cook—I'll eat out, I'll take out, I'll put out, but I ain't cookin'." Elayne Boosler (1984) describes the directions on "Soup for One: Heat it up, don't heat it up—who gives a shit? You're *alone!*" Rita Rudner (1991) observes that men like to barbecue because "they'll only cook if danger's involved," and notes that "Men don't live well by themselves—they live like bears with furniture." And Roseanne (1987) asserts: "The day I worry about cleaning the house is the day Sears comes out with a riding vacuum cleaner. . . . When my husband comes home at night, if the kids are still alive, I figure I've done *my* job."

Politics

This category features material about contemporary political personalities and events as well as overtly ideological material calling audience attention to issues of feminism, lesbianism, sexism (including harassment), and racism. Presidential elections generate a great deal of material for comics. Margaret Smith (1993) believes that it is "unfair that

Hillary had to give up law . . . when Bush was president, no one screamed at Barbara to get off the oatmeal container." Smith continues: "we want to know two things from politicians: Have you ever been unfaithful and have you ever smoked pot? Chances are they happened in the same night . . . only person I believe never smoked—Perot—'cause you don't pass it to the nerd—even if he *did* buy the bag."

Postelection presidential digs are also common. Brett Butler (1993) notes, "There are enough women here—I can do this," and asks, "Doesn't Clinton remind you of a guy that you meet in a bar who keeps tryin' to pick you up and every word out of his mouth is a lie, but you just don't want to go home by yourself?"

Sometimes the political humor of female comics is vitriolic. Robin Tyler asserts, "I think the Democratic emblem should be changed from a donkey to a prophylactic. It's perfect. It supports inflation, keeps production down, helps a bunch of pricks, and gives a false sense of security when one is being screwed" (Martin and Segrave 1986, 423). Some female comics speculate about a female president. For example, Angela Scott (1992) says, "I think a black woman should be president because you wouldn't hear, 'I don't know nothin' about runnin' no country.' I think you'd hear, 'Congress said *what?* Don't *make* me get up from this Oval Office and have to put my *heels* on and come on *down* there!'"

Political issues pertaining to women's rights are also occasionally addressed. Leah Krinsky (1991) describes a recent visit to a women's clinic during which she encountered 250 right-to-lifers protesting:

> It took me an hour and a half to fight my way through this mob of idiots—by the time I got through, I was so aggravated—I wasn't even pregnant—I had an abortion just to piss them off! What if men got pregnant?. . . . If men got pregnant, abortion clinics would have free beer, peanuts, dart boards, pool tables—they'd be open twenty-four hours, little cocktail waitresses running around in short skirts, "General anaesthetic or local? [giggles] It must be so tough what you're going through, you big, brave man, you—yeees." If you guys were smart, you'd wanna get pregnant . . . 'cause it would show the world you're gettin' laid.

Other ideological issues of racism, homophobia, and feminism also provide topics for discussion. Addressing racism, Angela Scott (1991) explains: "I grew up in Concord, Mass., and we were the only black family there. So, you know how when a subject comes up that may include you people tend to stare at you? Well, whenever they'd talk about Africa when I was in school, everyone would turn around and stare at me like I suddenly got a spear in my hand" (Gallo 1991, 82).

Discussing homophobia, Roseanne (1987) says, "I thank God for creatin' gay men 'cause if it wasn't for them, us fat women would have nobody to dance with." Suzanne Westenhoefer (1993) reports that when straight friends ask, "How do you get to be homosexual?" gays and lesbians should say, "We are chosen—first on talent, then interview, and the swimsuit and evening gown competition pretty much takes care of the rest." Lea Delaria (1993) says, that the "difference between a dyke and a lesbian" is "30,000 dollars." And Robin Tyler (1993) notes, "I hear that Hillary Clinton did have an affair with one of us in college, but don't worry—she didn't inhale."

Finally, commenting on feminism, Kate Clinton (1990) asks, "What is a feminist man? He plays Ms. Packman?" And Joy Behar (1988) says:

> Girls . . . I should apologize—it's 1988—we're not girls—we're . . . *men*. . . . I'm a feminist—not radical—I wear a bra . . . not because of politics, more because of Newton's laws of physics. . . . Let's solve it [miscommunication between sexes] now. . . . "Do we still have to pay?" Yes, you *do*. But that's the only thing that's the same. You don't have to light our cigarettes or pull out the chair, but pick up the check on a date? Yes, you *do*. And kill the big bugs in the kitchen? Yes, you *do*.

Popular Culture Phenomena

Topics in this category include television shows (past and present), commercials, print advertisements, films, books, music, consumer products and services, trends and fads (past and present), and New Age modalities (especially therapy—individual, group, and via self-help books). Some female comics talk a great deal about the influences of film and television. For example, Suzanne Westenhoefer (1992) claims that she knew she was a lesbian growing up because she "saw *The Sound of Music* 132 times." Carrie Snow (1991) recalls that "When I saw *Dances with Wolves,* I couldn't decide which Indian name I wanted for myself. It was a toss-up between 'Dry Scalp' and 'Touches Herself.'" And with her characteristic offbeat spin, Wendy Liebman (2001) asks, "Aren't movies expensive—when you forget to return them?"

Discussing the pervasive impact of television, Janeane Garofalo (1993) says, "I find it distressing that there's about six trillion bulimic, anorexic twelve-year-old girls feelin' bad about themselves 'cause they can't keep up with Shannon Dougherty's little buttock. . . . All I have to say is I'm glad that in my day it was *Welcome Back, Kotter.*" Marsha Warfield (1987) remembers "Captain Kangaroo—piece of shit . . . what was he before, *Lieutenant* Kangaroo? . . . Writers came up with names like Bunny Rabbit—I'm two, but I ain't *stupid!*" And Carol Leifer (1990) says, "I'm single, living in New York—every day I wake up and think, wow—I'm "That Girl"—I think I'll get way overdressed and fly a kite."

Television commercials and other forms of advertising are also frequently discussed. Lizz Winstead (1993) describes a beer commercial popular at the time: "What kind of delusional fantasy are men living in when they watch forty-five seconds of fiction on TV where Scandinavian women in butt thongs embark upon their smelly camping trip because they have *beer!* I'm thirty—I can buy my *own* beer— why don't *you* take a *shower?*" And Elayne Boosler (1988) talks about the use of breasts in subliminal advertising, speculating that perhaps the intent is for men to say, "Maybe I'll buy that car—maybe I'll buy two of 'em and park 'em real close together and put my face between 'em!" Even the way television is watched is joked about by female comics. Sue Kolinsky (1992) expresses her frustration with men channel surfing via the remote control, asking, "What are you looking for? Naked women *watching* sports?"

Current best-sellers are discussed by female comics as well. Diane Nichols (1993) asks: "Have you read *Vanna Speaks*? Did you *know* Vanna speaks? Well, apparently, she types also. Here's her big advice: 'Ladies, when taking a shower, open your mouth very wide, let the water rush in and strike your teeth—it acts as a water pik.' . . . *Wow* . . . I guess if I lean against the wall, I'm ironing my skirt . . . we must stop her before Vanna speaks again!" And Wendy Kamenoff (1992) describes the book *Do What You Love and the Money Will Follow,* predicting, "if it works out, by this time next year, I will have a quarter of a million dollars from masturbating and going to lunch with my friends."

A final topic in this category is therapy—self-help and otherwise. Joy Behar (1988) discusses self-help books, noting, "I didn't even know I hated men until I joined the Book of the Month Club—now

not only do I hate the men—I hate the women who love the men."
And Judy Toll (1992) shares a revelation she recently had in therapy:
"Apparently, I think I'm a piece of crap—that the world revolves
around."

Random Observations

This final catchall category includes material about restaurants, air-
planes, animals, school, sports, crime, holidays, professions, substances/
intoxication, laws, rules, friends (often focusing on gender differences
in same-sex friendships), and other minutiae of daily life. Rita Rudner
(1987) describes a restaurant so expensive that the menu had "no
prices—just different faces with expressions of horror." Taking the
phrase "Live every day as though it's your last" to heart, Amy Foster
(1990) says she decided to "Clear out my savings account, tell off my
boss, and have sex with twelve strangers." Margaret Smith (1992)
admits, "I wore a neck brace for a year—I wasn't in an accident or
anything—I just got tired of holding my head up." Laura Kightlinger
(2001) recalls, "I got asked to do a benefit for babies born addicted to
crack, and I said, 'Well, alright—I'll help you raise money for them,
but I think we *both* know what they're gonna *spend* it on.'" Finally,
Paula Poundstone (1999) explains:

> The state of Alaska's Department of Fish and Game is advising people to
> take *extra* precautions against *bears*. To . . . wear bells on their clothing and
> carry pepper spray, and to watch out for fresh signs of bear activity. And it
> *is* important to know the difference between black bear and grizzly bear
> dung. . . . Black bear dung is smaller and contains lots of berries and squir-
> rel fur, and grizzly bear dung has little bells in it and smells like pepper spray.

Gynecological Humor as Metaphor

After examining the preceding topical categories in the discourse of
contemporary American female stand-up comics, two important findings are apparent. First, although this investigation is not comparative
in nature, it is necessary and significant to mention that, for the most
part, male and female comics talk about the same topics.[2] Both male
and female comics focus, to a large extent, on issues pertaining to sex,
romantic heterosexual relationships, and the differences between men

89

and women, particularly in terms of communication. Both also perform a fair amount of material related to family and religion/ethnicity.[3] In general, female comics concentrate on issues of weight and body image (and occasionally housework) more than do male comics. Male comics tend to devote more material to sports, politics, and substances (alcohol and drugs) than do female comics. Male comics also perform numerous dick jokes (though female comics occasionally perform dick jokes—sometimes as a potentially subversive critique).[4] Both male and female comics spend a good deal of time discussing body parts, though not usually in the same way (for example, female comics often talk about the need to improve their own bodies, whereas male comics comment on female bodies from the perspective of consumers). The above are simply general distinctions; none of the material mentioned is exclusive to one sex. Clearly, female and male comics discuss the same topics differently, but so, too, do any two comics of the same gender. Indeed, as communication researchers frequently point out, there are as many differences within as between genders.

The second finding, however, deals with the only topic area that does appear exclusive to female comics—gynecological humor.[5] Martin and Segrave (1986) note that in the 1970s many female comics

> dealt with so-called women's topics like fashion, menstruation, weight, hygiene, being single, sex, and relationships. Sometimes these subjects were used in an almost self-deprecatory style, but mainly because these were areas in which women have been victimized or were vulnerable. Since humor was a way of dealing with pain, it was inevitable that these topics would crop up repeatedly. The politics were essentially personal (311).

The phrase "so-called women's topics" is relevant in this context. Today, with the exception of gynecological humor (menstruation, visits to the gynecologist, feminine hygiene, mammograms), none of the topics Martin and Segrave delineate are unique to the acts of female comics. Does this imply that, topically, stand-up comedy has become feminized or simply that—aside from gynecological humor—stand-up comedy has always been topically androgynous?

Although it is only one of eleven topical categories in the discourse of female comics, gynecological humor cannot be dismissed. By performing such material, female comics make choices at both stylistic and substantive levels—choices that may enlighten as well as entertain their audiences. Only female comics perform gynecological humor because this category features experiences that only women have. Why do female comics perform material about their menstrual periods and pelvic exams? Because it works. And why does it work? Because, as psychoanalytic theories of humor suggest, controversial or "taboo" topics allow audiences to feel naughty but not ashamed. Freud's notion of tendentious humor is helpful here; if gynecological humor is considered "obscene" by some audience members, then it obviously enjoys the reception of all other such humor. Still, gynecological humor is not the female equivalent of a dick joke, first, because it is not nearly as prevalent in comedic discourse and second, because it is not as universally accepted or appreciated by audiences. In my own experience performing this type of material, for example, it was the women in the audience who identified and therefore laughed the loudest. Depending on the audience composition (considering factors such as age and ideological position as well as gender) on any given night, I might choose to eliminate bits about yeast infections and feminine hygiene products. Hence, from a female comic's perspective, the decision whether to perform gynecological humor, like the decision about any particular joke or topic, is an inherently pragmatic one.

At a more substantive level, however, gynecological humor may serve as a means to address and express women's feelings of anger and victimization in a public context. Martin and Segrave's discussion of victimization may be useful in this regard. Perhaps a gynecological examination is a metaphor for violence toward women. Very few contemporary female comics perform jokes about rape, but the violation a woman experiences in a gynecologist's office (particularly if the doctor is male)—the sense of powerlessness combined with anxiety, fear, humiliation, at times physical pain, and always total objectification— may serve as a symbolic representation of the way in which women feel victimized by patriarchal culture. It is difficult to get most audiences to laugh at rape, but by using gynecological humor, a female comic may evoke identification from female audience members, enabling them to laugh at a shared indignity.

In fact, "indignity" is an understatement. In gynecological stirrups, a woman is defined solely by her sexual organs. She is in an uncomfortable and completely vulnerable position, penetrated by unwelcome instruments, and often treated with clinical detachment. The entire situation is constructed as both rhetorical and physical invasion.[6] Experiencing perhaps the ultimate objectification, represented synecdochically by a part of her body with which she may not even be comfortable but that nevertheless defines her as female, a woman in this context may not feel that she is viewed as a human being. As Adams (1991) explains, objectification is the first step in the insidious and dangerous cycle of violence toward women, in attitude as well as action. Once women are objectified, Adams suggests, they can then be fragmented, defined by body parts (for example, "piece of ass"), and ultimately consumed by a culture hungry for domination and control.[7] Although Adams's argument refers to the pornography industry, her discussion of objectification is applicable to gynecological exams. Even the feelings of dehumanization women may experience during these exams is fair game for comic material, however; for example, Joan Rivers, the comic who "introduced that filthy, twelve-letter word, 'gynecologist,' into the American stand-up's vocabulary" (Phillips 1989, 15), highlights this discomfort when she says, "gynecologists never look at a patient . . . met mine at a party . . . 'Hi, Doc'— he doesn't know who I am" [does a gesture of pulling her dress up to identify herself].

In a 1993 *Playboy* interview, Roseanne claims: "Comedy is the only chance I have to speak about what it's like to be a woman in this culture" (67). Perhaps performing material about gynecological examinations is the only chance female comics have to speak about violence and violation of women in this culture. Perhaps it is also one of the only public opportunities women have to express the discomfort they may feel with their own bodies (for example, Dumbrowski's cervix material quoted above) and their anger at the cultural values and norms that cause such discomfort. Eve Ensler's phenomenally successful play, *The Vagina Monologues* (2001) accomplishes much the same goal. Through the often humorous discourse of actual women Ensler interviewed, taboo topics such as feminine hygiene and, of course, gynecological exams are addressed. In one monologue, entitled "My Angry Vagina," the speaker rants:

> Then there's those exams. Who thought them up? There's got to be a better way to do those exams. Why the scary paper dress that scratches your tits and crunches when you lie down so you feel like a wad of paper someone threw away? Why the rubber gloves? Why the flashlight all up there like Nancy Drew working against gravity, why the Nazi steel stirrups, the

mean cold duck lips they shove inside you? What's that? My vagina's angry about those visits. It gets defended weeks in advance. It shuts down, won't "relax." Don't you hate that? "Relax your vagina, relax your vagina." Why? My vagina's not stupid. Relax so you can shove those cold duck lips inside it? I don't think so. (71)

Through passages such as the above, Ensler presents gynecological humor to diverse audiences, educating while she entertains.[8]

Like female comics, Ensler articulates women's experience. As part of the V-Day Campaign—a worldwide effort to raise awareness and funds to stop violence against women and girls—*The Vagina Monologues* foregrounds the culture of shame surrounding women's bodies, reclaiming the language used to describe them as well as the power inherent in such rhetorical reclamation. As the director of a recent (2002) production of *The Vagina Monologues,* I found that the humorous pieces (such as "My Angry Vagina") were those that audiences not only found most entertaining but with which they most willingly identified. In fact, Ensler does precisely what female comics do when performing gynecological humor—she disarms and relaxes audience members through comic discourse in order to teach them about what it means to be a woman in contemporary culture. In this way, gynecological humor may serve as a means of empowering comics and audiences alike. Clearly, the topic of gynecology is one derived from experiences unique to women; does this necessarily make it female or feminist humor?

Engendering Topics

Analysis of the material performed by contemporary American female comics suggests that, topically, there is nothing specifically "feminist" about the humor they create. If feminism means gender egalitarianism, then the existence of feminist humor seems highly unlikely. Indeed, it is impossible to fathom an "equal opportunity" humor of any kind, for one of the characteristics of humor (with the exception of wordplay and some observational humor) is mockery.[9] In almost any joke, some person or institution is derided or lampooned. Is a "feminist" humor one in which everyone is *equally* devalued?

Furthermore, topical analysis indicates that there is very little specifically "female" humor performed by female comics (with the significant exception of gynecology, the only topical category exclusive to women comedians). Instead, these comics perform women's point of view jokes, just as male comics perform men's point of view jokes. Horowitz (1997) notes that female comics are often criticized for being too "ghettoized" and overly concerned with "women's issues" (158); however, my analysis of the preceding topical categories suggests otherwise. As a phenomenon, humor does not appear inherently gendered; rather, it is the gender of the humorist that generates the label "women's humor." Similarly, "African American humor," "Jewish humor," or any other group's humor is so designated because of the joketeller's demographic frame of reference. The humor performed by white male comics is not called "men's humor," because the perspective these comics articulate is viewed as universal. As Horowitz observes: "The perspective that is thought of as neutral is usually that of the dominant group, i.e., male. Stand-up comedy is a personal, often autobiographical art form, and comics relate to broad issues through personal experience. When white male comics do this, their perspective is taken as the norm" (159).

Female comics are aware of this disparity, and some find it a personal challenge. For example, comic Emily Levine asserts: "Men think their version of reality is the reality. And I'd like my version of reality to be the dominant one" (cited in Horowitz 1997, 159). Explaining that onstage she asks the audience "to accept a different way of seeing things," Levine notes that in order to overcome the resulting tension, she must make her "version of reality" acceptable. Perhaps all marginal performance is a means of legitimizing alternate "versions" of reality. Analysis of the eleven topical categories evident in the discourse of contemporary female comics reveals the content of their particular versions of reality. Now that we know *what* female comics speak about onstage, we must determine *how* they speak. In other words, how do they rhetorically construct and perform their marginalized status as women before a variety of audiences? This question is explored in depth in chapter 4.

FEMALE COMICS: WALKING THE WALK

Whether discussing women's oral or written comedic discourse, very few scholars have sought a typology of female comic traditions. One exception is Judith Wilt; in her now-classic essay on women's humorous writing, Wilt (1980) discusses the "collision between comedy and feminism," arguing that this collision has resulted in two types of "women's comedy"—the matriarch, "knowing, sly, packed full of ripe experience, aware of the price being paid by all, capable of giving shocks" (179), and the maiden, "the virgin-mocker, the girl-hunter" who "exposes and deflates" (179–80). Wilt contends that the maiden's mockery is ultimately devoid of power, and the matriarch's—though subversive—has potentially dire consequences. She concludes that "Women may surely hesitate, then, before either of these two comic modes, wistfully wishing they could count more securely on a man's sense of humor" (194–95). Like most scholars of "women's humor," however, Wilt focuses on written rather than oral texts.

Since American female comics first took the stage in the nineteenth century, several traditions of female comic performance have been evident, but scholars have neglected to classify them thoroughly. Horowitz (1997) provides several labels such as "dumb blonde" and "wisecracking loser," suggesting that historically, to be funny, women could either be sexy/pretty and dumb or sarcastic/smart but unattractive. She claims that although most contemporary female comics reject the "dumb sexpot" vs. "smart spinster" model, many still retain elements of the "loser" persona of Phyllis Diller or Joan Rivers (14); she does not, however, provide examples of such comics.

Horowitz further describes historical precedents of "Dumb Doras" (for example, Mrs. Malaprop, Gracie Allen, Jane Ace, Lucille Ball, and Goldie Hawn) who "deny their intellect" and "Gawky Gertrudes" (for example, Marie Dressler, Judy Canova, Phyllis Diller, Lucille Ball again, Minnie Pearl, and Carol Burnett) who "deny their sexuality" (although she maintains that both types can transcend their labels) as well as "child" comic characters (Lotta Crabtree, Fanny Brice's Baby Snooks, Lily Tomlin's Edith Ann, and Whoopi Goldberg). Finally, Horowitz discusses "Wits" and "Wisecrackers," but does not truly distinguish between the two, later noting that female comics who use self-deprecation are "Gawky Gertrudes as wisecrackers" (144). Although some of her description is useful, the schema Horowitz provides is at times unclear and fails to encompass the full scope of female comic traditions. Suggesting that monologists like Dorothy Parker and Ruth Draper gave rise to "maternal" or overtly sexual comics like Mae West and Moms Mabley, for example, Horowitz conflates discrete types, muddying the historical waters in the process. Additionally, Horowitz fails to delineate comics from actors and does not provide contemporary analogues for the types she discusses. Indeed, a clear discussion of female comic traditions from their origins to the present is essential to any examination of marginal performance and fills a critical gap in the existing literature.

Ultimately, I believe that the female comic traditions evident since women began performing onstage in the nineteenth century evolved into five postures: (1) the *kid*; (2) the *bawd*; (3) the *bitch*; (4) the *whiner*; and (5) the *reporter*. These postures are rooted in female comic performance originating long before the genre of stand-up comedy as we know it today. Just as with topical categories, however, these postures are often conflated in female comic performance (even within the act of a single comic). This chapter provides examples of each posture by first describing the historical development, rhetorical functions, and stylistic elements of each, and next examining the five comedic postures in the context of strategic self-presentation, considering issues of combination of postures, interaction with audience, and analogous male personas.

Female Comedic Postures and Their Traditions

The Kid

This persona is desexualized and therefore nonthreatening.[1] The kid is playful and observant, offering honest assessments of people and situations. In the 1870s and 1880s, Lotta Crabtree, the "gold rush girl," was the highest-paid performer of her day. Aside from singing and dancing, she portrayed a child and was the "cause of more merriment than almost any other entertainer of her time" (Martin and Segrave 1986, 42). Early in this century, Irene Franklin was the most popular female vaudeville artist, known for songs, impersonations, and the child character she played. Perhaps the most famous female kid was Fanny Brice, star of both the legendary Ziegfeld Follies and radio as the character of Baby Snooks. As Martin and Segrave observe, "Brice . . . abandoned both her sex and her adulthood. As Baby Snooks she had become an asexual child" (115). A contemporary of Brice, Helen Kane, better known as "Betty Boop," used baby talk and her "Boop boop be doop" refrain as a way to project an innocent image while she sang on the vaudeville stage.

In the 1970s, Lily Tomlin became another much-beloved kid as the precocious Edith Ann, winning fans through her performances both on television's *Laugh-In* and on record albums. Ever the "wise fool," Edith Ann makes pronouncements about every aspect of life. On her Grammy Award–winning album, *And That's the Truth* (1972), for example, Tomlin-as-Edith Ann observes, "Baby Jesus has a light on his head so he can read comics in the bed." And on *Modern Scream* (1975), Edith Ann asks the audience, "Where do babies come from?" and receiving no answer, asks, "Don't you know either?" After explaining basic biology, Edith Ann urges the audience, "Try to tell as many people as you can in town."

The above are examples of the kid persona in American female comic performance since the late nineteenth century. And the kid is alive and well in the performance of contemporary female stand-up comics, most notably in the acts of Ellen DeGeneres and Paula Poundstone. In their acts, both women discuss animals extensively. Observing with wonder, DeGeneres (1992) offers:

> The scariest thing in the world happened to me. . . . I put my foot in my shoe . . . huge spider in my shoe . . . what if I would have put my foot in

the other shoe and there was a lot—like a snorkel of spiders or whatever it's called—that would be the scariest thing in the world, I thought—that would be . . . bad. . . . Or if you're on the beach and you're playin' frisbee. . . . and the frisbee goes flyin' past you and . . . you're like, "I'll get it," . . . and it goes into like a cave . . . and it's further down than you think, so you have to like spelunk down in there . . . and you go to grab for the frisbee and you're like, "Hey, how come my frisbee is squishy?" . . . and it's a bat—you're like squeezin' a bat . . . and it sets off thousands of bats and they all start comin' after you. . . . so you're like running, which is hard enough to run 'cause it's the sand and you've got heels on 'cause it looks good . . . with the swimsuit and so you're running and one of the heels breaks . . . so you're thinking, "I'll run into the water to get away from the bats . . ." and right when you're about to get in the water, a bat bites your ear off and so sharks can smell blood from miles away . . . and so the sharks are like comin' at you and the bats are at your hair and at your face, ya know . . . I just thought that would be the scariest thing in the world for that to happen.

Telling stories in the diction ("scariest," "squishy") and cadences of a child, DeGeneres constructs herself as the audience's playmate. DeGeneres wears very little makeup and performs a "wide-eyed" delivery; she also tends to speak in run-on sentences and, occasionally, the halting rhythms of a child attempting to remember every detail of a story. Throughout the above performance, the audience responds enthusiastically, apparently identifying with childhood fears.[2] Indeed, discussing DeGeneres's wide appeal, Fraiberg (1994) notes, "Quite simply, she tells what seem to be embarrassing stories about herself, but then sutures audiences into a mass position of identification with her" (321).

Paula Poundstone also employs the kid persona onstage. Performing in clubs since 1980, she is playful and exceptionally interactive with her audience, literally "playing" with audience members as everyone's funny friend. In a popular bit, Poundstone (1992) complains:

Pilots on planes always tell you to look out the window and you're always sitting on the wrong side, so you just know they're goin', "Pst—people on the left . . . don't tell the people on the right—there is the coolest stuff out your window right now. . . . We *hate* the people on the right . . . just look at them sitting there . . . I hate that . . . they're ruining *everything*. . . . You don't have to put your tray tables up if you don't want to. . . . If we go down, we're getting you out first."

Like DeGeneres, Poundstone projects an asexual innocence. She speaks in a child's idiom, using words like "coolest" and "stuff." Her speech is slightly slurred and frequently peppered with the word "um." She also refers to women in her audience as "ma'am" in a tone just sarcastic enough to suggest a naughty child.

Aside from her set material, Poundstone also interacts with the audience frequently, engaging in a good deal of playful teasing. For instance, after a lengthy discussion about an audience member's mother who "tore her face open on a lube rack" at a gas station, Poundstone spontaneously quizzes another audience member who has just returned from the restroom: "Apparently, there are special rules for Kara this evening. . . . um, Kara—when you're in a gas station, do you know what to be careful of? What a lovely face you have—hope nothing happens to it."[3] Establishing an intimate rapport, Poundstone refers to her audience as "you guys," assuming the posture of a mischievous pal. In a 1999 appearance, for example, she tells her audience, "I stayed at a hotel . . . I stayed in the Ernest Hemingway Suite— which was very embarrassing because he was in there and ya know, I haven't read all his books, so I didn't know what to say." As the kid, Poundstone presents a virtually androgynous persona, playful, non-threatening, and able to elicit strong audience identification. Indeed, within the kid tradition, female comics have long been adroit at entertaining without intimidating. The kid is mischievous but imminently likable. Most of all, devoid of overt sexuality, the kid is safe.[4]

Perhaps the most popular kid currently on television is Rosie O'Donnell. Although during her many years as a stand-up comic, O'Donnell generally assumed the "reporter" role, as a daytime talk-show host, her appeal to mass audiences seemed, to a large extent, based upon the wide-eyed nature of her nonthreatening, asexual persona. Laurie Stone (1996), a reporter from the *Village Voice,* refers to O'Donnell as "Joan Rivers without the self-loathing" and attributes O'Donnell's success to audience "affection for her big, smart, heartfelt, unembarrassed presence." Named "Entertainer of the Year" by *Entertainment Weekly* and one of *TV Guide*'s "Performers of the Year," both in 1996, O'Donnell has earned the sobriquet, "the Queen of Nice." Noting that she is "part brassy New Yorker, part perky den mother," *Time* reporter Ginia Bellafante (1996) sees O'Donnell as "the poster girl of the campaign to clean up daytime talk." Clearly, both the public and the media have been thoroughly charmed by O'Donnell's enthusiasm, sincerity, and penchant for clean humor. Interacting with her celebrity guests as just another starstruck fan, O'Donnell's engaging presence makes her everybody's pal.[5]

The Bawd

The antithesis of the kid, the bawd revels in sexuality and sensuality. The bawd uses her sexuality as a means of pleasure and control. She is sometimes portrayed as insatiable and always threatening, especially on the subject of male sexual apparatus and/or technique. Bawd comics tend to be physically large, often using their size to project a voluptuous image. Much more prevalent than the kid, the bawd tradition reached its apex in the climate of "sexual liberation" during the 1960s, ultimately giving rise to another posture, the bitch. The bawd comics of today assume a persona that dates back to the beginning of the twentieth century.

The first practitioners of this tradition included Eva Tanguay, who made her reputation in the first two decades of the twentieth century through the performance of sexually suggestive material (musical and otherwise).[6] Martin and Segrave (1986) note that Tanguay "and a few others symbolized a new aggressiveness in female comics"—that, indeed, "The groundwork for the aggressive and uninhibited woman comedian was laid ... by those like Tanguay but would never be fully realized until the late 1970s" (75). Others who helped to lay this groundwork included vaudeville bawds Lillian Shaw and Kate Elinore. Discussing these performers, Kibler (1998) explains that it was the tough, ethnic immigrant personas they adopted that made Shaw and Elinore acceptable to audiences accustomed only to male physical slapstick.[7]

An even greater license for female comic bawdiness onstage was physical size. Historically, many bawd comics have been large women who used their size in the service of their blatant sexuality. A famous early example was Sophie Tucker, the "Last of the Red Hot Mamas," a comic whose career spanned over half a century, including performances in numerous venues—from vaudeville to film. Tucker was physically large, a feature that added to her voluptuousness and provided humorous material in the form of "fat" jokes. This tradition continued with perhaps the most famous female comic bawd of all time—Mae West, an "American institution" (Martin and Segrave 1986, 173) who "opened up sexuality through humor and parody" (188).

Throughout a career that included singing, dancing, and acting on the Broadway stage, in clubs, and on radio and film, West was famous for acerbic lines like, "Come up and see me sometime. Come up Wednesday. That's amateur night" (190) and "Sex is a lot like snow. You never know when it's gonna come, how long it's gonna last, or how many inches you're gonna get" (*Laughtrack* 33).

Martin and Segrave describe West as "likely the most quoted woman in history" (190). At one time the highest paid entertainer in the country, West explained her own humor, noting: "I make fun of vulgarity. . . . I kid sex" (quoted in Martin and Segrave 1986, 182), and asserted, "I beat men at their own game. I don't look down on men but I certainly don't look up to them either" (189–90). According to Martin and Segrave:

> [West] presented women in a totally different light. With her characters women were always the winners. She took on and beat all male comers. She did it through a parody of the age-old femme fatale, a combination of humor and sex which hadn't been done before. At the same time she mocked the male. . . . Her importance to the women's movement, to female comedy, and to the self-image of women can't be overestimated. She was self-assured, flamboyant, and aggressive, an image of women that could only be presented through the softening effect of exaggerated comedy and satire, but she made her point. (74)

Noting that West was a true innovator in female comic performance, Martin and Segrave maintain, "She did what was impossible for a woman to do up until then—ridicule sex, while at the same time being sexual herself" (188).

Although overtly sexual, West was never graphic; her material was a combination of innuendo and double entendre, allowing her to be bawdy without being censored. The primary reason West became such a successful bawd, Ivanov (1994) argues, was her age and size. Allen explains that as West's sexuality became "unthinkable" due to these characteristics, she became "less and less threatening," ultimately, like many bawds, "authorized to be transgressive because, by their fusing of incongruent cultural categories [such as age and sexuality], they had been 'disqualified' as objects of erotic desire" (cited in Ivanov, 277). Because she did not meet societal norms and standards of sexiness and attractiveness, Ivanov maintains, West's sexuality was self-parody. Ivanov reminds us, however, that West was at least partly responsible for changing those same norms, introducing a more curvaceous and abundant figure as sexually desirable.

Another of the most famous bawds was the first female African American comic to gain national attention—Jackie "Moms" Mabley. Beginning on the black vaudeville circuit and continuing her career for over thirty years, Mabley released more than twenty-five recordings (her first album went gold) and performed in countless venues across the country, garnering her biggest success when she "was discovered in the 1960s by white audiences and reacclaimed by her ethnic community" (Williams 1991, 159). Presenting a unique persona that was simultaneously homespun and sexual, Mabley cast the audience as her children. Elsie Williams, who has written extensively on Mabley, maintains that "assuming the maternal pose provided Mabley with a vehicle for boundary setting, for controlling the relationship between herself . . . and the audience. . . . In addition, the adoption of the position "Moms" gave Mabley a natural platform for expounding folk wisdom, leveling world leaders and bigots, and instructing a society on what to teach its young" (164–65).

Yet, despite her "Moms" persona, Mabley was also overtly sexual, often telling risqué jokes and commenting on her desire for younger men. Her 1960 album, *The Funniest Woman in the World,* contains examples of this: "I'm old and like younger men . . . I'm guilty and I'm gonna get guiltier. . . . You got a fairy Godfather? No—I got a brother I ain't so sure about. . . ." After describing two "old maids" taking a walk, she quotes the first old maid: "I smell hair burnin'." And the second old maid: "Maybe you're walkin' too fast. . . ." To an audience member: "Take your hands outta your lap, son—you'll go crazy."

Occasionally more graphic, Mabley also performed material such as, "My brother is dead because one of those fairy tales they kept telling him . . . 'Ding Dong Bell/Pussy's in the Well . . . ' and he got drowned like a fool!" (Williams 1991, 165).

Mabley was perennially giving advice. For instance, explaining the way to attract younger men, she offers, "All you have to do is knock on their door and ask them: 'Say, doll, do you have change for a hundred dollar bill'" (cited in Martin and Segrave 1986, 290). Assuming the posture of an aging but still very sexual woman, Mabley endeared herself to audiences with precisely this paradoxical persona—a wise but lustful "Mom" whose sexual appetite was made comical by her advanced years.

Clearly the most famous African American female comic, Mabley helped establish the image of the African American woman as both maternal and hypersexualized. This image extends beyond the comic frame into numerous depictions of African American women in popular culture, particularly in film and television.[8]

The bawd tradition reached its zenith in the 1960s. Among the purveyors of occasionally "blue" material were several virtual unknowns such as Hattie Noel (described as a "copy" of Mabley), Lynn Robinson, Pearl Williams, and Bea Bea Benson.[9] The bawd of the sixties was often sexually explicit—much more so than the nineties bawd—focusing on body parts in great detail. Pearl Williams, for example, released "adults only" albums, performing graphic sexual material such as: "Definition of indecent. If it's long enough, hard enough, and in far enough, it's in decent! Definition of a cotton picker: a girl who loses the string on her tampax. . . . Hear about the broad who walks into the hardware store to buy a hinge? The clerk says, 'Madam, would you like a screw for this hinge?' She says 'No, but I'll blow ya for the toaster.'" When a heckler says "Pull your dress down," Williams responds: "Pull my dress down? To where? Which part of me do you want to see first? I got an awful lot here, honey. Take a good look. You could never handle this boy. You need eight guys, four to put you on, four to take you off. A night with me and you'll disappear for a month, ya dope ya. And how's he gonna find this thing, there's so many wrinkles around it! I'll have to urinate to give you a clue!" (cited in Smith 1988, 682–83).

Another little-known sixties comic was Bea Bea Benson, whose combination of stock jokes and graphic sexual imagery made her one of the bawdiest of bawds.[10] She also performed a surprising amount of material about rape. Her 1960s album contains the following: "Gee, but it's great after rapin' your date—draggin' the body back home. . . . The gal who didn't know she'd been raped 'til her check bounced. . . . So help me, I raped her . . . so rape her and I'll help you. . . . no such thing as rape—everyone knows a gal can run faster with her skirt up than a guy can with his pants down. . . . poon tang cocktail—very refreshing no matter *whose* joint you get it in."

One of the most popular singing bawds of the 1960s was Rusty Warren, who released eleven albums. Best remembered for the title track of her album, *Knockers Up,* Warren relied on sexual innuendo sprinkled with a few expletives. Her material includes lines such as:

103

before you were married [husband said,] "Marry me, baby, and I'll give it to you every morning, every afternoon, every night, and twice on Sundays!" Am I right, girls? After fifteen years you're lucky to get it! And when you do it's a present! He brought it all the way home from the office for you! On the bus! Under his hat! . . . [Introduces "Knockers Up" as:] a number for the young ladies to prove that we have something to give. . . . [Attempts to get women to sing along and march] Ladies—you're not marching. . . . I bet when you go *home*, you'll march right through your living room. . . . tomorrow at work . . . your boss will say, "Hot damn— Beatrice got her knockers up!"

Popular with both genders, her songs ("Wish I Could Shimmy Like My Sister Kate," "Gonna Get Some Poontang") and patter made Warren a memorable bawd.

"One of the most famous of the red hot mamas who told dirty jokes on novelty records of the 60s" (Smith 1988, 43) was Belle Barth. Like many of her contemporaries, Barth combined risqué songs with patter, performing lines like: "I always say the most difficult thing for a woman to do is try to act naive on the first night—of her second marriage. She hollers it hurts, and he's gotta tie his feet to the bed he shouldn't fall in and drown!" (cited in Smith, 43).

Beginning in vaudeville, Barth was "one of the first entertainers to use blatantly x-rated material" (Martin and Segrave 1986, 142). Her career spanned over four decades, reaching its apex in the sixties, but even her early material tested limits, for example: "When the world war broke out, I joined the WACS. . . . I figured, what the hell, at least I'll see a lot of action, and I felt as happy as the girl who got raped on Essex Street and thought it was Grand. But I had my disappointments in the service; I discovered that a 21–inch Admiral was only a television set" (cited in Martin and Segrave, 142). Known as a "female Lenny Bruce," Barth was one of the most popular bawd comics of her time.

A distinctive bawd who has been winning audiences with her unique brand of bawdiness since the 1970s is Bette Midler. Primarily a singer and, in recent years, a film actor, Midler uses camp and burlesque to construct her stage persona, the "Divine Miss M." Internationally acclaimed for her many successful albums and concert appearances, Oscar nominee Midler exudes sexuality onstage. She continues to entertain audiences with songs and references to her large breasts, such as "Two reasons why I didn't become a ballerina" (cited in Martin and Segrave 1986, 393). In fact, Midler has actually "flashed" audiences on more than one occasion. A clear inheritor of the Sophie Tucker/Mae West tradition, Midler assumes the bawd posture with great success.

Another bawd who surfaced in the 1970s was African American comic La Wanda Page. Before becoming known for her role on the hit TV show *Sanford and Son,* Page released an album featuring material such as: "[A whore in church:] 'One night I was layin' in the arm of a sailor. The next night I was layin' in the arm of a soldier. But tonight, I'm layin' in the arms of Jesus!' And the other whore jumped up and said 'That's right bitch, fuck 'em all!'" (cited in Smith 1988, 488).

Contemporary American female stand-up comics do not generally rely on songs or stock jokes. Rather, they perform original material in monologue form. As noted earlier in this discussion, they also do not tend to be as sexually explicit as their precursors.[11] Present-day bawds include Carrie Snow, Angela Scott, Stephanie Hodge, Adrienne Tolsch, Caroline Rhea, and Thea Vidale. Continuing the tradition of the African American bawd, Thea Vidale, former star of her own TV sitcom, *Thea,* and featured in the video *Comedy's Dirtiest Dozen,* has performed the following in her stand-up act: "I was married for 10 years and I can honestly tell you, ladies . . . I rate sex right up there with cleaning the oven and defrosting the refrigerator . . . so that's why I hired a maid and paid her 10 bucks just to be keeping the nigger offa me" (*Laughtrack* 26).[12]

One of the most overtly sexual contemporary bawds is Carrie Snow, who often jokes about her desire for younger men. In a 1985 performance on cable TV, for example, her material includes:

> I like young guys . . . I call 'em *tender vittles* . . . I've gotten very serious about them—I'm wearing this new Playdough cologne. . . . Sometimes, though, when they're really young, they're a little bit too frisky. So whatcha have to do is take 'em to the Sizzler, fill 'em full of beef to calm 'em down. Sometimes, if you're really lucky, they'll return the favor. . . . I do have a new boyfriend and I guess he's kinda young, 'cause I asked him how old he was and he said [holding up fingers of both hands] "*This* many!"

Acknowledging her own bawdiness, Snow explains:

> I talk real nasty and you guys think I'm not a nice girl and I want you to know I'm such a nice girl—I really am . . . I was a virgin until I was twenty and again until I was twenty-three. . . . I date a lot. . . . I've got a charge account at Planned Parenthood and everything. . . . [Referring to articles of

clothing men have left at her house:] I always have *one* sock—'cause I guess he was carrying his brains out in the other one. . . . I got crutches . . . I don't know who they belong to . . . there are a coupla things I'd like to know: First of all, Carrie, what were you doing with a guy on crutches, and second of all, just what did I *do* to him that he could walk out *without* them?

Blatantly sexual, making extensive use of innuendo, Snow exemplifies the contemporary bawd. In a 1991 performance (also on cable), she asserts: "We [women] think men are just vibrators with wallets . . . but I mean that in a beautiful loving way." Finally, in a 1992 cable appearance, Snow notes, "Some people treat their body like a temple—I treat mine like an amusement park." Then, with her hand at crotch level, she adds, "You must be this tall to go on this ride."[13]

Another performer who talks specifically about her desire for younger men is African American comic Angela Scott, as her 1992 material from a cable appearance attests:

One of the nice things about having a son that's six feet four and good-looking are his friends . . . young, *healthy* boys . . . come by to vi-sit . . . sometimes they come by to work out with my son on his weights . . . young, *swea-ty* boys . . . sometimes they wear those bold bright briefs . . . strong young healthy boys . . . and when they spend the night with my son, they have to pass by my room in the morning when they have to go to the bathroom . . . and you know how young boys are in the *mornin'* . . . they run by my room, they say, "Hey, Mrs. Scott—don't look, don't look, don't look." I say, "Oh don't worry, *bo-ys* [pretending to cover her face, but peeking through her fingers], I *won't*." . . . And they call me Mrs. Scott and I say, "Come on now boys, don't be so *formal*—just call me . . . Mrs. Robinson."

During this bit, Scott's facial expressions speak volumes as she rolls her eyes and licks her lips suggestively. Although not as physically large as many bawds, Scott uses expression and gesture in a highly sexualized manner and wears a tight-fitting leotard top. Strains of Mabley are evident in Scott's lascivious persona. Unlike Mabley, however, Scott does not cast the audience as her "children," but often performs material that focuses on the tension between her role as a mother and her own sexual desire.[14]

Indeed, sexual desire—especially for younger men—is a topic commonly discussed by bawd comics. This taboo lust is blatantly described by Adrienne Tolsch (1993): "I always liked younger guys— not *seven*—I'm not a *total* pervert—they weren't *that* young—they didn't have their little *mittens* still attached to their little sleeves . . . certainly not when they'd *leave.*" And Caroline Rhea (2001) confesses that, "Now, every time I see an eighteen-year-old boy, I'm like, 'Umm—breakfast.' I love the ones in the summertime on roller blades—I'm like, '*Oh*—meals on wheels, look!'" Much of Rhea's act is overtly sexual, including this bit directed at a male audience member: "You know what, sir? Your little bald head reminds me of something. . . . I was just recently gambling. . . . I heard this superstition when I was gambling—that if you rub a bald man's *head,* it's good luck—yeah—actually, I thought they said if you *give* a bald man head. So . . . *he* felt incredibly lucky, *I* won a lot of cash, and it's good to *see* you *again,* so there we go!" Like all bawd comics, Rhea flaunts her sexuality, unabashedly proclaiming her prodigious desire.

Perhaps the most "physical" of contemporary bawds, Stephanie Hodge oozes sexuality. In one particular bit, Hodge (1992) instructs women in flaunting their "femininity":

> Do you gesture, pulsate, undulate and throb? . . . You can get anything you want if you do that . . . all you have to do is learn to overenunciate everything you say so it all comes out like [gasps and quivers] "I need a cup of coffee . . . I need a cup of coffee *now* . . . cream and sugar? Oooh, *yeah!*" Now wait . . . 'cause you *know* once your lips get goin', your body's just gotta naturally follow. So if you start workin' on your lips about nine in the mornin', by noon that body's gonna be beatin' a native tattoo, gonna set those clothes on spontaneous fire—trust me! One o'clock tomorrow, you and me, we'll go to McDonald's, we'll test this out, alright? Walk in there sashayin' them butts just a little bit, wrigglin' them lips . . . place that order [quivering and gasping with pulsating gestures] . . . "Oh, your selection's so *big*—I don't know what I *want* . . . oooh . . . it's comin' to me . . . oh, I know, I'll have a McChicken sandwich, fries, and a chocolate shake." . . . It's embarrassing the first few times you do that . . . but you get your food for free, so who the hell cares?

Throughout this bit, Hodge "gestures," "pulsates," "undulates," and "throbs" in an exaggerated version of feminized sexuality. Clad in a tight-fitting dress, Hodge accentuates her ample physique and ensures that the audience sees each and every move. By providing metacommentary, however, Hodge renders her own sexuality less threatening. Essentially giving the women in her audience "lessons" in bawdery, Hodge also instructs them in performing their marginality in a way that "promises" increased resources and economic gain (free food).[15]

As discussed earlier, the bawd posture is always sexual, always threatening, and often deals with female desire for younger men. This female comic persona sends a double message. Although she can be quite intimidating, her sexualized demeanor frequently provides a palliative, simultaneously titillating the audience and inviting identification. The bawd says, in essence, "What you see is what you get—are you sure you can handle it?" Another female comedic posture threatening to audiences makes no attempt to ameliorate the intimidation she exudes; this is, of course, the bitch.

The Bitch

The bitch is the angriest female comedic persona. Blatantly (rhetorically) subversive, this posture uses "put-down" humor as a form of social critique, lampooning and lambasting individuals and groups. Often conflated with the bawd or the whiner persona, the bitch is caustic and sometimes overtly ideological. The bitch evolved out of the bawd tradition. The two diverge, however, as the bitch focuses solely upon speaking her mind and getting what she wants. This persona is not interested in pleasing her audience; rather, she frequently insults and offends them or rails out against social mores and cultural norms.

The prototype of this female comedic posture is Joan Rivers. Although she is commonly known for the self-deprecatory material that brought her to national attention in the early 1960s (making her an important figure in the whiner tradition as well), at least half of Rivers's reputation is based on her frequent put-downs of everyone from Elizabeth Taylor to unsuspecting audience members (the tendency for some female comics to switch personas frequently is discussed later in this chapter). Describing herself as the "meanest bitch in America" (cited in Martin and Segrave 1986, 344), Rivers became the highest-priced opening act in history by the end of the 1970s, and "Through the early and mid 1980's she was the most popular and highly paid comic in the country" (344). Rivers has released two comedy albums, written several books, written, directed, and starred in her own film, and hosted a successful TV talk show. On her 1983 album, *What Becomes a Semi-Legend Most?* Rivers performs the following: "Don't give me all this liberation shit—men like 'em stupid. All you need is a pretty face and a trick pelvis and you're home free. . . . [To

a female audience member who shows Rivers her engagement ring]
You're a Jew and you took that shitty ring? A piece of shit in four
prongs—is your mother alive?"

Rivers's loud and raspy voice coupled with her trademark gestures (for example, finger in mouth to indicate vomiting—usually
done when describing someone unattractive) provide powerful nonverbal bitch stylistics. She speaks rapidly, repeats her catchphrase (or
"hook"), "Can we talk?" and uses exaggerated facial expressions such
as an open mouth to strengthen her attacks on a variety of targets.[16]

Horowitz (1997) notes that Rivers maintains a dynamic tension
between her aggressive/male "insider comedy style" and "her outsider subject matter—victimized female" (103–4), that her onstage
persona is a Jewish American Princess—"a manicured rebel against
the cultural ideal of the self-sacrificing, subordinate female" (106).[17]
Describing Rivers's material, Horowitz discusses her use of the
"bitch" and the "tramp" (coding "tramp" as "sexually promiscuous
and stupid"). Rivers asserts, "I love being called a bitch. It means a
bright winner. Am I a tramp? Don't I wish!" (101). Horowitz points
out that Lenny Bruce did a routine on the rhetorical power of racial
epithets being linked to their suppression—that is, that saying them
deflates them. Discussing the way Rivers does this with "tramp" and
"bitch," Horowitz wonders if Rivers intends to strip the words of
their power as Bruce did: "We are left wondering where she stands.
Does she think that this kind of language is demeaning to women?
Does she think that women really are either respectable, clever bitches
or promiscuous sluts? Or does she just want to play the subject for
laughs—and enhance her career as an entertainer?" (103). That critics ask such questions is a testament to the power of Rivers's stage
persona. From a performance perspective, regardless of her actual
ideological beliefs, she is clearly doing what all comics do—attempting to elicit laughter from her audience.

Because the word "bitch" carries immense rhetorical power,
bitch comics often use the term to refer to themselves and/or other
women. For example, Marsha Warfield (1987) muses, "Why do men
think all good-lookin' men are fags? Women don't think all good-
lookin' women are dykes—they're *bitches*." And Judy Carter (1990)
asks the young women in her audience, "Were you at Woodstock? You
weren't born yet? *Bitch!*" Suzy Lowks (1990) notes:

pretty, young girls treat us women terribly . . . love *you men* . . . always wearing sexy little outfits—miniskirts [breathy] "Hi—can I help you find anything today?" [mimes pulling skirt up] . . . I love to tease other women . . . I'm talkin' about young girls—you older guys love 'em—on the street, they've got these attitudes . . . prancing around like they're little Shetland ponies—"Oh, hi" [tosses hair frenetically and whinnies]. . . . I shouldn't talk about 'em this way, but girls will be girls, so what the hell . . . anyway, the little bitches are *so* stupid.

The label "bitch" need not be negative, however, according to Pam Matteson. In a 1992 performance, she explains, "it's fun to be a bitch—it's an art form."

Comics who assume the bitch posture frequently make jabs at couples or other women. Wanda Sykes (2001), for example, opens her act by telling the audience, "I hate cute couples—I do—I could kick all of y'all right in your teeth." And Amy Foster (1990) extols her boyfriend's virtues and then dolefully intones, "I know as I'm tellin' you this, he's got some blonde bent over our coffee table." In this remark, Foster packs a double punch, ridiculing both her libido-driven boyfriend and the stereotypical "dumb blonde" bimbo. It is clear from her sardonic performance style that Foster is anything but a helpless victim in this situation.

Continuing the Rivers tradition, other female comics assuming the bitch posture also bash female celebrities. Joy Behar, like Rivers, speaks in a loud, raspy voice. Behar's face, in a perpetual sneer of displeasure, projects the bitch persona throughout her act. A comedy veteran prior to her success as one of the hosts of the popular TV show *The View,* Behar frequently performed the following bit:

> Does she [Heather Locklear] still have that commercial running? Where she comes out in that little string bikini? She comes out and says, "Are you ready for the competition?" I'll *smack* her! It's like, shut up, Heather! Go do something with your life! Go teach the handicapped, go save the whales, take care of the homeless, *get off my back!* . . . Cher has a fragrance out. And on her commercial she says, "I call it Uninhibited because there are so many people inside of me." Yeah—and they're all under *18!* (cited in Gallo 1991, 71)

Other bitch celebrity bashers include Carrie Snow (1991), who describes Nancy Reagan, noting, "she's not warm—ya just wanna say, 'Nancy—take the stick out and *live,* okay?" and Judy Tenuta (1992) who bellows, "Madonna—tell me she's not a mattress with a microphone!"

Perhaps most commonly performed by the bitch comic is material that criticizes and denigrates men at both the personal and cultural levels. Paramount among female comics who perform this type of material is Roseanne. Although much of her success is due to her popular TV sitcom, her stand-up act features her most acerbic material. In her first (1987) HBO special, Roseanne chews gum ferociously and portrays the bitch persona in cadences that can only be aptly compared to the whine of a dentist's drill.[18] This particular performance includes the following:

> [On prostitution:] If men knew how to *do* it, they wouldn't have to pay for it. . . . men drivers criticize your driving. . . . Sorry, I guess it just takes someone with that peculiar mix of testosterone and Aqua Velva. . . . [On a new Stephen King novel:] about a husband with a mind of his own—don't worry, ladies—it's a fantasy—it could *never* happen! . . . Husband's gettin' on my nerves . . . "Don't you think we should talk about our sexual problems?" Yeah—like I'm gonna turn off *Wheel of Fortune* for *that!* . . . men think the uterus is a tracking device. . . . "Any Cheetohs left?" Like he can't go lift up the sofa cushion like anyone else. . . . How many men here are impotent? Can't get your *arms* up either, huh? . . . Like a lot of people come up to me all the time. . . . They go " . . . Roseanne, you're not very feminine." . . . So I say, "Well, suck my *dick!*"

By choosing to end her act with the ultimate subversion of a dick joke, Roseanne simultaneously illustrates the preeminent power of the phallus in Western culture (and specifically in the genre of stand-up comedy) and lampoons this power by using the phrase as a woman—a woman who denigrates men. She is quite literally using the "master's" tool to mock the master's "tool." And in so doing, she exemplifies McWhirter's (1994) notion that "comedy, like all humanly, historically constructed social and aesthetic forms, is always contingent, always open to transformative reappropriation" (200–201).

Commenting on her own stage persona, Roseanne explains: "I realized I had to create a whole new kind of comedy called 'funny womanness.' But there wasn't any language to name women's experience and make it funny to men and women. . . . I felt I had to invent the language. . . . I knew that I could do what Richard Pryor did for himself—get inside the stereotype and make it three-dimensional from within" (cited in Horowitz 1997, 153).

The language Roseanne uses to articulate the experience of being an American "housewife" in the late twentieth century is often derisive. For example, in a 1992 cable special, Roseanne observes: "People say lesbians hate men—how could that be—they don't have to *fuck* 'em! . . . men are *not* complex . . . he *is* just sitting in his underwear drinking beer and watching TV. . . . men only want one thing and it's not even in our top ten and we *still* like it better than *they* do!"

Indeed, issues of sex and sexuality comprise the intersection at which the bitch and bawd postures converge. Making fun of male sexuality in either general or specific terms provides a substantial amount of material for both the bitch and the bawd. The two differ, however, in the level of overt anger fueling the words. Shirley Hemphill (1985), for example, assumes the bitch persona as she becomes downright vitriolic:

> You ever get so jealous you get in your car and you *follow* his ass? You go, "Wait a minute—*this* isn't the way to Seven Eleven—where the fuck he *goin'*? This better be a *short*cut—I'm gonna be pissed off here." Or you like wait 'til he's asleep and you check out his pockets? [She laughs in embarrassment] You feel like a *sleaze* bag when you do that . . . but it's somethin' that *needs* to be done [Wild cheers and applause from women in the audience]. . . . You can't do no real damage to a *real* man—you got to wait . . . best thing we got is that element of surprise . . . I like when you're sleepin' real good. . . . I ease up real close and grab his balls and go, "Baby—have I got your attention, *honey?* What does 'Ay-yi-yi' mean? What the hell does that mean? Huh? No, your nose ain't bleedin' so stop cryin.' Listen, don't you black out—I'll squeeze harder. . . . Okay, now listen to this [raises arm in the air several feet from where her partner's body supposedly is]—did you go to Seven Eleven yesterday? [Considerable audience laughter] Bring it in so you can think? Okay. Stick the spoon in your mouth—here we go again—did you *go?*" [More audience laughter] And sometimes, your ego works on you . . . you have his balls, you go, "Bark like a dog." "Ruff ruff." "Okay."

Whereas the bawd might describe sexual activity and even criticize male sexual styles, the bitch advocates a "hit him where it hurts" philosophy, truly aiming below the belt with her rhetorical weapon.

Many female comics assuming the bitch posture make cutting remarks about past or present relationships. Lizz Winstead (1988) notes, "I think, therefore I'm single," and recalls her response to an ex-boyfriend's desire for space, "Strap yourself to a fucking MX missile!" Similarly, Deborah Swisher (1993) explains that when her former boyfriend said, "I need more space—I can't breathe," she replied, "That's because there's no draft when your head's up your *ass!*" Several

112

female comics use the bitch persona to discuss and capitalize upon male fears. Leah Krinsky (1991) criticizes men whining about performance anxiety, asserting, "If I'm gonna earn 40 percent less in the workplace, you're *damn* right you're gonna satisfy me. As far as I'm concerned, this is my office and you can be replaced by a machine." Krinsky also contends: "Men hate women with short hair—you're afraid of us . . . 'cause you're afraid that if you find us attractive it means you like boys . . . you think that making love to a girl with a guy's haircut makes you gay—that doesn't make you gay . . . making love to a girl with a *penis*—that makes you gay!"

The most blatantly antimale of any contemporary female stand-up comic is Judy Tenuta. Although her "Petite Giver-Goddess" stage persona often seems to lean more toward performance art than traditional stand-up comedy, she performs in comedy clubs and is considered a stand-up comic by bookers, reviewers, and audiences. Tenuta's persona is very much a character, a "bitch" dressed in a diaphanous gown, flitting about the stage, speaking in a high-pitched lilt one moment and snarling along to an accordion the next. Known for calling the men in the audience "pigs," Tenuta plays the bitch as a cartoon—a larger-than-life version of female ire. Performing on an HBO special in 1987, Tenuta greets the audience with, "Hi, pigs! Soon you will all be my personal love slaves." She also offers the following:

> [Traveling on an airplane] to Europe with a guy who looks like a squid in stretch pants—yeah, like I'm ready to *spawn*. . . . tried to get me to *talk* to him—just because he paid for my trip! . . . Like I have time to get my feet bound for some *sperm whale* with a *Visa card!* . . . By now I'm sure you can tell that I'm the sort of woman who sits by the phone and waits for some *man* to call! [Spits gum at the audience] Crawl for it! Look at you stud puppets with your legs open like there's almost any hope! . . . I want to meet a . . . guy—like you but with a pulse. . . . To tell ya the truth, I was lookin' for someone a little closer to the top of the *food chain!*

Because her anger is so exaggerated, male audience members laugh—ostensibly in appreciation.[19]

The bitch posture in female comic performance extends to "out" lesbian comics like Lea Delaria.[20] In a performance at the Gay and Lesbian March on Washington (1993), Delaria, dressed in "male" attire and speaking loudly, remembers: "walkin' down the street . . . found myself trapped in a nuclear family . . . teenage boy said, 'You fuckin' bulldyyyyyyke!' and I thought, 'Oooh, what a smart man—he could probably tell I was white, too.'" Another lesbian comic, Robin Tyler, tells a heckler, "You can always be replaced by a tampax" (cited in Martin and Segrave 1986, 419), and when another heckler asks, "Are you a lesbian?" replies, "Are *you* the alternative?" (421).

Many contemporary female comics assume the bitch posture at some point in their acts. Being a bitch allows the comic to be strong, assertive, even overtly aggressive and intimidating. In fact, it is this persona most critics refer to with the label "feminist comic." Because her context is a comedic one, the bitch comic is afforded a unique opportunity—she can attain power and insult—even offend—her audience all in the name of a few good laughs. As with any of the five postures assumed by female comics, the bitch covers a broad spectrum of stylistic choices and may be combined with other postures within a single act. For example, as noted earlier, Rivers combines the bitch with another posture often perceived as its antithesis—the whiner.

The Whiner

Evolving out of the "dumb blonde" and "screwball" female comic personas popular in the first half of the twentieth century, the whiner uses self-deprecation to get laughs. Comics who assume this posture often send a double message: (1) they put themselves (and, by extension, women in general) down, often delineating their inadequacies (frequently based on body image); and (2) by performing the above in a comedic context, they subvert the status quo by calling cultural values into question.[21] By making herself the butt, a whiner comic creates a safe environment for her audience. Engaging in self-deprecation (as opposed to deprecating others), the whiner does not pose a threat to her audience in any way.

The whiner tradition of American female comic performance began in the late nineteenth century with "Madame Laughter," May Irwin, who entertained audiences for over forty-five years by singing and telling "fat" jokes about herself. Although she performed self-deprecatory material, Irwin believed that "Woman's sphere is the same as man's, and that is the world" (cited in Martin and Segrave 1986, 47). Another early whiner was Marie Dressler, star of vaudeville (and later film—both silent and "talkies"), who explained, "I was born homely . . . when everything else fails I get my voice down to the audience and make a face" (cited in Martin and Segrave, 55). Thus began the tradition of "mugging" and physical comedy that spawned the careers of later talents like Lucille Ball and Carol Burnett. A contemporary of Irwin and Dressler, Trixie Friganza, a singer/dancer and film actress, was another comic who assumed the whiner posture by making her weight the butt of her jokes.

The whiner tradition evolved not only from physical comedy, but from "ditsy" and "screwball" comics as well. Judy Canova, "Queen of the Hillbillies," starred in the Ziegfeld Follies (and later radio and TV), singing and performing comedy as a "ditsy" man chaser. Zasu Pitts made a forty-five-year film career playing the "addlepated spinster." And in the 1940s, Minnie Pearl created her hillbilly character, performing lines like, "I felt so at home when I got here. In fact, one feller told me I was the homeliest girl he'd ever seen" (cited in Martin and Segrave 1986, 212). The 1940s also saw the development of the "dumb blonde" stereotype, embodied in performances by Carol Channing in clubs and in films like *Gentlemen Prefer Blondes* and *Hello Dolly* as well as in the performances of the "dumbest broad of them all," Judy Holliday—a woman who actually possessed a near-genius IQ (226).

The tradition of female physical comedy continued with "rubber-faced" performers like Martha Raye and Imogene Coca, who began in vaudeville and later enjoyed successful television careers. Contemporary Joan Davis, whose act included slapstick and some self-deprecatory material, noted, "Laughs are based on other people's misfortunes—it's awful, isn't it? A good fall always gets a laugh" (cited in Martin and Segrave 1986, 212, 257). Certainly, the most famous female physical comic of all time was Lucille Ball. Her popular TV shows generally featured Lucy as a "scatterbrained housewife" who took countless pratfalls but somehow always retained control of the situation. As Karyn Kay, coeditor of *Women and Cinema,* notes: "Lucy, you were a voice of rebellion for a pre-liberation . . . group of women. You shared a big secret with us: that women do not necessarily want neat, orderly homes and spic'n'span lives, quietly serving their husbands. You rejected the expected, Lucy, and refused to behave correctly. You spoke a lunatic language of female discontent—you were an inspired clown in the dog days before feminist consciousness" (cited in Martin and Segrave, 272). Aside from her TV shows, Lucy was the first female head of a major film company, and was long considered the wealthiest woman in Hollywood.

The whiner tradition of "dumb blondes" of the 1940s and 1950s continued with Marie Wilson, a film, radio, and TV performer whose large breasts inspired many jokes. In the 1960s, Goldie Hawn popularized the "kooky blonde" character on TV's *Laugh-In* (later attempting to eschew this image by executive producing and starring in the film *Private Benjamin*). At the same time, Lucy's successor Carol Burnett starred in her own Emmy Award–winning TV show. Known as "Queen of the Zanies" and a "female Chaplin," Burnett capitalized on her elastic features, engaging in "self-uglification" because "I knew I wasn't going to win any glamour prizes. . . . I was going to have to establish myself as a slob" (cited in Martin and Segrave 1986, 327–29). Believing that both genders tend to view comedy as "unfeminine," Burnett grossed $1 million annually with her physical clowning. Explaining the origin of her self-deprecatory material, Burnett remembers: "Once someone in my television audience asked what my measurements were. I said '37–24–38—but not necessarily in that order.' It got a big laugh, so for a long time after that I would do put down jokes on myself. I wanted to strike first so nobody else would. It's a self-protective measure" (cited in Horowitz 1997, 68).

Horowitz (1997) agrees, maintaining that "Burnett's self-deprecating humor was typical of comediennes of the late 1950s and early 1960s, and it served to soften audience resistance to the notion of an assertively funny woman" (69). By the 1980s, however, Burnett turned to dramatic roles in film and television and rejected her whiner persona, claiming: "I don't think it does any of us any good to put ourselves down. If other people are going to have negative thoughts, that's their problem. I shouldn't add to it by substantiating what they might be thinking. It's anti-feminine" (cited in Martin and Segrave 1986, 334).

In the genre of stand-up comedy (as we know it today), the prototype for the whiner posture was, of course, Phyllis Diller. After telling jokes to other housewives at the Laundromat, Diller was urged to try stand-up by her frequently unemployed husband. Making her first professional appearance at the age of thirty-seven, Diller became a stand-up comic to support her five children. Once experienced in clubs, she appeared on *The Jack Paar Show* thirty times, establishing herself as "Killer Diller," delivering twelve punch lines per minute in the "set-up, pause, and pay-off" format used by her idol, Bob Hope. Additionally, Diller's material has always been punctuated by her trademark cackle to "prime the pump" (Martin and Segrave 1986, 341–42).

Ultimately earning $1 million annually, Diller considered herself a feminist, refused to wear pantyhose and maintained: "To make it on stage, I had to make fun of myself first. . . . I would come out on stage and put everybody down—myself, the children, the lady next door, the cops. Everybody has got to be bad. See, if everything is good, you've got Grace Kelly and that's not funny" (cited in Martin and Segrave 1986, 341). As Diller points out, aggression is inherent in stand-up comedy; whether the target is self or other, the comic acts out the anger most people repress. Whereas the bitch persona expresses this anger overtly, the whiner makes herself the scapegoat for societal discontent.

When examining self-deprecatory humor, many feminist critics fail to realize that Diller's jokes have always been precisely that—jokes. For example, a common source of her material for years has been her "flat-chested" figure—when in reality, Diller has had breast reduction surgery.[22] Based primarily on self-deprecatory material, Diller's career has spanned over forty years.[23] After countless TV appearances, albums, books, films, and even a performance at Chicago's Soldier Field for fifty-five thousand fans, Diller continues to perform the material that made her famous. As late as 1993, she was still performing in clubs— sometimes two shows a night—and as of 2003 continues to accept speaking engagements at the age of eighty-five. Believing that men possess an "attitude that a woman who is a comic has lost her femininity," Diller parodied this belief by posing for a pinup photo of "Miss Fun Fishing of 1973" in *Field and Stream,* wearing waders. Thinking of herself as a champion of housewives, Diller has claimed that she says what "they wanted to say but couldn't" (cited in Martin and Segrave 1986, 342–43). Diller also appealed to men who previously disliked female comics. As she explains: "They'd say, 'Ordinarily I don't like female comics, but. . . .' They were trying to tell me I was okay— possibly because I think I never lose my femininity. I may be hostile and aggressive, but I am still feminine. It's a spiritual thing. They'd feel it" (cited in Horowitz 1997, 55).

Comics assuming the whiner posture usually comment upon a physical characteristic or foolish behavior that makes them feel inferior to others. And because performers use "what works," Diller, like other whiner comics, created a basis for self-deprecation.[24] Wearing a "fright wig" and dressing in bizarre outfits, Diller caustically critiqued her appearance. As Horowitz (1997) points out, Diller's stage persona is "aggressively, comedically repellant—her sexual charms are absurdly inferior to those of any member of her audience"(48). Diller's rapid-fire delivery and intermittent cackle essentially "directed" audiences, telling them when to laugh. And laugh they did, charmed by her caricature and easily drawn into her distinctive comic rhythms.

Diller's popular 1960 album, *Are You Ready for Phyllis Diller?* includes the following material:

> I am the descendant of a very long line—my mother once foolishly listened to. . . . FDA declared my kitchen a disaster area. . . . When the beast comes home, the beauty better be ready. . . . Small chest condition—chronic. . . . someone danced with me backwards—"You idiot—those are my *shoulder blades!*" . . . I get so bad, I feel like putting them both together to make one *good* one. . . . I'm so tired of running on the rims—you've never known embarrassment until *you* have pulled into a Standard station and said, "Fill 'er up."

Diller's 1961 album, *Phyllis Diller Laughs,* also features a good deal of self-deprecatory material:

> these aren't wrinkles—I took a nap on a chenille spread. . . . Two weeks ago, my Playtex living bra died—of starvation. . . . wore apron and nothing else—you think *you've* seen a frightened Fuller Brush man—he didn't even come back for his *car!* . . . [In a Japanese restaurant] took off shoes—ten corn pads—with no shoes, I look like a typewriter . . . offered to take off everything else . . . [manager says:] "Please, lady—people are *eating . . .*" turned out to be the Fuller Brush man—still being treated for trauma.

In a 1969 appearance on *The Ed Sullivan Show,* Diller discussed her entrance in a beauty contest, noting that she "came in last and got 361 get well cards," and that she was on the "fourteenth year of a ten-day beauty plan." Finally, she recalled asking her fictitious husband, Fang, for a kiss: "he went and put on his work clothes." In 1972, when Bob Hope asked the reason for her facelift, Diller replied, "Well, I got sick and tired of having the dog drag me out to the yard and bury me." And on a 1985 Hope appearance, she asserted, "I have so many liver spots, I should come with a side of onions." Diller continued to perform some of her vintage material into the 1990s. She also updated her act, however, as evident in a discussion of her numerous facelifts

(1993):"my face has been pulled up more times than Jimmy Swaggart's *pants.*" The first American female stand-up comic with such widespread and enduring appeal, Phyllis Diller continues to influence contemporary female comics—whether or not they assume the whiner posture.

A few years after Diller began her career, another enormously influential whiner comic appeared on the comedy scene—Joan Rivers. Constructing herself as a "victim who struck back," Rivers has called self-deprecatory material "the sugar coating on the pill" (Martin and Segrave 1986, 344). Although, as mentioned earlier, Rivers also assumes the bitch persona, it is significant that the largest category in her "joke file" is one labeled "No Sex Appeal" (351). After a 1965 appearance on *The Tonight Show* with Johnny Carson, Rivers enjoyed great success performing in clubs and, by 1983, was earning $200,000 weekly; performances in Las Vegas, TV and film appearances, books, and her own talk show have continued to bolster Rivers's career. Rivers works constantly, replacing 60 percent of her material every three months. She claims that "you don't expect a woman to be funny. . . . Nobody likes funny women. We're a threat. I don't like funny women" (cited in Martin and Segrave, 351–52).

In a 1968 appearance on *The Ed Sullivan Show*, Rivers confided that her husband didn't know that "the hair he loved to touch he could take with him to the office." Deriding her own body image became a mainstay of Rivers's act. In a late 1970s TV appearance, she recalled that she was

> such an ugly kid . . . the doctor looked at me, said "She's not done yet," and shoved me back in. . . . they sent my picture to *Ripley's Believe It or Not*—he wrote back and said, "I don't believe it. . . ." When I was born, my mother looked at me, looked at the afterbirth, and said, "Twins! . . . "When you're ugly, your parents hate you . . . my mother used to say, "Take candy from strangers . . . ask the guy over there in the raincoat does he own a van?"

In a 1981 appearance on *The Tonight Show*, Rivers noted: "my body has had it. My boobies are dropping so fast . . . my left boob I now use as a stopper in the tub . . . if I was on the Matterhorn, I could nurse the villagers. . . . Last night I ran naked through the bedroom . . . he [her husband, Edgar] screamed, 'Who shaved the dog? . . . ' Oral Roberts saw me, put his hand over my face and said, 'Heal. . . .' Mother never told me the facts of life because she figured I wouldn't *need* 'em."

Although her self-deprecatory material may not appear empowering, Rivers considers herself a feminist. In fact, she took a class with Margaret Mead at Barnard College, and in the early days of her stand-up career, conducted survey research of club audiences, turning over the "data" (questionnaires) to Mead. Like all whiner comics, Rivers uses self-deprecation strategically. As she explains, "Talking about my unattractiveness relaxes the audience. There's a grain of truth in it, but I don't take it completely seriously. It's what women do. We put ourselves down to put each other at ease" (cited in Horowitz 1997, 99).[25] On her 1983 album, Rivers laments: "My body is falling so goddamn fast, my gynecologist wears a hard hat." Indeed, her early and continued use of self-deprecatory material makes Rivers a prominent member of the whiner tradition.

A comic whose career was based entirely on putting herself down is Totie Fields. Performing in clubs from her teenaged years, Fields became known for jokes about her physical appearance, particularly her weight. A 1963 performance at the Copacabana led to more than two dozen spots on *The Ed Sullivan Show* and ultimately, performances in Las Vegas and on many TV talk shows. In the 1960s, Fields rivaled Diller and Rivers, earning $200,000 annually. In 1970, Fields was called "the hottest comedienne in the country," and in 1975 dubbed "the number one stand-up comedienne on the saloon circuit" by *Playgirl*. On one occasion, while cohosting *The Mike Douglas Show*, Fields spoke after guest Arlene Dahl gave the audience beauty tips: "Why do you listen to her? Chances are you'll never look like her. Better you should listen to me because chances are you will look like me." Plagued by ill health, Fields underwent a mastectomy, suffered a heart attack, and had a leg amputated, yet continued to perform, earning the title "Entertainer of the Year" from the Sahara in 1978 before her death at age forty-eight (Martin and Segrave 1986, 321).

In a 1967 performance on *The Ed Sullivan Show*, Fields made fun of her physical appearance by telling jokes that clearly undermined it:

> That woman thought I was *Twiggy*. . . . Do you believe her dimensions? 20–20–20—my eyesight isn't even that good! . . . I've worked with three of the biggest writers in the country. They said, "Totie, it's so hard to write for you because in order to write for a comic, they should have something *physically* wrong with them. Jimmy Durante has a big nose, Martha Raye has a big mouth, Jackie Gleason's *fat*." [Pregnant pause followed by audience laughter. She gives the audience a dirty look] They said, "Totie, you're

too pretty to do comedy. You should have been a stunning girl singer—or a lady wrestler." . . . look at you men in the audience. I know what every one of you out there is thinking: "Take it *off,* take it *off!* . . . " it took me *four* hours to put it *on!* It was always like that . . . you know what it's like to go through life being a sex symbol? . . . It's a *curse.* . . . You women are all eating your hearts out, aren't you? Isn't it amazing when you're pretty? Look—I need *nothing.* I don't even wear hardly any makeup at all. . . . there are only two things I even use—silly putty and sandpaper. And exercise . . . that's how *I* stay *firm,* ya know? [Shakes flesh under arms] I have a wonderful tip for you ladies . . . I do this exercise for one hour every day [pats double chin with tops of fingers]—look how thin my *fingers* are.

Basing her entire act on the whiner posture, Fields made a career of self-deprecation. She put a unique spin on the whiner, however, by her use of irony. In the above material, Fields, short and round in a vivid green "baby doll" dress, speaks as though she is extremely attractive, using ironic comments like "You're too pretty to do comedy" to evoke her whiner image. Although her self-adulation is undercut with lines like "silly putty and sandpaper," it is her "serious" delivery of the ironic material that garners the biggest laughs.

Although there is no contemporary Totie Fields playing the club circuit, "fat" jokes are still a staple of the whiner posture. For example, in a 1985 cable appearance, Carrie Snow exults, "I just found out that I *do* have a thyroid problem . . . every fat person in the world wants one and *I* have one!" And Henriette Mantel (1992) says that if she is ever on life support, "I definitely want to be unplugged—but not 'til I get down to a size eight."[26] Other jokes about body image are popular as well. For example, in a 2001 *Letterman* appearance, Wendy Liebman notes that at her HMO, "they charge *me* for a self-breast exam—it's a flat fee." And Stephanie Hodge (1992) explains:

Women do not age pretty—we just fall the hell apart—happened to me— my butt fell last year . . . never forget that day . . . I walk out of the shower . . . it just hovered there quiverin' for a second . . . next thing I know—*BAM*— twelve and a half pounds of cottage cheese lyin' at my heels. . . . I catch a glimpse of myself bendin' over naked in my mirror in my bedroom, I'm thinkin', "Who *is* that man with the bad jowls sneakin' up on *me?*" . . . And the sad thing is, two months after your butt goes, your boobs just follow—they just see your butt layin' there on the floor, they think, "*My,* what a comfortable place to *be.*"

This material is met with considerable laughter from (especially female) audience members. Hodge's graphic description is particularly interesting in light of the body-focused material she performs earlier in the same act. As the bawd, Hodge uses her physicality to her advantage; as the whiner, she submits to physical inevitabilities. In both cases, however, she does what "works" to elicit laughter from the audience.

Interestingly, even female comics who are physically quite attractive by societal standards sometimes assume the whiner posture. A prime example is Rita Rudner (1987), who complains, "I diet, I exercise, but I still don't look anything like those women in *Playboy*—they're not from this planet and I'm glad because I don't want them here." At times, even female comics not apparently overweight perform jokes about weight loss. Anita Wise (1992) tells the audience that she is trying to lose weight in order to fit into her "skinny jeans," bought after a five-day stomach flu, noting that "whenever I want to lose some self-esteem, I try them on."[27]

Contemporary whiner comics perform self-deprecatory material in relation to issues of self-esteem (especially in a romantic context) just as often as they perform self-deprecatory material about body image.[28] For instance, in an interesting variation on the whiner persona, Wanda Sykes (2001) discusses women's desperation and denial in romantic relationships:

> Women are really nuts. . . . We *think* too much, we *overanalyze* everything. . . . A guy tell us something—we'll turn it around to mean something else. A guy tell us, "Uh, ya know, uh—I think we should see other *people*." And we'll go get with our girlfriends, start talkin'—"You know *what*? He's in love with me. *This* man has fallen in *love* with me—that's what it is. And my love is so *overwhelmin'* that he feels like he needs to *remove* himself from my *love* for a few minutes so he can get used to all this *love,* and so he can spend the rest of his *life* with me—that's what's goin' on—*that's* what he means." No, he doesn't mean that—he told you—"I think we should see other *people.*" In other words, "I am tired of screwing *you*—I would like to screw someone *else*—I suggest you do the *same.*"

Rather than denigrate only herself, Sykes berates all women for this failing, lapsing into the bitch posture in her acerbic critique.

A more traditional whiner, Karen Haber (1985) also laments her romantic woes:

> I walked up to this one guy and he wasn't so great and I said to him, "Look—if you would take me out . . . you could keep my car." And he said, "What kind of car do you have?" . . . [On playing hard to get:] In the

morning, I made him breakfast and I shined his shoes and I painted his apartment and he said, "I hate you, you're stupid, get outta here." I said, "That's okay, 'cause I'm busy Saturday night anyway," and *I* left. But . . . I broke down and I called him up and I begged him to come over later. And he said "Maybe," like if I would pay for the gas in his car. You know what I told him, this cheap idiot? "*No*—who do you think I am? The Bank of America? I'll come pick you *up*." In the morning, he said, "I hate you, you're stupid, get outta here." I said, "But this is *my* house," and *I* left.

Haber perpetually denigrates herself, both as a whole and by specific body parts. In a cable appearance (1990a), she tells the audience that her mother says, "If you want a man, you have to lay a trap for him," and notes, "I did, but the last guy almost chewed his own leg off trying to get away." Haber further explains, "I've been playing subliminal tapes in my bed when guys sleep over. They go, 'Marriage is *good*. Family is *good*. Small breasts are *plenty*.'" Finally, Haber (1990b) claims, "I'm really good in bed—unless I'm *with* someone." Haber literally "whines" much of her material; her physical posture is often slumped, projecting a defeated demeanor.

Another comic who assumes the persona of a perennial underdog is Cathy Ladman. Like Haber, Ladman truly whines and assumes a defeated physical posture. In a cable performance (1992a), she notes that as a child she did not own a Barbie doll but "Tammy," a doll that "came with her own low self-esteem." Ladman also observes that on Halloween, she had to use a print sheet for a costume, "The Martex ghost . . . empty-handed and degraded again." Ultimately, Ladman (1993a) admits that for her, good days occur "when I get the lint screen off in one piece." Acknowledging ignorance of office protocol in her distinctive and unique rhythms, Wendy Liebman (2001) confesses that in a recent job, "I got fired because I thought casual Friday meant I could come in on Monday." And, summing up the whiner posture on a 1984 HBO special, Elayne Boosler discusses dining out alone. When the hostess asks, "Just one tonight?" Boosler responds, "No—I've been a loser all my life."[29]

Audiences of all kinds appreciate the whiner. She is the schlemiel, the underdog, the reminder of the hapless, anxious, disgruntled part of all of us—the part with which we identify, but which we also often conceal. Indeed, the whiner posture remains integral to contemporary American female comic performance. Whether she is mocking her own physical appearance or simply complaining about her lack of romantic prospects, a comic assuming this posture usually receives positive audience response. Because she is not at all threatening, the whiner enables audiences to laugh safely, often unaware of the double message sent by such discourse.

The Reporter

This final posture assumed onstage by contemporary American female comics is, like the kid, relatively androgynous. The reporter persona is clearly opinionated, but because she offers sociocultural— and occasionally political—critique through an observational lens, she does not appear threatening. The reporter directs her dissatisfaction at general targets (that is, society) through commentary peppered with questions like "Did you ever notice?" This persona also muses, often telling humorous anecdotes as a way to voice mild irritation, frustration, or incredulity. Because the reporter evokes a sense of community ("We're all in this together"), this posture is extremely popular with a variety of audiences. Whether it is Jerry Seinfeld or Margaret Smith (see chapter 3 for examples of Smith's observations, political and otherwise), the reporter simply observes the human condition, and reports her or his observations as a mild form of social critique.[30] As with all of the comedic postures, the reporter is easily conflated with others.

The first real female reporter comic was Jean Carroll.[31] A true monologist, Carroll performed material about domestic life, making mild jabs at her husband "like any moderate 50s comedian . . . would gag about his wife" (Gallo 1991, 124). Indeed, the jabs were mild, including the following material from a 1959 appearance on *The Ed Sulllivan Show:* "[On honeymoon:] got all ready . . . went in [to husband] . . . he looked so nice, I hated to wake him. . . . 'Honey, it's your *wife*'—he said, 'Quick—*hide* me!'" Although she did not assume the bitch persona, Carroll was criticized for performing material such as: "The other day he [husband] woke up with a headache . . . I felt sorry for him. I would like to help him but I can't. I told him so many times. When he jumps out of bed—feet first" (cited in Gallo, 124). To her detractors, Carroll responded, "I can't say I'm fat, I can't talk about my mother, my husband, my child. You know, there is really very little left to say" (cited in Martin and Segrave 1986, 295). Moving from her vaudeville (singing and dancing) roots to "droll commentaries upon everyday situations" in clubs and on radio and TV, Carroll was very popular both in the United States and England. Ultimately, her American TV series was short-lived because, according to Martin and Segrave, she did not portray conventional women like the "ditsy housewife" or the "man chaser," but rather "a stronger woman, one in control, a dominant female able to manipulate without whining, pleading or hysterics" (296).

What Carroll did do, however, was build a foundation for future female reporters. In the 1970s, Lily Tomlin took up the baton. Launching her career with television's *Laugh-In,* Tomlin went on to release several albums (one of which earned a Grammy) and enjoy great success in film and television. When asked in 1981 if the women's movement had had an impact on her career, she responded, "If it hadn't been for the Women's Movement, people would call it my hobby" (cited in Martin and Segrave 1986, 372). Although she is best known for characters like the precocious Edith Ann and Ernestine, the telephone operator, Tomlin's 1975 album, *Modern Scream,* includes the following reporter observations:

> I worry about being a success in a mediocre world. . . . The average person spends four hours of the 4,69,500 hours of a lifetime experiencing orgasm . . . 62 percent is self-inflicted. . . . If the formula for water is H_2O, is the formula for ice H_2O squared? . . . Isn't it weird to think that one day bean bag chairs will be antiques? . . . Why is it that when we talk to God it's called praying, but when God talks to us, it's called schizophrenia?

Commenting on life and lifestyles, reporter comics often elicit a great deal of audience identification.

One comic who has successfully assumed the reporter posture since the 1970s is Elayne Boosler. Occasionally assuming mild versions of the bitch, bawd, and even whiner postures, Boosler generally performs observational material. In a 1984 HBO special, for example, Boosler imagines a "restaurant for singles" with no chairs, in which patrons "eat standing over a sink," and later notes that "the only time you ever see a penis in a movie is if a pervert sits down next to you." Like many female comics, Boosler resents the label "female comic," preferring to focus on her reporter role and to be called simply a "comic." Asked in 1979 about using "feminine wiles" in her act, Boosler maintained, "It's true . . . in the middle of a heavy political bit

I get an urge to clean up the stage, to line the audience up in neat rows" (Martin and Segrave 1986, 410).

Another veteran comic often assuming the reporter posture is Carol Leifer. Active on the comedy circuit since 1978, Leifer includes the following in a 1990 cable appearance: "[On annulment of marriage:] talk about denial . . . how do you explain your wedding album? Oh— that was just some play I was in." And in 1993, she notes that New York is the only city in the country featuring radio requests such as, "Yeah, this is for Tina—I'm sorry I stabbed you." Laura Kightlinger (1991) also describes a distinctly "New York" experience: "I sat in a coffee shop and I drank half a cup of coffee before I noticed there was lipstick on the cup. And then I went to wipe it off with a napkin and there was wadded up gum and lipstick on the napkin . . . and I must've been sitting in that woman's lap for . . . I don't know . . . fifteen minutes."

Female comics assuming the reporter posture frequently perform (but are not limited to) observational material; as discussed in chapter 3, this type of material comprises a wide range of topics. Commenting on a televised history lesson, for example, Janeane Garofalo (2001) recalls: "I was watching a documentary about Hitler . . . and they profiled Eva Braun, Hitler's girlfriend . . . they had her diaries, and *this* was her problem with Hitler. . . . He was *uncommunicative.* He was a little *cold.* Didn't return phone calls quite as quick as she'd like. The other stuff not so *much,* but . . . he was just not emotionally *available* for Eva, and that was *her* problem with *him.*"

Discussing a topic with which all audiences can identify, Rita Rudner (1987) marvels at the wonders of sleep: "you get to be alive and unconscious at the same time." Jann Karam (1992) describes her sister as "suicidal but really health conscious," taking an overdose of Sleepytime tea that did not kill her, but did make her "really relaxed." And Karen Haber (1990b) explains that she is dating a "pseudo-vegetarian" who "only eats animals that only eat vegetables."

Marsha Warfield (1987) notes that "smoking pot . . . everything becomes work . . . 'I don't mind changing the channel, but I'd have to get up . . . I'm not into that.'" Carol Siskind (1993) tells men in the audience that they experience less stress than women do because "What you're wearing tonight will be in style for the rest of your lives." And Kathleen Madigan (1992) recalls boarding a bus and wanting to call *Unsolved Mysteries* to say, "I found everyone." Finally, in a

1992 *Tonight Show* performance, Sue Kolinsky (who also occasionally assumes the bitch posture) performs the following: "Don't you feel different when you borrow money from a relative? To me, that doesn't count. Come on, it's your family—they don't get it back in a week, it's a gift. I have one brother I've borrowed so much money from he's like a human credit card. I can walk into a store with a picture of him and say, 'Ya take Fred?'"

Acerbic in her social critique, the reporter nevertheless remains nonthreatening to audiences—she may be a critic, but she is also always a reporter, simply sharing "the facts" as she perceives them. Indeed, it is precisely this delicate balance of "reporter" and "critic" that gives the reporter her mass appeal. Like the kid and the whiner, the reporter is safe.

As with all of the comedic postures, the reporter varies stylistically with each individual performer. Margaret Smith uses a deadpan delivery, whereas Carol Leifer speaks energetically and loudly, and Rita Rudner is generally smiling and soft-spoken. Certainly, a comic's choice of material is related to the posture she assumes onstage. Material does not dictate posture, however, as (for example) reporter comics may discuss sexual topics without necessarily assuming the bawd persona. Topical variety, however, is characteristic of the reporter; for example, Margaret Smith's material ranges from presidential politics (see chapter 3) to explanations like, "I don't go home for the holidays 'cause I can't get Delta to wait in the front yard" (1993). Although quite similar to the kid in her androgynous, observational manner, the reporter does not specifically use a child's idiom or behavior; in fact, the reporter typically discusses topics at the "adult" end of the observational humor continuum.

The preceding discussion of the historical development, rhetorical functions, and stylistic elements of the five postures reveals the ways in which contemporary American female comics perform (or do not perform) their marginality in a comedic context. As discussed in chapter 1, sociological marginality cannot help but be performed (in the sense that it comprises physical characteristics seen by the audience), whereas rhetorical marginality is a choice. Thus, when comics assume the bawd, bitch, or whiner postures, they generally foreground their marginality rhetorically by performing various gendered behaviors. When comics assume the kid or reporter postures, however, they de-emphasize gender and therefore do not perform their marginality rhetorically. The remainder of this chapter focuses on strategies of self-presentation in relation to the rhetorical construction of marginality.[32]

Female Comics and Strategic Self-Presentation

Self-Presentation Strategies

Particularly relevant to the discussion in this chapter is the notion of "strategic self-presentation" developed by Jones and Pittman (1982). As social psychologists, Jones and Pittman are interested in "those features of behavior affected by power augmentation motives designed to elicit or shape others' attributions of the actor's dispositions" (233). Jones and Pittman call this phenomenon "strategic self-presentation," and offer a typology of five strategies commonly employed in human interaction: (1) ingratiation (I want you to like me); (2) intimidation (I want you to think I'm dangerous); (3) self-promotion (I want you to think I'm competent); (4) exemplification (I want you to think I have integrity and moral worthiness); and (5) supplication (I want you to think I'm weak and powerless and therefore feel compelled to help me). Although exemplification and self-promotion are not salient to this investigation, the remaining three strategies—ingratiation, intimidation, and especially supplication—provide a useful framework for analysis of postures that contemporary American female comics typically assume onstage.[33] Because the reporter is less overtly strategic than the other four postures, Jones and Pittman's strategies are not as directly applicable to this stance.[34] The remaining four postures, however, employ strategies of ingratiation, intimidation, and supplication respectively.

The kid posture is based on ingratiation. Kids want to be liked and the playfulness they exhibit endears them to others. DeGeneres, Poundstone, and O'Donnell are examples of kid comics who elicit not only audience identification, but who are enormously well liked by diverse populations. The kid can be naughty and irreverent but, by remaining a kid, assures that she will be perceived as merely a teasing, nonthreatening "pal." Just as the "class clown" in school delighted and amused her classmates with playful and mischievous behavior, the kid comic delights and amuses audiences, ensuring that she will be liked in the process.

Intimidation is the strategy employed by both bawd and bitch comics. In the bawd tradition, performers like Caroline Rhea, Stephanie Hodge, Carrie Snow, and Thea Vidale use their sexuality in an aggressive, often threatening manner. These comics may be threatening to both male and female audience members because the comics portray themselves as insatiable, manipulative, or critical, all in the context of sex and sexuality. A comic who is obviously in control of her sexuality may appear to be in control, period. Because the bawd is often conflated with the bitch posture, it is not surprising that the bitch is based on intimidation as well. Comics like Roseanne, Leah Krinsky, and Judy Tenuta represent extreme examples of this strategy. Clearly aggressive, often angry, the bitch comic critiques male sexual technique and apparatus as well as male inadequacies in intimacy and communication. Whereas the bawd may seduce and titillate male audience members, the bitch seems unconcerned about being liked by them. To the contrary, in fact, the bitch may go out of her way to insult and offend them. Whereas the bawd may champion female sexuality, the bitch represents female autonomy. (Hence jokes about penis size and preference for vibrators, though sexual, are tools of the bitch rather than the bawd persona.) Rowe's (1995) notion of "the unruly woman" applies to both bawd and bitch comics for, as Rowe explains, "the unruly woman can be seen as a prototype of woman as subject— transgressive above all when she lays claim to her own desire" (31).

Finally, Jones and Pittman's strategy of supplication is employed in the self-deprecatory manner of the whiner comic. Asserting that "Supplication—the strategy of advertising one's dependence to solicit help—works best when there appears to be an arbitrary or accidental component in the power differential" (for example, race and gender), Jones and Pittman offer the following example of this strategy:

> The classic female . . . is nearly helpless in coping with the physical world. She cannot change a tire, understand algebra, carry a suitcase, or order wine . . . the supplicant female influences the male to expend energy on her behalf; to do things for her that she would like to have done. She accomplishes this at the small cost of being considered totally incompetent by her vain and dedicated husband or suitor. (247–48)

The female stand-up comic who uses strategic self-deprecation clearly exhibits these same characteristics: Either she is domestically inept or unattractive in the Diller/Rivers tradition or, in the language of contemporary female comics like Cathy Ladman and Karen Haber, unable to obtain a commitment or even a date from a man. Although the issues of attraction and commitment are less overt examples of supplication than Jones and Pittman's, they are, nonetheless, attempts by the self-designated powerless to win the acceptance—and, more important, the support—of the powerful.

Supplication is a specific use of self-deprecation. As Barreca (1991) explains, self-deprecatory humor functions strategically by making the powerful comfortable: "If we tell these jokes about ourselves, we'll make the straight, white, patriarchal man our pal, because he finds these jokes funny too" (25). Disarming through humor is important because it is, of course, the straight, white, patriarchal man who controls economic resources in our culture. Strategic supplication must be used with care, however, because "To be a woman and a humorist is to confront and subvert the very power that keeps women powerless, and at the same time to risk alienating those upon whom women are dependent for economic survival" (Walker 1988, 9). Appearing helpless and inferior in order to win the trust of the powerful may be a particularly insidious subversive strategy. Supplication can be a risk, however; Jones and Pittman (1982) note that "There may be heavy costs to one's self-esteem in acknowledging or even advertising one's helplessness and incompetence" (248). Although it is potentially damaging, Jones and Pittman further explain that supplication may be "a highly effective way of avoiding the negative reaches of others' power when one's own power resources are limited" (258).

Sullivan and Turner (1996) describe four strategies that women use to communicate in the political sphere: (1) denying: women assume the moral boundaries of the political arena are nonexistent or permeable—that is, success comes from following the rules; (2) confronting and (3) accommodating: best used in combination because if women only confront, they remain outsiders, and if they only accommodate, they remain silent (whereas deniers assume the playing field is level, confronters/accommodators assume it is not and that they must learn the tactics necessary to play the game); (4) revisioning: unlike the above strategies, which all reify patriarchal values and assume the world is rational, revisionists recognize boundaries but are unwilling to work within them because they disagree with the value system underlying them; rather, they seek to redraw the boundaries altogether (47).

Although Sullivan and Turner refer specifically to American female legislators in the political arena, their schema is useful when examining the way female comics communicate their marginality. Certainly, both the kid and reporter comics seem to deny or at least ignore any gender boundaries in the world of comedy. By downplaying their gender, these comics simply follow the rules and present noncontroversial material and personas. The whiner accommodates and simultaneously subtly confronts the culture that welcomes this accommodation. And bawd and bitch comics both confront and revision, boldly challenging cultural norms and values by transcending boundaries with every punchline. Regardless of the label, however, at the core of all strategic self-presentation in the performances of female comics is the manner in which "woman" is constructed by each comic. Whether she seems to be saying, "Pay no attention to the fact that I'm a woman" (the kid, the reporter), "I'm a desirous and desirable woman—maybe more than you can handle" (the bawd), "I'm a woman whether you like it or not" (the bitch), or "I'm just a stupid, unattractive, or helpless woman" (the whiner), a female comic constructs her rhetorical marginality early in her act, and this construction shapes the message she sends to both male and female audience members.

Combining Postures

As mentioned throughout this chapter, female comics often combine postures, assuming several even within a single act. Why? Because as performers they use what "works" (the notion of what "works" in relation to audience is discussed further in chapter 5).[35] For stand-up comics, the goal is to elicit audience laughter by whatever means necessary. And sometimes comedic success depends on the performer's ability to switch postures instantaneously, such as when spontaneously creating material in order to pursue a premise that has just received a laugh, recover from a joke that "bombs," or deal with hecklers. Several of the comics discussed in this chapter switch postures within their prepared material, however; this tendency has implications for the performance of marginality. Most comics project a central, identifiable onstage persona, only occasionally switching postures. For example, when Karen Haber performs the "pseudovegetarian" line, although it is not specific to her whiner posture, it is mentioned in the context of dating—a topic central to her self-deprecatory style. Other comics, however—most notably, Joan Rivers and Stephanie Hodge—perform a substantial amount of material in at least two comedic postures.[36]

As discussed earlier, Rivers is known for her portrayals of both the bitch and the whiner. Although some critics see her solely as one or the other, clearly, Rivers is both. The connection between the two personas seems to be anger. Whether Rivers is targeting others (for example, celebrities or audience members) or herself, she is caustic, even explosive. Stephanie Hodge portrays both bawd and whiner. Hodge (1992) also plays the bitch, as evident in her unprovoked "attack" on a female audience member: "look at *you*—*God* . . . you'd never do anything that mean, would you? Make fun of *old* people, 'cause you're so *pretty* and *feminine*—I'm gonna push you *down* . . . I can't do the *feminine* thing—I tried it once, it threw my back out, I just had to *give* it up . . . I bet you can wrinkle your nose too, can't you? Yes you *can*—you just did it—you little *tramp.*" As discussed earlier, in Hodge's performance the connection between postures seems to be physicality. Whether her description entails "undulating" as the bawd, "quivering" as the whiner, or "pushing" an audience member (rhetorically) as the bitch, Hodge emphasizes physical action. When female comics switch postures within a single act (for reasons other than audience response), a connection between postures is both significant and—for purposes of consistency—necessary.[37]

Responding to Hecklers

Regardless of which posture(s) a female comic assumes onstage, she must interact with the audience. Stand-up comics deal with hecklers on a nightly basis, and though mentioned briefly in relation to the bitch persona, the way female comics respond bears additional commentary. An adept comic can respond to a heckler without deviating from whichever posture she assumes. Cathy Ladman, for instance, maintains her whiner posture when a male audience member at a show on the *USO Comedy Tour* (1993b) yells, "Take it off!" Ladman responds, "Take it *off?* Oh, man—you need *liberty.*" Although her retort pokes fun at the heckler's psychosexual state, it is also a comment on Ladman's own inherent sex appeal or lack thereof. Because of their aggressive, often assaultive nature, however, most "squelches" come from a bitch persona. For example, a stock heckler line sometimes used by female comics (to respond to male hecklers) is, "Sir—next time you come to a comedy club, stop at the drugstore first, buy a condom and put it on your head, 'cause if you're gonna act like a dick, you may as well dress the part." Indeed, effectively "squelching" hecklers often requires all female comics to assume the bitch posture. Sandra Bernhard who, like Tenuta, is difficult to classify as a traditional stand-up comic, asks a heckler, "Do I have to fuck you to get you out of my life?" (cited in Zehme 1988, 118).

An interesting variation in responding to hecklers occurs when a female comic plays the role of apologist, qualifying her own material by positing a fictitious heckler—essentially, "self-heckling." An example is Carrrie Snow who, in a 1985 cable performance, asserts that she knows the men in the audience are saying, "Make me laugh, bitch," and later, after saying that she likes younger guys, notes that the older guys are saying, "That bitch." Similarly, in a 1993 cable appearance, Pam Stone tells the audience, "You guys are like, 'Aww—another chick—they probably ovulate together—bring on a guy.'" Both of the above are representative of the apologist posture used occasionally by contemporary female comics. Whereas comics of both genders construct themselves as critics, teachers, and bullies, male comics do not seem to apologize for gender in this manner. By apologizing to men in the audience, comics who use this strategy may undermine their own material. Ironically, in their attempt not to alienate half of their audience, they risk alienating the other half. In their diction and tone, even bitch or bawd comics like Snow and Stone seem to be saying, "I'm sorry I'm performing so much material about (and potentially for) women—I'll get to the important stuff in a minute." In a rhetorical move that can only be construed as meta-self-deprecation, female comics who apologize for their gender foreground any incipient audience discomfort related to that issue.

Analogous Male Comedic Postures

As illustrated throughout this chapter, the kid, the bawd, the bitch, the whiner, and the reporter comprise present-day analogues of traditions established in the late nineteenth and early twentieth centuries. Most prevalent today are the bawd, bitch, and whiner postures, with the conflation of the first two accounting for most current female comic performance. The bitch posture alone is twice as common as any other posture as female stand-up comics have become more overtly aggressive in the last decade.[38] Although this is not a comparative study, it is important to mention that male comics assume postures comparable to the kid, bawd, bitch, whiner, and reporter. These are (1) the *kid* (Emo Phillips); (2) the *stud* (John Mendoza); (3) the *rebel* (Gilbert Gottfried); (4) the *loser* (Richard Lewis); and (5) the *reporter* (Jerry Seinfeld). Additionally, contemporary American male stand-up comics increasingly perform a type of "sensitive New Age guy" (SNAG) material (as either the loser or reporter), engaging in a sort of emotional self-deprecation as they explain to audiences that men are simply not as deep as women and that the macho act is precisely that—an act. For example, when discussing "women's lib," Bill Maier (1993) perfectly illustrates Jones and Pittman's notion of supplication, noting: "In the old days, women played dumb and we bought it because we *are* dumb. Women just let men go around being stupid, macho guys . . . because they knew there was a lot to be gained by being underestimated—women actually got men to say to them, 'No woman of *mine* is gonna work.' Pretty good deal to me—'Honey—you stay home and relax—I'll bust my ass every day 'cause *I'm* the *smart* one.'"

Tim Allen (1989), on the other hand, feels compassion for women: "Boy, women, I have no idea who cut your deal. 'Okay, Women: You'll bloat, you'll bleed, you'll have a large object come out of a small space which will cause you incredible pain. Men, you'll shave. What's that, not fair? Okay, they'll go bald, too, but that's as far as it goes'" (*Laughtrack* 25).

Jerry Seinfeld (1991) observes, "guys watch women, yell 'Ow!' from trucks . . . women wonder what we're thinkin'—nothing." Tony Edwards (1991) explains, "We like waitresses because they are the only women who have to talk to us." Rich Shydner (1992) says that when women ask men how they feel, men do a quick inventory: "Not hungry . . . not tired . . . I feel okay." Bob Nickman (1991) reveals that "guys *have* to like sports—or have an excuse—'No, can't play—gotta go put a transmission in a stripper's car.'" And finally, Jeff Stillson (1993) asserts that "plumbing the depths of the male psyche is like hunting for Easter eggs—there are only a certain number of eggs buried" and maintains that gender differences can be summed up as follows: "A woman wants *one* man to satisfy all her wants and needs and men want *every* woman to satisfy his one want and need." Clearly, many of the above lines are the male counterparts to female comics' musings about gender differences. Regardless of gender, however, the posture a comic assumes onstage is integral to the overall rhetorical effect of any performance.

After examining the five postures that female comics assume onstage and the traditions these postures represent, we must ask: Are these postures distinctly "female" or, more specifically, "feminist?" Although they are performed by women, as suggested above, each of the postures has a male equivalent. Although the bawd and the bitch foreground gender, the stud and the rebel accomplish much the same task from a male perspective. Are the labels "male" and "female" truly useful in this (or any) context? As discussed throughout this investigation, all humor (except certain types of observational humor and wordplay) mocks a particular target, whether an individual, group, or institution. Thus, whether delivered by a bitch or rebel persona, "putdown" humor is prevalent in contemporary comic discourse. When women affirm their own experience onstage in a comedic context, it is usually at the expense of individual or collective males. Indeed, it is generally the bitch persona that is considered "feminist," whereas the whiner is sometimes perceived as antifemale.[39] In fact, what is called "feminist" humor seems to be: (1) humor simply performed by a female; (2) sexist humor directed at males; or (3) "marginal" humor.

Marginal humor deserves special consideration. As discussed in chapter 1, defining characteristics of marginal humor include the use of self-deprecation and blatant rhetorical subversion. Humor performed by women and minorities is, therefore, inherently similar. Rather than simply focus on the differences between so-called feminist humor and other types, the similarities between humor created and performed by women to that of other marginal groups must be addressed. And marginal humor itself must be examined as part of a larger rhetorical class—a rhetoric of victimage. Contemporary female comic performance targets the self (whiner), others (bawd and bitch), or everyone (kid and reporter) as objects of and sources for humor. Having explored the topics that contemporary American female comics address onstage as well as the postures they employ, we can now consider the implications of performing marginality in terms of genre and power relations in a broader cultural context.

THE POLITICS OF PERFORMING MARGINALITY

How do contemporary American female comics perform their marginality onstage? What does this performance of marginality reveal about the existence of a genre called female or feminist humor? And what does this performance reveal about power relations in a broader cultural context? As discussed in chapter 4, the humor most frequently cited as "feminist" is usually humor simply performed by a woman (hence the "female" and "feminist" confusion), humor that is sexist toward men, or "marginal" humor (that is, humor performed by members of marginal groups). Although Barreca (1991), Walker (1988), and other scholars insist that there is a definable literary genre called "women's humor" and, even more specifically, "feminist humor," it seems more apt to call this genre "literature written by women" or "literature written by feminists." The same applies to the genre of stand-up comedy. A self-designated feminist performing humorous material does not necessarily make the material "feminist humor." Indeed, ideology is in the mind of the beholder.

The defining characteristics of African American, female, gay/lesbian, and Jewish humor, therefore, are inherently similar. And marginal humor sometimes seems to be a subset of a larger rhetoric—the rhetoric of victimage. Because of the "us against them" nature of marginal humor, marginal comics often construct themselves as victims. In so doing, however, they may subvert their own status by embodying the potential power of powerlessness. Their social critique is potent and, because it is offered in a comedic context, safe from retribution as well. In this sense, female comics, like so many others, perform their marginality in an act simultaneously oppressive (by using demeaning stereotypes) and transgressive (by interrogating those very stereotypes through humorous discourse). Ultimately, with the exception of wordplay and the observational humor performed by comics like Jerry Seinfeld and Elayne Boosler of the "Didja ever notice?" variety, humor functions by making fun of someone or some group. There is no "equal opportunity" humor.[1] If feminism is defined as gender egalitarianism, then there is no "feminist" humor. Female comics deride patriarchal culture; Jewish comics deride WASP culture; African American comics deride white culture; gay and lesbian comics deride straight culture. As noted in chapter 4, it is the similarities between humor performed by women and humor performed by members of other marginal groups rather than the differences between so-called female or feminist humor and traditional (that is, male) humor that can be most fruitfully examined. In order to explore issues related to the rhetoric of victimage such as the objectification inherent in humor, the potentially subversive use of self-deprecation (the power of powerlessness), and the rhetorical construction of victims and butts of jokes, this chapter discusses the problematic nature of scholarship regarding feminist humor, examines the politics of performing marginality, and considers the role of the audience in comic performance.

Problems with Studies in "Feminist Humor"

As discussed at length in chapter 1, the very terms "feminist," "women's humor," and "feminist humor" are ill defined and used in confusing, sometimes contradictory ways. Furthermore, existing analyses of feminist humor are extremely limited—the critical investigations are usually confined to examination of women's writing (Barreca 1991; Bunkers 1985; Dressner 1988; Sheppard 1986; Toth 1984, 1985; Walker 1988, 1991a, 1991b), and the empirical studies use small, unrepresentative samples and present unsupported conclusions (Levine 1976; Stillion and White 1987; White 1988). Specifically, in the context of female comic performance, the issue of women's use of self-deprecatory humor appears repeatedly (Auslander 1993; Barreca 1991; Dolan 1989; Horowitz 1997; Martin and Segrave 1986), yet is most often subject to oversimplified, even myopic analysis. Whether they are writing about female comics for academic or popular audiences, critics unanimously condemn women's use of self-deprecatory humor as negative, suggesting that it merely reinforces stereotypes, reinscribing patriarchy in the process.

Although some of these same critics explain that female comics who used self-deprecatory humor in the past can be forgiven because this was their only means of defense given sociocultural parameters (Auslander 1993; Horowitz 1997; Levine 1976; Martin and Segrave 1986), others view self-deprecatory humor as the antithesis of feminism. Barreca (1991) for example, asserts that "nearly all women's humor is in some way feminist humor (with the exception of those early, self-deprecating 'I'm so ugly ...' jokes associated with the very earliest comedians)" yet adds almost immediately that "anytime a woman breaks through a barrier set by society, she's making a feminist gesture of a sort, and every time a woman laughs, she's breaking through a barrier" (182).

In the above statements, Barreca succinctly articulates the paradox apparent in much feminist criticism, known in some circles as the "Madonna question": power—obtained by whatever means necessary—is desirable, yet self-objectification as a means of obtaining power (whether through the self-deprecatory humor of Diller or the explicit photo opportunities of Madonna) is unacceptable. This paradox is central to feminist, Marxist, and postmodern criticism; indeed, when critiquing cultural representation—from pornography to MTV videos, from prize-winning literature to weekly sitcoms—the issue of power—where it resides and how it is negotiated—is key. Is Madonna the ultimate feminist, completely in control of her economic resources, or a mere tool of the patriarchy, perpetuating misogynistic stereotypes? And, similarly, is a female comic who uses self-deprecatory humor insidiously subverting the status quo or affirming oppressive cultural beliefs?

Clearly, it is up to the audience to interpret any form of cultural representation. And to assume, as many critics do, that all self-deprecatory humor will be passively accepted at face value is as ludicrous as assuming (as many critics do) that every audience member laughs for the same reason (Lutfiyya 1990; Merrill 1988). Equally presumptuous as claiming to know with certainty the reason(s) audiences laugh is claiming to know the reason(s) a performer behaves in a particular manner. At best, the critic can describe what the performer does and, like any audience member, offer an interpretation. Yet critics frequently seem to believe themselves omniscient, making unfounded assertions about performances that impede rather than facilitate analysis. Such assertions undergird analyses of "feminist" humor that posit an "internalized anger vs. externalized anger" binary in the work of female comics. For example, Bunkers (1985) contends that "female humor turns inward, back on the joke teller, while feminist humor turns outward, directing itself toward others" (89). Dolan (1989) notes that "At last, women have turned comic perspective outward, away from dingbat and self-deprecatory humor, toward comment on their world." Finally, Auslander (1993) maintains: "Clearly, whatever anger may be implicit in the self-deprecatory comedy of Diller and Rivers has been turned inward onto the female subject herself, rather than outward onto the social conditions that made it necessary for Diller and Rivers to personify themselves in this way in order to have successful careers as comics" (327).

All three of the above critics fail to consider two important points: that self-deprecatory humor may be construed as cultural critique, and that comics who use self-deprecatory material do not necessarily believe themselves to be the personas they project onstage.[2] Ironically, many critics of humor seem to forget that they are analyzing jokes—humorous discourse that reminds the audience not to take it (or themselves) seriously with every punchline. As discussed in chapter 2, humor is a rhetoric unique in its ability to undermine its own power with the "only joking" disclaimer. Critics, especially those most adamantly opposed to self-deprecatory humor, however, appear to overlook the fact that these are the jokes, folks! An excellent illustration of the two points enumerated above can be found in the performances and careers of Phyllis Diller, Roseanne, and Brett Butler.

As discussed at length in chapter 4, female comics may assume more than one comedic posture, even within a single performance. Phyllis Diller is a case in point. Although she devoted a fair amount of her material over the years to put-downs of her fictitious husband, Fang, as well as of other women, it is always her use of self-deprecatory humor for which Diller is noted. The critics who view Diller only as a comic limited to self-deprecatory humor, internalizing anger in an attempt to please patriarchy (Auslander 1993; Barreca 1991; Horowitz 1997; Martin and Segrave 1986; Merrill 1988) fail to recognize that all of Diller's jokes about her appearance were precisely that—jokes. Diller never truly believed she was grossly unattractive but donned a fright wig to amuse audiences. Neither did she ever feel flat-chested, but, in fact, had breast reduction surgery.

Although initially her self-deprecatory material may appear demeaning (toward herself and/or women in general), a closer scrutiny reveals that Diller's jokes accomplish what all marginal humor accomplishes—it calls cultural values into question by lampooning them. Whether she mocks her domestic routine of putting ironing in the refrigerator and hanging a turkey out the window (1960) or her newly reconstructed appearance (1993), Diller always mocks society as well. From being on the "fourteenth year of a ten-day beauty plan" (1969) to being "so wrinkled I could screw my hats on" (1993), Diller uses herself as the butt to make fun of culture at large. Through self-deprecatory material, a comic ridicules the society that creates ideals for appearance and behavior as well as individuals who subscribe to those standards. The subtle social critique inherent in this material serves an important function, as Diller and her successors have used it successfully to voice women's discontent with cultural norms and expectations.

Diller is still performing self-deprecatory material. She tells jokes about her many facelifts, illustrating that although she may have invested a great deal in cosmetic surgery, she maintains the ability to laugh at herself and—by extension—the culture that created facelifts. She is, in essence, laughing at the human condition—its frailty and foibles (as well as at the cosmetic surgery industry for its "solution" to aging).[3] Indeed, self-deprecatory humor can be viewed as subversive if given more than a cursory interpretation. As Walker (1988) maintains, "Self-deprecation is ingratiating rather than aggressive; it acknowledges the opinion of the dominant culture—even *appears* to confirm it—and allows the speaker or writer to participate in the humorous process without alienating the members of the majority" (123; my emphasis). Apparently unaware of its subversive potential, critics continue to dismiss self-deprecatory humor as negative. Comics themselves are aware of the bad reputation this type of humor has. Diller explains: "Of course, I was accused of being self-deprecatory. I've got to be. . . . Comedy is tragedy revisited or hostility. It is mock hostility, of course, or it would be ugly" (cited in Martin and Segrave 1986, 341). What Diller is saying is something that all performers know—use what works! Hence, the real question to be asked here is not, "Why do female comics use self-deprecatory humor?" but "What is it about contemporary American culture that makes this type of marginal humor "work" with diverse audiences?"

Has Diller been a feminist all of these years? She thinks so! Recall that her entrance into the world of professional stand-up comedy was economically motivated—she needed to support her five children. With male role models, particularly Bob Hope, she entered a male-dominated profession and, within the male-defined parameters of stand-up comedy, told jokes that she knew would "work," making millions of dollars in the process. And she is still going strong.[4] Yet, Barreca and others do not consider Diller's brand of comedy "feminist."

They do, however, accord that privilege to Roseanne. Like Diller, Roseanne was a "housewife." Unhappy with her blue-collar surroundings, in the early 1980s, she began to vent her anger onstage in vitriolic stand-up monologues. Her 1987 HBO special, *The Roseanne Barr Show,* launched what would become a multimillion dollar career, replete with one of the most popular shows on TV for eight seasons, films, and books. As discussed in chapter 4, Roseanne is to the bitch persona what Diller is to the whiner persona. Roseanne has always highlighted her anger in her comedy, yet she acknowledges Diller's legacy. In a *Playboy* interview along with then-husband, Tom Arnold (1993), Roseanne describes her humor:

> Instead of espousing political theory I changed it into women's point-of-view jokes. But it wasn't just role reversal. I didn't want to have a husband named Fang, because that had already been done—and very well. Men became the butt of my jokes, only I tried not to be mean-spirited. I joked about how we women thought instead of how we looked, about our hypocrisy. As for packaging, I used the cover of being everyone's fat mother, fat neighbor. I used a funny voice. (68)

In the above statements, Roseanne contradicts herself, both claiming not to base jokes on female appearance and immediately admitting that her own weight and voice are the features that made her safe and funny. As Tom Arnold notes, "If an insecure man looks at Roseanne, instead of having to deal with who she is, he says, 'She's crazy and she's fat.' That way he doesn't have to deal with the fact that she's powerful, intelligent and brilliant" (68).

Using her weight, Roseanne objectifies herself. If others dehumanize her—see her as a "thing"—then they will not be threatened and will be able to laugh. In the *Playboy* interview (1993), Roseanne complains: "I've talked about this stuff [feminism] to the media for years, but it never gets printed. The media only want to hear about how much I eat because it's threatening to read about a woman who has a vision and a fucking brain.... I'd like it to be about my body of work, not just my body" (67). And yet, she makes "it" (her act) about her body. Auslander (1993) contends that "Whereas the Diller and Rivers personae make their own supposed physical unattractiveness a source of humor, Barr insists on her right to be overweight, making those who are not the object of her humor" (327). To illustrate his point, Auslander quotes material from Roseanne's 1987 special: "If you're fat, just like be fat and shut up. And if you're thin—fuck you!" By failing to see the way in which Roseanne self-objectifies in order to tell the preceding joke, Auslander, like so many others, mistakes anger for feminism.

Roseanne considers herself a feminist. But does this make her humor "feminist humor?" And why does the overt anger that she and other so-called feminist comics use seem to fuel critics' desire to apply this label? Clearly, Roseanne is only able to perform the "if you're thin—fuck you!" punchline because she is speaking as someone who is not thin. She tells "fat" people simply to "shut up," and saves her real venom for the "thin." True, she never says, "I'm so fat that . . . ," but does she really self-objectify less than Diller? Is the internal/external anger binary truly applicable?[5] In their acts, Diller and Roseanne talk about themselves, men, and the comedy of the quotidian. They both perform lines about male vs. female driving habits. They both ridicule domestic tasks. They both offer social critique in the form of stand-up comedy. Yet Roseanne is often considered a feminist comic and Diller is usually acknowledged as a precursor, forgiven for doing the best that she could. Both academic and popular critics lack a sense of cultural history by imposing current feminist standards on 1960s feminist practices. The message seems to be: If Diller made fun of herself, then she did not perform feminist humor because to be a true feminist by contemporary standards requires overt rather than subtle anger.

Auslander (1993) cites Roseanne's "Suck my dick!" line,[6] calling it an example of "the comic woman's most overt challenge to phallocentrism . . . humor that altogether usurps the traditional male prerogative" (330). Acknowledging that the line also functions as a dick joke designed to shock the audience, Auslander explains: "By claiming to possess a metaphoric penis . . . [Roseanne] claims her right to the comic stage and challenges the cultural values that assert that women are not supposed to be aggressive and funny, are not supposed to have access to the power that humor represents."

As mentioned in chapter 4, Roseanne's line is both an effective appropriation and subversion of a standard dick joke. Most critics would probably consider this an example of feminist humor. Another example of Roseanne's humor, however, is a line not performed in the 1987 special. Noting that "It's gonna piss everybody off," she includes it in the *Playboy* interview at Tom's urging: "I used to be a feminist, until the first time Tom grabbed me by the hair, threw me up against the wall and fucked me in the ass." After a brief interchange with Tom, she adds, "That's every guy's fantasy—that his wiener saved your life" (67). Clearly, critics who condemn female comics' use of self-deprecation would likely be horrified at the above joke. To be horrified, however, is to fail to recognize it as a joke. By articulating these words in a humorous context, Roseanne is subverting the status quo. She is not saying that all a woman needs to be happy is to be sexually dominated and abused by a man. On the contrary, she is lampooning this belief. In the *Playboy* interview, Roseanne asserts that "Everything comics do is to expose hypocrisy and dishonesty" (60). And this is exactly what she accomplishes in the wall joke. She is not advocating or valorizing violence against women. Neither is she suggesting that becoming a "real" woman requires disavowing feminist ideology. Rather, she seems to be asking, "Can you believe women who drop their best friends when a guy calls for a date?" or, in this case, "who drop their ideology for a good time?" Roseanne clarifies her view by adding the lines about "every man's fantasy." She makes explicit her intent—to ridicule the people who believe that a woman's place is on the end of a man's penis. And she does this constantly, describing it as "telling the truth—a revolutionary act" (67). In this sense, the wall joke is a case of the ends justifying the means. "*How* I got there is not the issue," Roseanne seems to say, "but *that* I got there."

On her second *Tonight Show* appearance, Roseanne performed the following material: "Men are here for one reason only: to serve me, to bring back food and build a comfortable hive for me and my larvae, to willingly move on when it's time for a younger drone with more stamina. Oh, call me old-fashioned" (quoted in Roseanne 1993, 67). Roseanne does not perceive any of her material to be sexist toward either gender. In the above lines, she mocks traditional sex roles by parodying domesticity with a bawdy spin. The "queen bee" metaphor is a classic symbol of female power. And the punchline, "Oh, call me old-fashioned," reminds the audience that it is precisely "old-fashioned" mores that are being mocked, and hence challenged, through humor.

Does Roseanne's blatant attack on hegemonic culture make her humor more "feminist" than Diller's? And what of Roseanne's material that puts down specific groups of women, like those with eating disorders? Is her 1987 line, "Hey—I eat the same amount of food that *you* eat—I just don't *puke* when I'm done!" affirming women's experience or is she simply relentless in her quest to unmask hypocrisy wherever it resides? Is she the quintessential feminist who will use whatever means necessary to retain power? Has Roseanne taken her metaphorical penis too literally? Certain critics would undoubtedly delight in relegating her "nonfeminist" material to the "male" model she must emulate in order to succeed within the genre of stand-up comedy.

Another female comic called feminist by some is Brett Butler. Like Diller and Roseanne, Butler began her comedy career performing for other women. Her audiences were residents of women's shelters, people who shared her experience of having been a battered wife. After considerable success as a stand-up throughout the 1980s, Butler landed her own sitcom, *Grace under Fire,* in 1993. Described as "the brazen, shoot-from-the-lip, feminist stand-up comic poised for Roseanne-size stardom"(Krupp 1993, 185),[7] Butler often performs material that puts men down. Using frequent jokes about her "redneck" ex-husband, Butler simultaneously critiques the "good ol' boy" mindset and her own naivete, as in the line, "I was so young when I got married, I thought a battered wife was the kind you dipped in bread crumbs and deep fried" (cited in Gallo 1991, 100). Although she mocks both specific males and patriarchal culture in general, Butler also employs self-deprecatory humor when commenting on her past relationships. She often combines this with put-downs of other women. For example, when performing material about young girls in department stores spraying "Obsession" perfume on passersby, Butler (1992a) addresses the girl in question: "You're seventeen, I'm thirty-three—you don't know what obsession is yet . . . it's not in a bottle. Come over here, you little baby-sitter, let me tell you what obsession is. Obsession is roaming around in the bushes outside a married man's house at midnight with a machete in one hand and a jar of Vick's Vapo-Rub in the other—now go tell your daddy that. . . . And tell him to call me." What begins as a patronizing diatribe against intrusive and oblivious young women ultimately becomes an admission of anxiety and self-doubt. But it is important to remember that this self-deprecatory discourse is performed in a comedic context.

Does Butler actually roam the bushes obsessively? Not according to her discussion of a blissful marriage to a New York Jew. And within that frame, she momentarily adopts the perspective of her in-laws (1993): "A divorced older southern gentile comedienne who bleaches her hair—why didn't you just shoot us in our sleep?" It is far too simplistic to note that by enumerating the above characteristics, Butler demeans herself. Rather, she offers a broad sociocultural critique in which all participants are butts.

Finally, Butler (1992b) performs material with the same potential effect as Roseanne's wall joke. Discussing a briefing by the Republican State Department spokesperson, Margaret Tutweiler, she offers the following: "'Good afternoon, my name is Margaret Tutweiler. I'm the State Department spokesperson. I'm a forty-eight-year-old debutante, my eyes will never leave this page, nor will the inflection in my voice vary one iota because I'm a frustrated, conservative woman in dire need of a big sweaty-bellied man pounding my head against the backboard of . . . ' Margaret—you need to figure out the other knob on the shower massage." This material may be interpreted by some as antifemale, suggesting that all a woman needs to become actualized is a "big" man to dominate her. A closer look, however, reveals that what Butler actually attacks is the culture that espouses that value. By lampooning conservative "repression," Butler critiques twelve years of Republican hegemony. Furthermore, by interrupting her own impersonation at the "climax" in order to advocate sexual autonomy, Butler makes a liberatory statement. So by some definitions, her humor is most definitely "feminist."

Butler explains: "Some people just want fluffy observational comedy; I have an aversion to it. I want people to know that a woman of substance is up there" (cited in Krupp 1993, 186). Responding to her continued comparison to Roseanne, Butler suggests that the promo for her show be, "Hi, I'm Brett Butler—the new bitch at ABC." Waters (1993) notes that "This would be slighting her talent. But considering how well the last woman to suffer this title [Roseanne] has done, it isn't such a bad rap to take." Essentially, Waters is saying that the end justifies the means. Do Roseanne and Butler actually consider themselves to be bitches? And, more important, when critics of popular culture equate bitchiness with feminism, where does power ultimately reside?

Perhaps Phyllis Diller, Roseanne, and Brett Butler are merely putting everyone down. Perhaps the true feminist—or more aptly, humanist—comic is one who devalues all people equally. Auslander (1993) notes: "A growing strain of feminist literary theory . . . suggests that humor and comedy may be valuable as empowering 'feminist tools,' especially when motivated by the anger women need to express at the social and cultural limitations they confront" (316). This theoretical strain seems to endorse a very particularized notion of feminist humor. The acceptable equation seems to be: female anger + male target = funny. Anything else appears to be a betrayal of feminist ideals or, worse, complicity with patriarchal oppression. Indeed, the hypocrisy inherent in any antidogmatic dogma is in itself humorous. Avowed feminist theorists who condemn patriarchal culture for its intractable mandates and then proceed to create a new set of mandates (often while simultaneously enumerating the reasons that feminism is not monolithic) are themselves likely targets of humor—"feminist" or otherwise.

Both academic and popular critics suggest that there is a distinct women's or feminist humor characterized by its lack of put-downs, its connectedness, and its affirmation of women's experience—its reclamation of female subjectivity (Auslander 1993; Dolan 1989; Finney 1994; Fraiberg 1994; Jenkins 1986; Kibler 1998; Kolbert 1993; Merrill 1988; Stillion and White 1987; USA Today 1990; White 1988). Although some studies focus on women's writing or humorous discourse in conversational settings, even those specifically examining stand-up comedy (Auslander 1993; Dolan 1989; Fraiberg 1994; Horowitz 1997; Kolbert 1993; Merrill 1988) depict female or feminist humor as less abusive than traditional male humor. And the popular press perpetuates this image as well. According to Donna Kauffman, quoted in USA Today (1990), for example, contemporary

female stand-up comics do not bash men or other women but simply make fun of relationships. Roseanne's Cheetohs joke from her
1987 HBO special ("men think the uterus is a tracking device. . . .
'Any Cheetohs left?' Like he can't go lift up the sofa cushion like anyone else") is used as evidence that female comics do not use put-down
humor. True, Roseanne's joke deals with human nature, but her
impression of her husband asking for the Cheetohs, replete with finger up her nose, clearly makes him the butt.

Since her success began in the late 1980s, critics have lauded
Roseanne precisely because of the sexism inherent in her material.
Phillips (1989) notes that Roseanne, "though several kids, years, and
pounds beyond Dating Standard, does not tell fat jokes: she tells lean,
mean, husband jokes with cheerful vengeance. On hearing that a
woman has stabbed her husband thirty-seven times, Rosie offers, 'I
admire her restraint'" (17). Perhaps "cheerful vengeance" is another
manifestation of what some critics dub "feminist" humor.

It is evident that many female comics do use put-down humor.
It is also evident that many female comics resist the feminist label. As
Kauffman observes in *USA Today* (1990): "They say they're not feminists, yet they challenge the traditional role of women. Their humor
raises consciousness, but it does so in a non-threatening way. Humor
might, in fact, be a force that could bring about social change. And
that's nothing to laugh at" (9). With the exception of Kate Clinton,
lesbian comic and self-designated "fumerist" (combination of "feminist" and "humorist," cited in Pershing 1991), in fact, very few female
comics willingly wear the feminist mantle. Some, like Elayne Boosler,
have even gone so far as to disavow the label emphatically, claiming,
"I'm a woman who's a comic, not a woman's comic" (quoted in Martin
and Segrave 1986, 410).[8] Ellen DeGeneres and Paula Poundstone also
view humor as a genderless phenomenon—not surprising, given their
success with androgynous kid personas.[9]

Perhaps female comics are simply representative of the many
American women who, regardless of sympathy toward feminist issues,
refuse to designate themselves feminists. According to Wolf (1993), a
1989 poll indicates that twice as many women support the goals of
the women's movement as are willing to call themselves feminist (224).
And in February 1994, Friend reports that in a Time/CNN poll, only
37 percent of American women consider themselves feminists and "in

yet another poll, a mere 16 percent of college women embraced the term" (52). In its own 1994 poll, *Esquire* finds that only 34.1 percent of the one thousand eighteen- to twenty-five-year-old women queried claim to be feminists (67). Friend explains that "Feminists have usually attributed this discordancy to the media's having loaded feminist with a crippling, pejorative burden: ugly, hairy, humorless, bra-burning, ball-busting bitches" (52). Given this description, it is certainly not surprising that female stand-up comics eschew association with an ideological label that is likely to brand them "humorless."

Dolan (1989) asserts that "Today, women are telling jokes and a broad, sweeping female humor is emerging" (5). In that "broad, sweeping" statement, Dolan neither considers the rich history of female comics nor defines "female humor." Later, however, Dolan maintains that female comics are "at the very edge of our democratic discourse . . . demanding that we think about issues not only through the prism of male perspective but from the female point of view" as well (5). The statement is accurate, although it assumes that there is a single "female point of view." As noted earlier, Roseanne (1993) has characterized her humor as "women's point-of-view jokes" (68). She has previously likened her material to "having coffee with your neighbor—the way you talk before the husbands come in" (cited in Dolan, 5). Perhaps Roseanne's description can be applied to much of the material currently performed by female stand-up comics.

The mistake critics of such discourse frequently make is the assumption that the way women talk in single-sex groups is devoid of vitriol and sexism directed against men (even if the anger is manifested as humor). As discussed in chapter 2, the generic constraints of stand-up comedy make it an inherently aggressive form; hence, any notion of dialogic intimacy and support-seeking behavior is generally precluded by the monologic construction of the act. Indeed, the characterization of women's humor and feminist humor (specifically as it relates to stand-up comedy) discussed thus far is problematic for two reasons. First, it places women in a win–win situation; either we are inherently superior to men because our humor is based on support and affirmation rather than abuse and humiliation, or we are aggressive and "bitchy" only because by performing stand-up comedy, we are forced to operate within a male-defined genre. This type of feminist rhetoric is inherently sexist toward males.

Second, the present investigation indicates that contemporary American female stand-up comics are extremely similar to their male counterparts in both form and content. Data do not suggest that—either at topical or stylistic levels—contemporary female stand-up comics are performing material that is particularly nonthreatening and nonabusive (see chapter 3). To the contrary, most assume the "bitch" posture at some point in their acts. Perhaps this is necessary because, as Wolf (1993) points out, "it is only the master's tools that can dismantle the master's house; he hardly notices anyone else's" (224). Does this mean that in order to perform stand-up comedy successfully in America today, a comic must assume "male" characteristics?[10] As discussed in chapter 2, hard-and-fast male and female distinctions usually preclude rather than encourage further discussion and investigation. Instead of making the oversimplistic assessment that all humor is inherently aggressive—and therefore inherently male—we need to consider the nature of the subject-object relationship fundamental to all humor.

Humor and Objectification

As noted in chapter 2, with the exception of wordplay and some types of observational humor, there is no "equal opportunity" humor. Some individual, group, or institution is always the target of humor, especially marginal humor. Comics deal with generalizations, with types. Comics say, "Women are . . . " or "Men are . . . " or "Construction workers are . . . " or "Doctors are . . ." Comics may even say "Comics are . . . " and "Audiences are. . . . " The "All" before the subject is implicit—comics speak in absolutes. Humor, especially stand-up comedy, is based on reduction and superiority. In fact, the very form of stand-up comedy may be said to undermine its content. The form features the use of stereotypes—superficial, generally negative characterizations of individuals and groups, characterizations of individuals by group membership. Stereotypes are reductive, inherently objectifying as they define human agents unidimensionally, seizing upon a single characteristic or behavior. Stand-up comedy may thus be considered a "conservative" act—one that builds on preconceived types, as comics base their acts on generalizations.

Stereotypes are objectifications. Yet, scholars of marginal humor believe that using the type in order to explode the type may be

150

considered a subversive act (Boskin 1979; Dorinson and Boskin 1988; Levine 1977; Mintz 1988; Walker 1988). As Levine explains: "Marginal groups often embraced the stereotype of themselves in a manner designed not to assimilate it but to smother it. . . . To tell jokes containing the stereotype was not invariably to accept it but frequently to laugh at it, to strip it naked to expose it to scrutiny" (336).[11]

Stereotypes are part of the currency of stand-up comedy. Comics constantly type themselves and their targets. The question arises: Are comics' motives "pure?" Are they attempting to educate their audiences through the use of stereotypes or are they simply using what "works" in order to get laughs and, ultimately, dollars? And, more important, what is it about stereotypes that "works" for most audiences?

Cohen (1999) believes that jokes only work because they are predicated on truths—not truth about the object but truth about the far-reaching influence and impact of the stereotype. To illustrate, he uses a joke about black men and basketball, explaining that the joke reveals "not truths about black men, but truths about how black men are thought of" (80). Disturbed by claims that offensive humor based on stereotypes is not funny, Cohen argues that "if there is a problem with such jokes, the problem is compounded exactly by the fact that they are funny. Face that fact. And then let us talk about it" (84).[12] And Davies warns against taking comic stereotypes too seriously, suggesting: "ethnic jokes in general are not a good indicator of the joke-teller's feelings toward the butts of their jokes, which may range from dislike and hostility to amity and affection. People do not necessarily dislike those whom they disesteem, and the throwers of custard pies do not regard their targets in the same way that those who hurl rocks or grenades do" (cited in Gruner 1997, 78).

Clearly, stereotypes elicit audience laughter, but can they be instructive? Margolis (1998) asks whether stereotypes can combat stereotyping without offending, and whether the strategy of using the type to explode the type works for all marginalized groups and all audiences. She explains that "stereotypes establish boundaries separating those being stereotyped from those whom the stereotype identifies as other. Two elements in understanding how a stereotype works must be who employs the stereotype and the degree of power or powerlessness attributed to the Other" (200). Asserting that "No [comic] tradition exists for women comparable to that . . . existing for more than a century in African American culture" (214), Margolis argues that without a comic tradition, women have internalized sexist stereotyping more deeply than African Americans have racial stereotyping (and that therefore it is more difficult for women to use the type in order to explode the type). With this unsupported generalization, Margolis fails to consider the long and diverse tradition of women's comedic discourse discussed in chapter 4.

Ultimately, she maintains: "To undercut the negative stereotype, the artist must be able to hail the audience so that it recognizes the subject/Other relations that the negative stereotype calls into play" (215). If this is successful, Margolis contends, "Broadly, comedy enables negative stereotypes to be used to undermine negative stereotypes." She issues a caveat, however, pointing out that "negative stereotypes are rarely simple images of race, class, or gender in isolation, and the use of stereotypes to counter negative stereotyping is less likely to succeed if this mixed quality is not kept in mind." Certainly, in order for stereotypes to be transgressive, the audience must recognize the strategy undergirding their use. To adopt the holistic, context-driven view Margolis advocates, however, we must ignore the fact that stereotypes are inherently reductionistic; to humanize the Other, they must become multidimensional and hence no longer stereotypes.

Some performers see a danger in the use of stereotypes. Performance artist Eric Bogosian, for example, believes that "It's very easy to incite an audience toward more prejudice when you're trying to discourage prejudice" (cited in Bernstein 1990, H1). Nilsen (1993) supports this view, noting, "Jokes based on . . . stereotypes become even funnier when we think that the stereotypes are being broken in the jokes, but we later discover that the stereotypes aren't being broken at all" (222). To censor humor, however, may be equally dangerous and ultimately ineffective. As Davies suggests, "to become angry about such jokes and to seek to censor them because they impinge on sensitive issues is about as sensible as smashing a thermometer because it reveals how hot it is" (cited in Nilsen, 219). Clearly this debate, which for the past several years has been located within the cacophony of the "political correctness" controversy, continues to fuel arguments concerning the use of stereotypes in public discourse—comedic and otherwise.

The link between stereotypes and objectification is well documented in scholarship from numerous academic fields, including communication, English, sociology, and women's studies. Said (1978) contends that when the "other" is culturally represented not only as different but as foreign—a "thing" to be despised and feared—the result is a systematic objectification, devaluation, and dehumanization of the other. Collins (1986) asserts that "defining and valuing one's consciousness of one's own self-defined standpoint in the face of images that foster a self-definition as the objectified 'other' is an important way of resisting the dehumanization essential to systems of domination" (518). In other words, being dehumanized begins with allowing someone else to define who we are (and who we are not). According to many feminist theorists, avoiding or escaping such domination requires claiming or reclaiming subjectivity.

Modleski (1991) notes that the "most useful" type of criticism is that which "analyzes male power, male hegemony, with a concern for the effects of this power on the female subject and with an awareness of how frequently male subjectivity works to appropriate 'femininity' while oppressing women" (7). To experience subjectivity, Modleski (and others) imply, is to eschew oppression. Discussing her concept of "feminist" humor, Merrill (1988) contends: "To refuse to see the 'humor' in one's own victimization as the 'butt' of the joke or the 'object' of ridicule, while seizing and redefining the apparatus of comic perspective so that it is inclusive of women's experience is a necessary and powerful gesture of self-definition" (279–80). What Merrill and others fail to consider is that all humor requires a butt. With the exception of wordplay and certain types of observational humor, jokes are always told at someone's expense.

The focus of this investigation has been upon the performances of female stand-up comics. Data suggest that these performances are examples of marginal humor, sharing characteristics with the humor performed by members of other marginalized groups such as African American, gay/lesbian, and Jewish comics. The issue of subjectivity is central to marginality. Specifically, critical discussions of feminist humor designate this category as one that affirms women's experience and grants them subjectivity. What these discussions fail to recognize is that this subjectivity is only won at the expense of another's subjectivity—usually a male's. For marginal humor to exist in public discourse, there must be a butt. And the butt of most so-called feminist humor is generally a man or male culture. Some critics attempt to

153

evade this problem with claims that are tenuous at best. Kaufman argues that feminist humor does not create stereotypes of men the way misogynistic humor does of women—that although male actions are sometimes stereotyped, there are no father-in-law jokes equivalent to mother-in-law jokes told by male comics (cited in Walker 1988, 145). White (1988) maintains that whereas antiwoman humor "denigrates women on a universal level as women," feminist humor "is generally limited to attacks on specific men and/or the abstract cultural notion that men are superior" (85). These assertions are weakened by the fact that much of what passes as feminist humor is humor performed by female comics that uses men as targets.

Indeed, objectification is at the heart of stand-up comedy. As Burke observes, "the comic frame should enable people to be observers of themselves while acting" (cited in Levine 1977, 321). By performing in a public space, the comic is exposed, made vulnerable before the audience. With every action, every utterance, she calls attention to herself—as art, as entertainment, as commodity. Sometimes, she makes herself the butt of her jokes; at other times, she targets individuals or groups, reducing them to stereotypes. The audience identifies—sometimes with the comic, sometimes with the target (indeed, sometimes the audience is the target). Yet in marginal humor, no subject-subject relationship exists. Within the context of marginal humor, to treat someone comically is to deny subjectivity. In order to make someone the target or butt of a joke, it is necessary to make that person a thing, an object; only then is it permissible to laugh at him or her. By laughing at someone else, we elevate ourselves; this is the classic superiority theory of laughter and humor conceived by Plato, extended by Aristotle, and ultimately developed most fully by Hobbes (Morreall 1987, 19).[13] As Boskin (1979) explains:

> Because of its aggressive aspect, humor is one of the most effective weapons in the repertory of the human mind. It was for this reason that Thomas Hobbes conceived of laughter in relation to power. . . . Hobbes offered an explanation of social rivalry. The passion of laughter was nothing, he argued, save the "sudden glory" emanating from the realization of "some eminency in ourselves, by comparison with the infirmity of others," or with our own former position. (256)

This is the essence of put-down humor. Putting the object or butt of a joke down raises the subject or teller of the joke up.[14] Although its influence is evident, some contemporary scholars find Hobbes's theory limited. Holland (1982) for example, prefers Burke's belief that the purpose of laughter is "not so much a glorifying of the self as a minimizing of the distresses menacing the self" (45). Regardless of differing interpretations, however, superiority theory offers an incisive explanation of much humor, specifically marginal humor.

Another major theorist contributing to this perspective on humor is Bergson. As discussed in chapter 1, Bergson believed that laughter was inherently social and required a "momentary anesthesia of the heart"—that is, a suspension of sympathy toward the human subject: an objectification. Boskin (1979) further notes:

> "Something mechanical encrusted on something living" was a central notion in Bergson's view of the comic. He formulated the image as an axiom of humor: "We laugh every time a person gives us the impression of being a thing." To illustrate his concept, he pointed to the antics of two circus clowns. As they bumped and collided with each other, gradually, "one lost sight of the fact that they were men of flesh and blood like ourselves; one began to think of bundles of all sorts, falling and knocking against each other." (258)

Once a person has been rendered insensate, we can laugh at the newly ascribed "thingness." As Boskin suggests, "This . . . is the connection between stereotypes and aggressive humor" (258). Because of the objectification inherent in and necessary for humor to occur, even when the audience identifies with a comic taking a literal or figurative pratfall, the identification is with the "object" status of the comic—the butt of the joke. If the audience identifies with the comic as joketeller, the audience, like the comic, is placed in a subject position only at the expense of the object. In order for a joke to work, the audience must "get it." And in order to get it, identification or "disidentification" (see chapter 1) must occur—the audience must see itself in order to construct its identity as either subject or object.

Hence, the message sent by critics who valorize feminist humor as that which reclaims female subjectivity is: We must deny male subjectivity in order to experience female subjectivity. Therefore, if we use the term "feminist" to mean gender egalitarianism, then "feminist" humor is an impossibility. Horowitz (1997) wonders if stand-up comedy will ever become a "sexually neutral profession" (160). Nietz posited such an occurrence in 1980, longing for an ideal state in which "men and women can both tell jokes, and can both laugh together . . .

155

with neither needing to assert superiority over the other through their jokes, or in other patterns of interactions" (222). Indeed, this is an idealized state. Certainly, it is not a "humor" state. If the inferiority/ superiority dichotomy undergirds all marginal humor, then the use of the "master's tools" is inevitable. This "turnabout is fair play" rhetoric must be recognized as such before claims for a humor that escapes "traditional" or "male" constraints can be made.

Hierarchy is essential to most humor. And historically, because they have been perceived as powerless, women have been objectified through humor as in other forms of cultural representation (Barreca 1988). Mellencamp (1986) notes that "In his study of jokes, particularly tendentious or obscene jokes, Freud assigns woman to the place of object between two male subjects" (91). From Legman's assertion that "there is no place in it [the "dirty joke"] for women except as the butt" (cited in Mitchell 1978, 23) to countless male comics' performance of dick jokes that objectify women, humor in American culture has traditionally depicted women as objects. Film theorist Laura Mulvey (1991) maintains that in traditional cultural representation, "women are simultaneously looked at and displayed, with their appearance coded for strong visual and erotic impact so that they can be said to connote to-be-looked-at-ness" (436). Perhaps women have also typically connoted to-be-laughed-at-ness.[15] Perhaps Mulvey's notion of the "male gaze" can be applied to the "male guffaw," a means of denuding women of dimensionality, of constructing them as mere objects of scorn and derision, as what Barreca (1988) calls "the unlaughing at which men laugh" (15).

A feminist humor, suggests Merrill (1988), is one that "posits a female spectator" (279). Throughout her discussion, Merrill, like many feminist critics, seems to equate "female" with "feminist." Phyllis Schlafly is a female spectator, but probably not the one Merrill has in mind. When female comics disparage other women in their acts, is it because they are not positing a female spectator but, having internalized patriarchal values, are playing to an audience of "universal males" (that is, constructing a "male" spectator)? Is denying male subjectivity the only way to posit a female spectator? Might comics of either gender posit a feminist spectator (of either gender)? Auslander (1993) contends that during their acts, female comics create a "community" with female audience members and that

> In the hands of the most skilled practitioners this community becomes a strategic community, a moment at which a shared subjectivity that excludes men is created under our very noses . . . placing the men in the audience in the position women have traditionally occupied as comedy spectators . . . the articulation of the comedian's performance as cultural text . . . can produce circumstances within the context of the performance that run counter to the social norm, circumstances in which women may find a sense of empowerment through a sense of shared subjectivity. (321)

This description of female comics and female audience members exemplifies the subject-object paradox of marginal humor. For men to assume the traditional "woman's" position necessitates a loss of male subjectivity. Hence, when Anita Wise advocates "contraceptive beer" as "something we women could be sure you [men] were taking," when Lizz Winstead says that "Every time I see a guy around forty in a Corvette, I just want to scream out, 'Sorry about your penis!'" or even when Rita Rudner observes that men like to barbecue because "they'll only cook if danger's involved," the male is objectified as the target of humor.

Whether female comics truly subvert patriarchal norms through their discourse is, of course, contingent upon audience interpretation. Certainly, female comics *invert* the "traditional" stand-up comedy scenario to the extent that male and female exchange subject-object positions as the hierarchy is turned upside down. As Mo Gaffney, former host of *Women Aloud,* a comedy/talk show on HBO, maintains, "Comedy has always been what men thought was funny; now we have women's perspective" (cited in Horowitz 1997, 159). In this configuration, female comics are just as capable of sexism as their male counterparts. Rather than construct a feminist vs. sexist humor dichotomy, therefore, it seems more appropriate to examine humor in terms of female vs. male "point of view" jokes.[16] And rather than limit discussion to issues of gender, it is important to explore the larger category of marginal humor.[17]

Self-Deprecation and Subversion

Most studies of marginal humor focus on Jewish and/or African American humor, frequently noting the similarity of these two traditions. Levine (1977) suggests: "The need to laugh at our enemies, our situation, ourselves, is a common one," but points out that it is often strongest "in those who have the most objective reasons for feelings of hopelessness" (300). Discussing Jewish humor, for example, Shapiro

(1999) explains that the laughter of this particular group is "an integral dimension of a culture intent on resisting the spiritual and emotional suffocation that can be the lot of a people afflicted with so much pain"—that ultimately, "Humor dissolves the overwhelming facticity and solidity of a threatening world" (25).[18] As noted in chapter 1, a primary feature of marginal humor is the use of self-deprecation. As Boskin and Dorinson (1987) observe, "Mocking the features ascribed to them by outsiders has become one of the most effective ethnic infusions into national humor, particularly by Afro-Americans and Jews" (116–17).[19] Grotjahn illustrates the reason for self-deprecation in the tradition of Jewish humor: "one can almost see how a witty Jewish man carefully and cautiously takes a sharp dagger out of his enemy's hands, sharpens it so that it can split a hair in mid-air, polishes it so that it shines brightly, stabs himself with it, then returns it gallantly to the anti-Semite with the silent reproach: Now see whether you can do half so well" (cited in Gruner 1997, 99).[20]

As discussed throughout this investigation, self-deprecation may also be subversive. Dorsinson and Boskin (1988) describe the humor of African American comics as "Inwardly masochistic, indeed tragic, externally aggressive, even acrimonious. . . . Theirs is the connection between subserviency and humor and the use of humor to overturn roles and position" (174). In this way, Dorinson and Boskin suggest, jokes function as the Freudian notion of "mini-rebellions" (176). Lincoln maintains that oppressed groups have three options: acceptance, avoidance, and aggression (cited in Dorinson and Boskin, 181). Clearly, marginal humor is an aggressive response to domination. Although it is not always overt, the aggression in marginal humor may be discerned as cultural critique. Discussing self-deprecation as "a major subversive device of the domestic humor of the 1940s and 1950s," Walker (1987) asserts: "By denigrating her [female comedic subject's] own ability to live up to societal standards of domestic excellence, she appears to take the blame for her failure, and thus to accede to those standards; but the underlying message is that the standards—and those who seek to enforce them—are at fault" (125–26).

Indeed, when self-deprecation is strategic, its subversive effect may be to send a subtle double message, Bakhtin's "double-voiced discourse," used by Little (1991) and discussed by Finney (1994) as one "which often interweaves elements of a subversive discourse into the language of the status quo—the discourse of power and control—using the former to ridicule, subvert, or deconstruct the latter" (7). At times this double message may become a type of supplication, an embodiment of the power of powerlessness.[21]

Marginal humor may also be overtly aggressive, launching blatant attacks on the dominant culture for the entertainment of the dominant culture. African American comic Dick Gregory noted the irony of this situation in the 1960s: "I'm getting $5000 a week—for saying the same things out loud I used to say under my breath" (cited in Levine 1977, 361). Gregory's words illustrate what many scholars believe—that marginalized individuals speak from the position of outsiders, alienated and excluded by the dominant culture (Cohen 1999; Collins 1986; Harman 1988; Ortner 1996; Stonequist 1937). Yet, as discussed in chapter 1, it is precisely this alienation—the "outsider within" status—that affords marginalized individuals a unique vantage point and produces a unique humor.[22] In recent years, humor created by women has been compared to that of other marginalized groups. Walker (1988) maintains that the humor of women "employs the same subversive strategies as does the humor of racial and ethnic minorities, camouflaging with laughter the pain of the outsider who is denied access to power and must live by someone else's rules. Yet the situation of women is more complex because of their close involvement with members of the dominant group, which has blurred the boundaries between 'us' and 'them'" (137–38). Indeed, the us/them distinction is central to marginal humor as it creates victims and butts—not necessarily one and the same.

Certainly, there are more high-profile female comics working today than ever before, many of whom assume the bitch persona at some point in their acts. Mo Gaffney believes that "Today, there's less women's self-deprecating humor, and women can be both attractive and funny. The fact that there are more women comics puts a check on men's sexist humor." This serves female comics well both onstage and off, Gaffney, notes, as "Now men have to work with women, go backstage and see a woman who is as powerful and funny as they are" (cited in Horowitz 1997, 159). The acceptance of female comics by audiences is an ongoing process, however; as Alison Field of Sensible Footwear observes, "It's threatening for women to have a sense of humour and it's doubly threatening if it's not the sense of humour turned on yourself but turned out to other people and other groups" (cited in Hengen 1998, 259).[23]

In order not to alienate their audiences, some female comics still adopt the whiner posture. And, as discussed earlier, the self-deprecatory humor often employed by comics like Diller, Haber, and other marginalized individuals may send a double message: its objectifying use of reductive stereotypes may fuel the fire of racist, sexist, or other "ist" rhetoric; the less overt message, however, may be construed as a subversive critique of social norms and cultural representation. Because of the first message, self-deprecatory humor is a "safe" and effective means of both entertainment and social control.[24] Self-deprecation is safe entertainment because it does not abuse or offend the audience—in fact, it *appears* to reaffirm hegemonic values. It, like all marginal humor, is effective social control because it accomplishes what professional fools have always accomplished—critique with impunity—impunity granted, of course, by the status quo. Ironically, in the context of public comic performance, the status quo is perpetuated because it has institutionally "allowed" a potentially subversive discourse to be voiced. As Eagleton notes, "carnival" only occurs due to "a permissible rupture of hegemony" (cited in Stallybrass and White 1986, 13). And Stallybrass and White point out that kings and queens were actually crowned during carnival, a time of officially sanctioned comic chaos.

Victims and Butts

Whether the victim is the same as the butt in marginal humor depends entirely upon audience identification and interpretation. For example, when Karen Haber performs the material about her dating debacle (see chapter 4), her whiner persona may appear to construct her both as the piteous victim and the hapless butt. An alternate interpretation, however, sees Haber as victim and her boorish date as the butt. In other words, although she quite literally whines as she describes her ridiculous attempts to please her arrogant date, her descriptions and paraphrases of this man depict him as a self-absorbed brute—clearly an object of scorn and ridicule. In this scenario, neither victim nor butt emerges unscathed, but it is important to recognize that they are not necessarily one and the same. In fact, when comics play the victim—whether of an individual or of society—they do what professional fools have always done—become "fool makers." Indeed, being wise enough to play the fool suggests the ability to make others the butt or target of humor in a variety of ways not always immediately apparent. Even overtly hostile marginal humor does not necessarily construct victim and butt as the same individual.[25]

In Roseanne's wall joke, for instance, she may appear to be both the victim of domination and abuse by her husband and the butt of the joke—the joke being her own ideological sellout. Another possibility is to see Roseanne as victim and all feminists, even all women, as the butt—easily placated by a good time. A final interpretation, however, places women, specifically feminists, as victims and American culture itself as the butt. Any society that actually finds this (a woman being raped—ideologically or otherwise) natural and appropriate, Roseanne may be saying, needs to have its collective unconscious radically interrogated. It is important to remember, however, that Roseanne offers this critique in a comedic context. Like all jokes, this one depends upon audience interpretation to determine its effect. And like all jokes, the extent to which this one works determines its inclusion in the comic's act.[26]

The above discussion is not meant to suggest that in marginal humor victim and butt are never the same. Although the victim/butt dichotomy is at the heart of the us against them nature of marginal humor, only audience identification can designate victims and butts. Hence, if a male in Roseanne's audience feels victimized by her impotence jokes, he can conceivably construct himself as both victim and butt of the jokes. Indeed, it seems that the more overtly hostile the humor (for example, much material performed by comics assuming the bitch posture), the more clearly victim and butt are distinguished or conflated. A direct attack appears strategic and certainly less ambiguous than the more sophisticated social critique embedded in other forms of humor. Thus, when bitch comic Judy Tenuta calls Madonna "a mattress with a microphone" or tells a male audience member that she was "lookin' for someone a little closer to the top of the food chain," victims and butts are easily seen as one and the same. When whiner comic Henriette Mantel says that she only wants to be unplugged from life support after getting "down to a size eight," however, Mantel may be seen as the victim and the society that promotes this type of thinking as the butt.

As discussed in chapter 4, even Diller's use of self-deprecation can be seen as much more than merely self-ridicule. By self-scapegoating, Diller and other whiner comics substitute self for society; the social critique is, therefore, implicit rather than explicit. Indeed, it is precisely the failure of many feminist critics to recognize the *difference* between victims and butts that prevents them from viewing self-deprecation as a potentially subversive rhetoric. Clearly, issues of objectification, subversion, and the construction of victims and butts lie at the very heart of any rhetoric of victimage—comic or otherwise. When considering power relations in the context of public comic performance, however, we must examine the role of audience.

The Role of Audience in Comic Performance

Audience plays a critical role in any type of comic performance. As Freud (1960) explained, "An urge to tell the joke to someone is inextricably bound up with the joke-work" (143).[27] In fact, when humor is performed in public, it requires the legitimation of laughter in order to be recognized as humor (Gilbert 1996). As noted in chapter 1, comic George Carlin maintains that audiences essentially "vote" with their laughter, determining whether any given joke will "kill" or "die." And stand-up comedy is a unique performative genre precisely because of its interactive nature. Although the comic's material is monologic, the audience can interrupt or be interrogated at any time; hence, a comic's act is always in process—the "rehearsal" becomes a "performance" only as it is legitimized by audience laughter. In this way, comics create some of their material spontaneously onstage. A spontaneous, contextual response to a heckler that works during a particular performance may ultimately become part of the comic's act. One of the cardinal rules of stand-up comedy, after all, is: Keep what works! Clearly, unlike its function in any other performative contexts, audience plays a crucial role in the creation and legitimation of public comic performance.

Taking a Bergsonian position, Merrill (1988) maintains that "humor always implies shared values" (276). This statement affirms Bergson's notion of a "secret freemasonry," a complicity between laughers. It also assumes that members of a given audience all laugh for the same reason(s). The double message inherent in much marginal humor, however, suggests that people in the same audience experiencing the same performance may laugh for very different reasons. Cultural values shape our responses to humor; as Holland (1982) notes, "It is as though our ability to laugh, like our ability to speak, is innate, but we learn our particular culture's way of doing it" (68). In the context of marginal performance, this notion is particularly relevant to male and female cocultures.[28] For instance, a male audience member may laugh at a female comic's self-deprecatory humor because his values (beliefs that women are inferior) are affirmed, whereas a female audience member at the same performance may laugh because her values (beliefs that patriarchal culture is absurd) are equally affirmed.[29] In order for an audience to laugh, some form of identification (or disidentification) must occur.[30] Whether an audience member identifies with the butt of a joke (and thus engages in self-objectification) or with the comic as victim (and thus laughs at society in general or one group in particular), some identification is made at the instant the joke is performed.

An interesting question regarding identification arises in the context of marginal humor: Why do men laugh at sexist jokes directed toward them by female comics? Certainly, the reason seems different than that motivating the "nervous laughter" of accommodation that women have traditionally manifested at sexist jokes directed toward them by male comics (Barreca 1988; Merrill 1988). Indeed, men appear to laugh appreciatively at jokes that attack them, often overtly. Perhaps by laughing a man is saying, "I'm a straight, white male—I am hegemony—hear me roar. No amount of joking, no matter how well done, is about to unseat me from my power position any time soon." Perhaps the laughter is precisely because he is *not* threatened. Members of the dominant group in any culture know that names can never hurt them. Marginalized groups like women and minorities, however, may feel threatened by humor that seems to perpetuate existing structures of oppression. For example, when Roseanne notes that "only the male mind could conceive of one inch equaling a hundred miles," both men and women in the audience laugh. Although men are both butt and victim, as members of the dominant culture they are not truly threatened. When comics such as Andrew "Dice" Clay insult women, however, centuries of real domination may prevent women from finding this type of humor amusing.[31]

Raskin argues that communication consists of either "real talk" or "unreal talk" (play frame, humor). He claims that people with no sense of humor treat every topic as "real" talk, and that conversely, some individuals can make fun of any topic. In the middle, he contends, are "those who choose not to see a comic script in some topics" such as feminists and members of certain religions (cited in Gruner 1997, 91). Indeed, feminists are often accused of being humorless when they do not find jokes that objectify women funny. Self-designated feminists are not the only people selective about which topics are off-limits, however; as discussed above, any marginalized individuals who have been victimized by dominant cultural practices may feel threatened when they become the target of jokes made by members of a group that historically has oppressed them. Undeniably, humor is a powerful rhetorical weapon, whether in the hands of dominant or marginalized groups. The question we must ask is: Can marginal humor actually transform social conditions? Boskin (1979) does not think so, maintaining that humor can be political as long as it does not "enter into the sanctified halls of action" (64). The very phrase "That *made* me laugh" implies a certain passivity on the part of the audience. Indeed, comic Jerry Seinfeld asserts, "To laugh is to be dominated" (cited in Borns 1987, 20). To "make" someone laugh indicates that the act is, at some level, involuntary. The extent to which we consciously *choose* to laugh or to refrain from laughing may be the extent to which humor actually affects social reality.[32]

Humor disarms audiences, entertaining and even relaxing them; "comic activism" is, therefore, unlikely to occur. This is not meant to suggest, however, that audiences have no volition. Indeed, audiences are comprised of individuals, each an embodiment of social and political experience, each capable of constructing and reconstructing his or her own discursive space—of negotiating and renegotiating identity. The question remains, however: Is discursive empowerment truly liberating? Although marginal humor may be rhetorically transgressive, does that necessarily make it politically transgressive? According to Dollimore, "It would be wrong to associate the exhilarating sense of freedom which transgression affords with any necessary or automatic political progressiveness" (cited in Stalllybrass and White 1986, 201). At the end of the day, if most of the power and most of the economic resources are still controlled by the dominant culture, has the performance of marginality on the comic stage really accomplished any political work?

The "master's tools" may never dismantle the "master's house," but the master's cover charge and two-drink minimum might help to build another very nice house. In other words, a female comic who has temporary control of the hegemonic wallet may, indeed, be performing a political act. Perhaps it is the commodification of performed marginality that makes it subversive. Perhaps a female comic who quite literally lives by her wits and her marginality is in a unique position vis-à-vis the dominant culture. If, for example, an African American female comic can say, "I may be excluded from your culture, but I am going to show you how absurd this exclusion is. I am going to make you laugh (maybe even at your own expense) and you are going to pay me for it," then perhaps a chink has been made in the hegemonic wall after all. By performing marginality onstage, a comic is doubly empowered—first by foregrounding difference, and second by commodifying and ultimately profiting from that difference. In this way, social stigma may function as a rhetorical means to a political end. As noted in chapter 1, performed marginality is enhanced by its "cumulative" nature. In other words, the more marginalized the comic, it seems, the funnier the comic. And the funnier the comic, the more successful she or he is economically.

The tacit understanding of the power of performed marginality among comics results in countless attempts at self-marginalization (often through self-deprecation). For example, Todd Glass, a white male comic, begins his 1993 cable performance by commenting on his clean-cut appearance. Because there is nothing particularly unattractive or anomalous about him, Glass jokes that he is on the way to a fraternity party, receives only minimal audience response, and then comments on his bad haircut, noting that he looks like "the offspring of Fred Flintstone and Ollie North." Again, the audience is relatively unresponsive. Because Glass is not sociologically marginal in any way, his attempts to become rhetorically marginal result in humor that seems forced and therefore fails. The more "always already marginal" a comic is sociologically, then, the better chance he or she has of capitalizing on difference. Although their difference may result in discrimination on a daily basis for many marginalized individuals, this same "premarginalization," by some immutable, congenital feature, affords the marginal comic an edge on the competition. Comics always use what works. Hence, an

African American female comic like Ellen Cleghorne foregrounds both race and gender in her act.

It is important also to consider the demographic composition of comedy club audiences in this regard. Given that women are a marginalized majority in this country, comedy club audiences are themselves 51 percent "marginal." Clearly, without data, it is impossible to know exactly who comprises comedy club audiences, but certainly, the extent to which they are, in fact, already marginal must affect comics' rhetorical construction of performed marginality.

As discussed earlier, in a comedic context the dominant culture, not threatened by any real challenge to its power, sanctions its own comic "abuse." A significant question arises here, too: Which groups are officially sanctioned "targets" for attack and which are not? And, as licensed social critics, are comics the only individuals allowed to attack these groups? Meyrowitz believes that the "sensitivity" to difference prevalent since the 1960s has culminated in both political correctness and the public desire to hear subversive views expressed by socially sanctioned critics. Although a Freudian interpretation suggests that all humor results from the need to express repressed drives and desires, Meyrowitz contends that contemporary comedy creates a "safe" context for the actual hostility and frustration Americans feel toward various groups, specifically because of the "politically correct" parameters imposed on public discourse. Given the continuing climate of cultural sensitivity, Meyrowitz maintains, "It is . . . safer now for blacks to make fun of whites or for women to make fun of men than the other way around" (cited in Bernstein 1990, H34).

Certainly, comics push the envelope, often performing material guaranteed to offend marginalized groups, as in the controversial act of Andrew "Dice" Clay. Clearly, political correctness—indeed, any form of "correctness"—is antithetical to the very nature of humor. Kay notes that Lucy entertained audiences and raised feminist consciousness by refusing to "behave correctly" (cited in Martin and Segrave 1986, 272). Perhaps this is the best description of all marginal humor—a refusal to behave correctly. How are marginal comics and their audiences affected by this misbehavior? When a woman is paid for performing her marginality in a comedic context, where does power reside? Certainly, the comic is empowered both rhetorically, by being the joketeller, and economically, by receiving money for the performance. Audience empowerment is more difficult to discern. As discussed earlier, identification and interpretation determine audience experience, including the experience of power or the lack of power.

This investigation suggests that power may reside in such unlikely places as the self-deprecatory material commonly performed by marginal comics. As Auslander (1993) observes, "although . . . recuperative mechanisms . . . may have the effect of domesticating women comics for male spectators, they may not succeed in inhibiting female spectators from being empowered by the comics' representations" (325). The key question remains, however: Does discursive power necessarily entail political power? Stallybrass and White (1986) assert that "Only a challenge to the hierarchy of sites of discourse, which usually comes from groups and classes 'situated' by the dominant in low or marginal positions, carries the promise of politically transformative power" (201). Hence, although discursive power is by no means synonymous with political power, the discursive power of marginalized groups—in the form of a challenge to the hegemonic culture—must certainly precede any political power ultimately obtained.

What are the politics of performing marginality? They are social. They are economic. They are rhetorical. When a female comic performs her marginality, is she challenging the existing power structure? Yes. By the very act of standing onstage, speaking about any topic and getting paid, a female comic is empowered rhetorically and economically—by most standards, a "feminist" triumph. Does her behavior change existing power structures in any way? Perhaps not visibly—not immediately. No single joke is likely to precipitate the decline of prevailing ideologies. Still, given the inherently subversive power of humor, jokes may be a place to begin.

CONCLUSION

Kelly Leonard, executive producer of Chicago's famed Second City Theater, believes that "Often, what's bad for the state of the country is good for the state of comedy" (Simon 2001). This assertion is congruent with psychologist Samuel Janus's 1981 observation that Americans are in "psychosocial crisis," that professional comics are contemporary court jesters providing commentary on "national and international tragedies," and that "comedy has become an essential catalyst for emotional release and identification. It now provides the essential stabilization of the public's mental state" (162). Indeed, humor serves a critical function in society. Stand-up comics, like their ancestors, the professional fools, speak truths with impunity by virtue of their license as social critics. And when comics—specifically members of marginalized groups like women and minorities—get paid for "performing" their marginality and attacking the dominant culture, they provide a unique context for examining power relations in public discourse. In order to explore the construct of performing marginality in relation to issues of humor, gender, and power, this investigation sought an answer to the question: How do contemporary American female comics perform their marginality onstage? Additionally, the following two questions were posed: What does this performance of marginality reveal about the existence of a genre called "female" and, more specifically, "feminist" stand-up comedy? What does the performance of marginality reveal about power relations in a broader cultural context?

My analysis of the discourse of contemporary American female stand-up comics at both substantive and stylistic levels suggests that material alone does not generally constitute a performance of marginality. Rather, female comics, like male comics, mainly address "universal" concerns in order to entertain the widest possible audience. Only female comics perform gynecological humor, however; this topic is generated from experiences that only a woman can have, such as gynecological examinations, mammograms, pregnancy, and childbirth.[1] This material—particularly that pertaining to gynecological exams—often serves as a metaphor for violence to women. Still, the category of gynecological humor is only one of eleven topic areas female comics discuss. Consequently, their performance of marginality is best examined in terms of the comedic postures they assume onstage.

Female comics historically have assumed one or more of five distinct postures onstage: kid, bawd, bitch, whiner, and reporter. Regardless of which posture(s) she assumes, a female comic performs her marginality by constructing her femaleness—either by emphasizing her "difference" from male comics with the bawd, bitch, and whiner personas, or de-emphasizing her difference with the "de-sexualized" or androgynous kid or reporter personas. As noted in chapter 4, whether the comic seems to be saying, "I'm a woman whether you like it or not" (the bitch) or "I'm just a stupid, unattractive, or helpless woman" (the whiner), she is performing her marginality by performing her "femaleness." Even if she sends the message, "Pay no attention to the fact that I'm a woman," as with the kid or reporter, a female comic is performing her *sociological* marginality—she is simply choosing not to perform her *rhetorical* marginality by de-emphasizing biological sex and gendered behaviors (see chapter 1).[2]

Very few female comics assume only the kid or reporter posture (for example, kid comics like Paula Poundstone and reporter comics like Margaret Smith assume whiner or bitch postures at times). Although the kid and reporter postures are certainly "safer," the prevalence of the bitch persona in the acts of contemporary female comics suggests that this might be one of the most effective ways for a woman to perform her marginality onstage today. Perhaps anger—whether performed by a bitch or rebel comic (the equivalent comedic posture for males)—is a feeling with which most audiences identify but that they fear expressing. As Janus (1981) maintains, after a comedy performance, the audience "walks away with a sense of catharsis and relief that someone has publicly verbalized that which they secretly fear" (167).

The genres of "female" and "feminist" stand-up comedy, often conflated and frequently assumed without clear definition or delineation, are extremely problematic. Comics are usually labeled feminist because (1) they perform material from a female perspective (hence the confusion between "female" and "feminist"); (2) they perform material that is sexist toward men; or (3) they perform material characteristic of all marginal humor. As addressed at length in chapters 1 and 5, all marginal humor uses rhetorical strategies of subversion—whether in the subtle form of self-deprecation, using types to explode the types, or the more overt form of attack that targets the status quo. In this way, what is called "female" or "feminist" humor is actually part of a genre of marginal humor. And, by its inevitable use of an "us against them" premise, marginal humor is part of a rhetoric of victimage. This is not to say that all female comics perform such a rhetoric—indeed, comics like Poundstone and Smith who assume the androgynous kid and reporter postures do not generally perform a rhetorical marginality at all. It is not these comics, however, that critics have in mind when using the labels female and feminist; rather, it seems to be the bitch comics like Roseanne who are thus labeled.[3]

Clearly, the performative speech act (in the Austinian sense) of standing onstage and speaking can be construed as "feminist."[4] A woman onstage taking up time and space and getting paid is rhetorically and economically empowered. But is what she says and how she says it necessarily feminist? Ideology is in the mind of the beholder; the audience has the last laugh, quite literally, in the context of public comic performance. As in any performance, the psychology, ideology, and life experience of the performer funds and informs female comic performance. Unfounded categorizations and essentialist assumptions, however, hinder more than help analysis of such performance. Indeed, it is the tendency to attack patriarchal essentialist assumptions with feminist essentialist assumptions that undergirds much of the confusion and frustration generated by contemporary feminist scholarship in general.[5] As cultural theorist Teresa Ebert (1993) explains, feminist discourse frequently "valorizes what the dominant order denigrates—but it does not overthrow the system underlying oppressive dichotomy. It merely reverses its privileged terms without touching the structure that produces the binarism" (26).[6]

Indeed, many critics who discuss "feminist" humor seem to want it both ways: They object to the humor created by women being ghettoized by the label "women's humor" but seek to replace it with an even more differentiated label, "feminist humor"; they object to male privilege but wish to replace it with female privilege. In short, these critics do not wish to eradicate hierarchy; they simply wish to invert it. Certainly, no hierarchy is "natural," regardless of which sex is "on top." And any ideological perspective that advocates true equality should find the very notion of hierarchy untenable.

This investigation has illustrated that within the genre of stand-up comedy, no genuinely "feminist" humor exists. As the superiority theory of humor (discussed in chapter 5) explains, humor always entails hierarchy; if feminism is defined as "gender egalitarianism," therefore, it is not present in the discourse of contemporary stand-up comics, male or female. Indeed, the phrase "comic egalitarianism" is an oxymoron. If, as the above suggests, no "liberal" feminist ideology is discursively created in the performances of female comics, then certainly no "radical" feminist ideology can exist in this context. The very nature of humor is antithetical to action. First, it functions as an "anti-rhetoric," always negating its own potential power by being "just a joke." More important, humor renders its audience passive. It disarms through amusing. Laughter is not generally a galvanizing force toward political action. What critics who discuss the subversive nature of "feminist" humor miss is the fact that humor disarms *all* audiences—it does not discriminate between hegemonic and marginalized individuals. Although it may send a double message, if it is successful, humor produces laughter. And laughter does not constitute a radical politics.

Little (1983), however, offers a cogent explanation of the potential of marginal humor: "While feminist comedy is not the same as feminist political action, it is not surprising that feminist comedy would use for its imagery the 'holiday' actions which have sometimes historically emerged into the everyday, into political action, into revolutionary movements that could envision the possibility of a new world" (187). Acknowledging that the comedy of women (in Little's case, women writers) does not constitute activism, Little nevertheless explains the way the carnivalesque inversion often employed in marginal humor might influence actual social conditions. And Horowitz (1997) asserts: "A laugh is a vote of understanding that no one can deny. In that vote is, eventually, a revolution" (161).

Stand-up comedy is an inherently aggressive genre. Nearly all humor objectifies. It assaults. Someone, some group, or something is targeted and attacked. As Borns (1987) explains, "The premise for every joke is that something is wrong—with you, with the country, with your mother. . . . If nothing is wrong it's not a joke, it's making conversation" (29). Just because humor is inherently aggressive, however, does not mean that it is inherently male. Although stand-up comedy, as a genre, has traditionally been dominated by men, female comics are not being "male" by being aggressively funny. The "supportive" and "connected" nature of so-called women's humor is not relevant to the genre of stand-up comedy (even some of the characteristics of "women's speech" are at times, specious claims). A performer onstage with a microphone before a live audience is rhetorically powerful, regardless of biological sex or any other marginalizing features. The comic's function is not to "nurture" or "affirm" audience members but, rather, to amuse them—usually at any cost.

The essentialist labels "male" and "female" are not useful for discussion of contemporary comic (or other) discourse. Certainly, female comics are *different* from male comics, but they are also *different* from one another. And it is the *individual* characteristics that distinguish a comic—whether or not these include marginal features—and account for her (or his) unique perspective. This investigation indicates that topically, with the exception of gynecological material, female comics display little difference from male comics in terms of what they talk about onstage; additionally, the five comedic postures women assume onstage have counterparts in male comic performance. These findings do not suggest that all comics are exactly alike. Rather, they suggest that the labels "female" and "feminist" humor are problematic. Rhetorically, the humor created and performed by female comics is inherently similar to the humor of other marginal groups. It seems more apt, therefore, to call the discourse performed by female comics—specifically, that which (whether insidiously or overtly) attacks the dominant culture—"marginal" humor (itself often part of a larger rhetoric of victimage). Horowitz (1997) notes that: "As comediennes dispute old, sexist ideas about what is funny or real, everyone is challenged. Both male and female comics are challenged to be more honest and original. Audiences are challenged to listen to new, sometimes radical ideas—and laugh at the stupidity of accepted ways of thinking" (161). Indeed, the humor of women, like all marginal humor, may serve as a lens through which important social issues can be scrutinized. As M. H. Abrahms said of literature, humor may function as both a mirror and a lamp, simultaneously reflecting and illuminating cultural phenomena.

It is evident that with its distorted lens, humor often provides an accurate view of the flaws and foibles that make us fully human. At a basic level, humor may serve as a dependable, albeit rough-hewn, form of theory. As Olsen (1990) notes:

> Theory is a process of abstraction, and abstraction is a process of categorization . . . we cannot think or communicate or probably even survive very long without categories; because through them, we make sense of our existence. There has to be a little bit of Aristotle in us all to help us get along from day to day. . . . We must, therefore, do two things simultaneously: We must realize that we are drawing road maps and that without road maps we are bound to get lost; and we must recognize that road maps *are* road maps and that we can't drive *on* them but *with* them (and that we *still* might get lost). (33)

Le Guin (1989) maintains that "When we women offer our experience as our truth, as human truth, all the maps change" (160). Perhaps the melding of experience with theory, the articulation of truths through humor, can help us move forward. Perhaps we can become cultural cartographers, remapping the ideological terrain so as to "unlearn" the untruths that keep us in stasis.

Clearly, more research on performing marginality is needed. Kibler (1998) calls for more examination of power and identity issues such as ethnicity in the scholarly treatment of female comedy—analyses that move beyond the current limited focus on the way female comic spectacle undermines gender roles.[7] As Fraiberg (1994) points out: "Stand-up becomes a matter of agency when cultural critics begin to account for what the laughs mean, where they are coming from, and who is included. Cataloguing and accounting for the specifics and differences of these patterns offers feminist cultural criticism a strategy for turning a sense of comic relief into a matrix for agency grounded not just in contextualized social frames, but in a sense of pleasure as well" (329).

Indeed, stand-up comedy offers a unique template for exploring the discursive construction of identity, power, and culture. The humor of marginal comics (female or otherwise) provides a compelling glimpse into the "borderlands" these individuals inhabit. As

Ortner (1996) contends: "The attributions and claims of difference (how much, what kind, how significant) is one of the things up for grabs in the borderlands, but difference and identity (or identities) are not the only cultural things under negotiation. Rather, whole issues of meaning and style, forms of practice and forms of relationship, are in play and in question" (182–83).

Examining marginal humorous performance affords insight into just such issues. Further research in this area may extend the notion of marginal humor as resistance to hegemonic strictures. Clair (1998) asserts that "we must be open to *multiple practices as resistance,* but we may also need to look at practices that provide alternatives in addition to survival, *which convert oppression into expression and hold the potential for change"* (156; my emphasis). Perhaps marginal humorous performance is precisely such an alternative practice. Undoubtedly, the study of contemporary American female comic performance of marginality teaches us much about what such marginal performance accomplishes.

Performing Marginality Is Performing Culture

In a 1993 cable television appearance, comic Deborah Swisher asserts, "I'm black and Jewish *and* a woman—so *every* joke offends me." In twelve words, Swisher both encapsulates and embodies the essence of performing marginality. Foregrounding her sociological marginality (race and sex), she proceeds to construct her rhetorical marginality through a series of jokes about her multicultural background. In other words, by *performing* her race and sex, Swisher voices those features that make her marginal—in the act of performance, she "rhetoricalizes" her marginality. In the line cited above, Swisher calls attention to her own demographic features and simultaneously comments on white male hegemony. In short, Swisher does what all marginal humorists do: She simultaneously features margins and "re-reveals" social and political centers. And in so doing, she provides a template upon which power relations between disenfranchised and hegemonic groups in contemporary American culture can be explored.

Indeed, the act of performing the rhetorical construction of marginality for an audience in a comedic context provides a site where, through humor, cultural values are both affirmed and interrogated. As embodiments of culture, marginal comics open up a space for "safe" discussion of taboo topics. Contemporary audiences can go to a comedy club and hear about race/ethnicity, sex, sexuality, death, and numerous other subjects deemed unacceptable in "formal" contexts and controversial in others. More important, audiences can participate in the construction of victims and butts—an endeavor that entails examination of self, society, and the way power is negotiated and renegotiated. Although audience members may laugh unthinkingly, they are nevertheless participating in cultural performance. And together with the performer, they create a carnivalesque atmosphere reminiscent of "those ancient, decorated caves that still give evidence of singing and dancing, people celebrating fertility in risky, sexy, violent, collective, playful ways" (Schechner 1977, 110).

Performing Marginality Is Performing Transition

Stand-up comedy is a unique genre. The contemporary comic functions as a cultural barometer; as she "performs" culture, she reflects the values and beliefs of the day. Stand-up comedy provides a vocabulary for discussing societal ills; as part time bomb and part time capsule, the comic relays sometimes volatile information. The contemporary comedy club (or cable or network television appearance) provides a context for "trying out" subversive rhetoric. In this sense, the discourse of marginal comics functions as "a rehearsal for the revolution" (Boal 1985, 122). Although other contemporary forms of art and entertainment may serve this purpose, only humor creates a transitional rhetoric. By bridging the interstices between events and interactions in our social fabric, humor serves as a transition from one cultural moment to the next. And because of its interactive nature, stand-up comedy incorporates audience contribution into its very substance.

Phyllis Diller, for example, continues to perform material that has served as a transition between various cultural periods and events. She is still making fun of herself, but through the years, jokes about her looks became jokes about her plastic surgery, always including timely, topical references ("my face has been pulled up more times than Jimmy Swaggart's pants"). Although her career has not yet lasted as long as Diller's, Roseanne, too, performs a transitional rhetoric, both critiquing traditional male fears and targeting specific audience members through her jokes about impotence. Throughout elections and Olympics, even in the face of national and international disasters, comics continue to connect us—to events and to each other.

Always reminding us both of universal human truths and of the latest news, comedy is at once cultural artifact and cultural critique. The comic is one of society's vanguard, both participating in and observing human interaction, telling the audience, as did Yeats's famous bird, "Of what is past, or passing, or to come" (1977, 192). In this way, stand-up comedy affords us unique insight into ourselves, our world, and each other. Truly, comics are "the abstract and brief chronicles of the time" (Shakespeare, cited in Harbage 1969, 949). Like the ancient bards Havelock (1963) describes, comics are the singers of tales, the makers of fools, the "tribal encyclopedia" (66). When we laugh at their jokes, we move to the rhythms of history.

Performing Marginality Is Performing Power

This investigation has illustrated the paradoxical nature of marginal humor: By voicing their powerlessness in a comedic context, marginalized individuals are temporarily in control of an audience and thus *rhetorically* empowered. Marginal stand-up comics participate in an extraordinary cultural phenomenon—they get paid for articulating subversive messages, paid sometimes by the very people they lampoon and lambast. Indeed, by commodifying their performed marginality, comics are *economically* empowered. As Veeser (1989) explains, "symbolic exchanges have cash value" (xv). Furthermore, comics are *politically* operative. Although they do not allocate resources or single-handedly transform existing social structures, by performing a subversive discourse they depict and exert pressure upon existing social conditions. Through humor, they call attention to cultural fissures and fault lines.

Humor itself is paradoxical. Because it functions as an "anti-rhetoric," always disavowing its own subversive potential, humor provides the performer with a unique guarantee—the opportunity to critique with impunity. Ironically, it is precisely this feature of humor that ensures the "safety" of the status quo; humor, no matter how subversive, will never be taken "seriously." Therefore, whether Carrie Snow calls men "vibrators with wallets" or Karen Haber lampoons the dominant culture by berating herself, whether comics target specific audience members or generalize about groups, their jokes can be dismissed as harmless "fun." And yet, like any powerful rhetoric, humor produces real social and psychological effects. Through this particularized discourse, marginal comics are able to underscore power imbalances in contemporary American culture. And by the act of laughing—regardless of the reason—audiences affirm the comic's perspective.

Indeed, stand-up comedy is an inherently *democratic* enterprise. It is "the people," after all, who quite literally have the last laugh. As audience members, they "vote" with both laughter and dollars, legitimizing humor *as* humor and determining just how large the comedy coffers will be. Additionally, much of the humor created and performed by contemporary comics is itself democratic; it is distinctly "American," the sound of multivocality—of marginality. The performance of marginal humor is also *modern*. Olsen (1990) maintains that "the impetus of postmodern humor is to disarm pomposity and power" (18), but so too is the impetus of *all* humor. Although the disruption, dislocation, and subversive potential of marginal humor make it a likely candidate for postmodern critique, humor *requires* a hierarchy in order to *subvert* a hierarchy. Superiority theory (discussed in chapter 5), which continues to help us explain countless jokes, necessarily entails stratification. As Olsen notes, "The dominance of conservative attitudes oscillates with the dominance of subversive attitudes" (149). In other words, we cannot have one without the other.

By performing marginality, comics perform power—which is to say, they depict for us how social relations could be transformed if their viewpoint were to prevail. Clearly, the subversive effect of marginal humor is *primarily* rhetorical. Like any discourse unaccompanied by coalitional rearrangement or changed economic circumstances, humor is limited in the extent to which it can achieve major political change.[8] Failure to recognize these limitations can be dangerous. When, as Ebert (1993) notes, "the affirmation of already existing differences . . . is largely seen as in itself an effective mode of social resistance to the hegemonic" (7), we risk replacing action with critique. Action must *begin* with critique, however, and humor—specifically marginal humor—is a powerful form of such "prefatory" social influence. As Little (1983) notes, the "lack of resolution" inherent in "feminist comedy" (that is, marginal humor) "transforms holiday into politics, and makes celebration the imagination's prelude to action and perhaps to new variations on an open human history in which all things are possible" (188).

In order for humor to succeed, its critique must be tempered by its ability to elicit laughter. Indeed, more than any other performative or rhetorical genre, stand-up comedy abhors ideological purity. Quite simply, "true believers" are usually at odds with the comic spirit. The moment at which a comic allows ideology to supersede humor is the moment she risks "losing" her audience. As this investigation has illustrated, the discourse of contemporary American female comics testifies to the power of genre; the generic constraints of stand-up comedy mandate that a comic must be adaptive, that she must be aggressive, and that most of all—regardless of her "message"—she must be *funny*. Performing marginality is, therefore, an exercise in power negotiation. The humor performed by women and other marginalized individuals involves performer, audience, and culture itself in a continuing conversation, one that encompasses a constellation of psychological, rhetorical, economic, and political effects and one that, if successful, leaves everybody laughing.[9]

NOTES

1. An example of this, Sella maintains, is Gore's September 2000 appearance on David Letterman's *The Late Show,* when "Relaxed and apparently having fun, Gore . . . read the Top 10 list, which contained one item that went: 'Remember, America— I gave you the Internet, and I can take it away. Think about it.'" (75).

2. See chapter 2 for a more detailed discussion of the comedy industry as big business.

3. Indeed, two of the most talked about women on television are former stand-ups O'Donnell and Ellen DeGeneres—both featured in media from *TV Guide* covers to numerous Web sites, and both engaged in specific performances of marginality. O'Donnell, a single (and only recently publicly acknowledged lesbian) mother, and DeGeneres, a lesbian who made television history by having her character Ellen (on the show of the same name) come out publicly as she did in her offscreen life, have brought mainstream attention (and to an extent, acceptance) to the groups they represent.

4. Although California (sixty-three clubs), Florida (forty-one), New York (thirty-seven), Massachusetts (thirty-five), Illinois (thirty-one), and Ohio (twenty-four) top the list, even a state as small as Rhode Island is home to three comedy clubs. The only states without a single comedy club listed in this particular directory are Hawaii, Montana, and Wyoming.

5. According to Betsy Borns, author of *Comic Lives: Inside the World of American Stand-Up Comedy* (1987): "The distinction between a dick joke and sexual joke lies in what makes the joke funny: if people laugh because the word "fuck" is used, that's a dick joke (and an easy laugh); if people laugh in reacting to an insightful observation about sex, that's a sexual joke" (15).

6. Koziski (1984) addresses this point, noting that an MC warms up an audience by conducting ethnographic research (asking questions like, "Where are you from?" and "What do you do?").

7. Kramarae (1981) notes that "As Edwin Ardener points out, no researcher could come back from a study of any culture having talked only to women and about men and be considered an authority on that group. Yet the reverse happens frequently," adding, "ironically, it is likely that women are more aware than men of the world models of both groups" (63).

8. Clair summarizes Aptheker, noting that Aptheker draws from Adrienne Rich's work.

9. Auslander (1993) claims that only 10 percent of professional stand-up comics are female, but relies on 1987 and 1989 data for support.

10. Michael (2001) suggests that the boom era of stand-up comedy was between 1986 and 1993. He claims that in 1975, there were only ten comedy clubs nationwide, but that there were hundreds by 1986. Michaels attributes the closing of 25 percent of U.S. comedy clubs by 1993 and the concomitant decline in stand-up comedy (he mentions 1995 as significant because in that year, the famed Improv closed its clubs in New York, San Diego, and Chicago) to three factors: (1) headliner comics like Robin Williams, Rosie O'Donnell, and others' departure from stage to screen; (2) the glut of televised stand-up comedy (both network and cable), specifically Comedy Central (formerly the Comedy Channel); and (3) the censorious effect of political correctness on the acts of comics.

11. Although their opportunities may still be more limited than those of their male comedic peers, some female comics believe that conditions for women in comedy have improved. Veteran comic Susie Essman, for example, asserts: "I'm treated more equally now. . . . My group of comedians . . . broke a lot of barriers. I took the discrimination as a challenge. I became so good that they couldn't deny me—and now they don't" (cited in Kaplan 2002b, 17)

12. I was first introduced to this term by Dr. Roderick Hart of the University of Texas at Austin. Throughout this book, my usage refers to the act of creating a victim with a subversive rhetorical intent (i.e., by making fun of herself, a comic actually critiques the culture at large as when Phyllis Diller mocks her own appearance, calling into question a culture that judges women primarily on their appearance).

CHAPTER 1

1. For my definition of rhetoric, I draw upon both Aristotle's classical notion of "all available means of persuasion" and Hart's conception: "The art of using language to help people narrow their choices among specifiable, if not specified, policy options" (1997, 2).

2. Schechner discusses entertainment, on the other hand, as spawned from theater, enacted for fun, and involving the audience solely in the role of spectator/appreciator.

3. Although his distinction is similar to Schechner's, Turner adds the construct of commodification: "[Liminal phenomena] are centrally integrated into the total social process [whereas liminoid phenomena] develop apart from the central economic and political processes, along the margins, in the interfaces and interstices of central and servicing institutions. . . . The liminoid is more like a commodity—indeed, often is a commodity, which one selects and pays for. . . . One works at the liminal, one plays with the liminoid" (54–55).

4. Prior to Stonequist's introduction of the term "marginality," however, Simmel (1921) published "The Sociological Significance of the 'Stranger'" in Park and Burgess's *Introduction to the Science of Sociology*. Always cited as the precursor to discussions of marginalized individuals, Simmel's notion of the stranger is one that con-

flates "nearness and remoteness" because of the unique positioning between cultures. According to Simmel, the stranger's mobility, objectivity, ability to serve as confidante, freedom from convention and abstract relations afford this individual special insights and opportunities.

5. When referring to the rhetorical construction of marginality, I am using the word "rhetorical" in a broader sense than simply "persuasive" or "agenda-driven;" here, I refer to the process of creating an identity through language.

6. Although any of these features can be surgically altered, the sociologically marginalized individual generally does not take such a drastic step (and if she or he does, especially in terms of sex, the "change" must be artificially maintained).

7. For a discussion of "passing" vs. assimilation, see Stonequist (1937, 185).

8. Throughout this investigation, the term "gender" refers to a rhetorically and socially constructed performance; the term "sex" refers to a biological designation.

9. It is important to note that a number of the theories discussed apply to more than one dimension (for example, Freud is the progenitor of psychoanalytic humor theory but also related to superiority theory); I have chosen to feature major theories within the category to which they most extensively apply.

10. Freud's description is as follows: "in addition to the one who makes the joke, there must be a second who is taken as the object of the hostile or sexual aggressiveness, and a third in whom the joke's aim of producing pleasure is fulfilled" (1960, 95).

11. Certainly, there are exceptions, such as wordplay and some types of observational humor (as noted later in this investigation), but most humor—especially "marginal humor"—is aggressive.

12. Related to this is Turner's (1982) discussion of the way in which "play" democratizes.

13. For an extensive discussion of the fool tradition, see chapter 2.

14. Indeed, the rich tradition of Jewish humor has, at its core, an ongoing relationship with oppression. According to comedy writer Larry Gelbart: "Whatever makes us what we are, that's what worked its way in—that sense of irony, a sense of caustic wit, of defensive wit, offensive wit, all the tools that three thousand years of getting kicked in the yarmulke will instill in you." And humorist Carl Reiner asserts that "the combination of being downtrodden and smart, those two things make you funny" (both cited in Kaplan 2001, 3).

15. Lenny Bruce discussed this phenomenon in an early routine: "To me, if you live in New York or any other big city, you are Jewish. It doesn't matter even if you're Catholic; if you live in New York you're Jewish. If you live in Butte, Montana, you're going to be goyish even if you're Jewish" (cited in Kaplan 2001, 3). The comic equation, then, is as follows: Jewish = urban = American. As comedy writer Nora Ephron recalls, "What happened to [my generation] didn't seem to me particularly 'Jewish' in any way. Urban, yes. New York, even. But Jewish, no" (cited in Kaplan 2002a, 8). As Jews assimilated into American culture, infusing it with their distinct brand of humor, they also became more "American." As Waldoks suggests, post–World War II humor "became 'de-Jew-ified . . .' to reach out to a larger audience. From a sociological point of view, in many ways this shift represents the beginning of America becoming more Jewish and Jews becoming less Jewish" (cited in Kaplan 2001, 2). Clearly, the

equation works both ways—in fact, rather than a linear reality, the relationship between Jewish and American humor (much like the relationship between Jewish and American identity) is a circular one, fraught with ongoing tension.

16. Janus (1981) also found that although Jews comprised only 3 percent of the American population, they comprised 80 percent of all professional comics. A demographic survey of all professional comics currently working in this country would provide an indication of the prevalence of the comedic performance of marginality.

17. Jewish humorists, in particular, are aware of the risks of too much self-deprecation. As comedy writer/performer Carl Reiner explains, pre–World War II Jewish humor emphasized "humiliating self-caricature," but once Hitler gained power, "all of the Jewish accents disappeared, because we realized we were giving fodder to the enemy" (cited in Kaplan 2001, 1). This historical note provides a useful frame for considering the preceding discussion.

18. See chapter 2 for a definition of Ardener's "muted group theory," upon which Kramarae's perspective is based.

19. The figure of the "wise" or "sage" fool—in reality a "fool maker," is discussed at length in chapter 2.

20. In fact, it can be argued that Letterman is himself part of the "establishment." Certainly, his highly publicized courtship by and subsequent move to CBS from NBC and his multimillion dollar contract are not generally perceived as marginal to the status quo. Letterman can even appear to function as the network "gatekeeper," as he did when attempting to censor Madonna during her infamous 1994 appearance. Still, Letterman's quirky persona and innovative parodies (for example, having his mother report on the Winter Olympics in Norway via satellite) keep him on the slippery brink between mainstream (for example, *The Tonight Show*) and a more progressive or alternative cultural milieu.

21. Handelman was referring to Letterman and Johnny Carson, but might just as well have been referring to Carson's replacement, Jay Leno, another enormously popular comic.

22. The phrase "sense of humor" is extremely problematic. Rarely defined, it is usually used to suggest the capacity to appreciate rather than generate humor—hence, the common accusation that women do not have a sense of humor when they do not laugh at jokes they do not find funny.

23. Dresner (1988) refers to this as a "double-edged irony" used extensively in humor created by women "from Bradstreet's use of the deferential pose to the self-mocking stance of domestic humorists and even the more aggressive posture of feminist humor" (152).

24. Although the terms "women's humor" and "feminist humor" generally appear without quotation marks throughout the rest of the book, I am, nevertheless, continuing to question whether such categories necessarily exist.

25. Walker further suggests that political upheaval set the cogs of the humor machine in motion—that "the decades just before and just after passage of the woman suffrage amendment in 1920, and the women's movement that began in the 1960s— gave rise to a distinctly feminist humor" (1991b, 69).

26. Empirical research supports this notion, however; for example, Mitchell (1978) reports that women tell hostile and aggressive jokes for the same reasons as men—to entertain, create cohesion, show sexual interest, and embarrass or "put down" men. And, agreeing with Zillman and Stocking's (1976) claim that "The traditional masculine ideal of dominance and infallibility may make it more difficult for males to laugh at their own expense," Moore, Griffiths, and Payne (1987) conclude: "While it is unlikely that sexist jokes will become unfunny as a result of changes in traditional definitions of masculinity and femininity, it is possible that the preferential bias for female-disparaging jokes will eventually disappear and the use of male-disparaging jokes will increase" (529).

Although the authors use the term "sexist" to mean male sexism toward women, they acknowledge the presence of and potential for increase in male-disparaging humor. (It is interesting to note that, like Zillman and Stocking, the authors believe that it is more difficult for men to laugh at their own expense than for women to do the same. This is paradoxical, given traditional masculine beliefs about women's lack of a sense of humor—often assessed as the ability to laugh at oneself.)

Empirical research typically measures variables in controlled environments or, occasionally, in naturally occurring conversation; although these contexts are quite different from that of a comedy club, conclusions about the relationship between biological sex and humor preference are relevant to the study of humor and power in society.

27. Female comedic postures and the traditions they represent are discussed extensively in chapter 4 of this volume.

28. This issue is addressed in considerable detail in chapter 5 of this volume.

29. Perhaps this is why audiences do not display the same discomfort or resistance to other marginal comics, such as Jews and African Americans. In fact, Jewish humor and Jewish humorists are more widely accepted as mainstream today than ever before. According to Kaplan (2002b), in the 1990s, "Jewish performers in the '70s and '80s who had been largely relegated to supporting roles now emerged as the leads in popular sitcoms such as *Seinfeld* and *Friends*. . . . The public's acceptance of this phenomenon affirmed that 'Jewishness' had finally become an integral part of America's pop-culture landscape" (11).

30. Although the education as well as entertainment of audiences is practiced by many comics, because their audiences invariably hold prejudicial views about marginal groups, marginal comics in particular face this double duty onstage.

31. Many audiences all over the world are still unaccustomed to seeing female comics. As Alison Field of Sensible Footwear observes of her experience in Britain: "Even if people like what we're doing it's kind of, 'but of course it's peculiar they're all women.' You have people who are booking a building going, 'I can't have you on that night because I've already got a woman and we have to spread it out evenly.' It'd be like, 'I've got someone with three heads that night'" (cited in Hengen 1998, 259).

32. Additionally, four male and two male/female comedy teams made a total of twelve appearances, twenty-two male comic actors made a total of sixty-six appearances, and fourteen female comic actors made a total of nineteen appearances. (I have

included in the designation "stand-up comic" only those performers who, for a substantial portion of their careers, have been known primarily as stand-up comics. Hence, performers like Jerry Lewis, Carol Burnett, and Marsha Warfield are classified as comic actors.)

33. Smith's roster runs the gamut from Jean Carroll to Judy Tenuta and includes many funny women who never did traditional stand-up, from Mae West to Whoopi Goldberg. In fact, many of Smith's entries are for women who sing funny songs peppered with comic patter. Further, Smith includes "artists" of questionable stature and ability—some for whom there is no biographical information, simply a name and one album (for example, Bea Bea Benson, a sixties "bawd" whose album I found at a used record store), usually produced by an obscure record label. The only widely recognized female comic "celebrities" included in Smith's guide are: Phyllis Diller, Joan Rivers, Totie Fields, Moms Mabley, Lily Tomlin, Gilda Radner, Whoopi Goldberg, Judy Tenuta, and Sandra Bernhard. (This small group of "stars" have been rewarded for their talents: of her four albums, one of Tomlin's received a Grammy Award and two others were nominated, Rivers and Radner each received one nomination, and Goldberg received a Grammy for her only album—a recording of her highly acclaimed Broadway show.)

34. Dick jokes are discussed at length (so to speak) in chapter 2.

35. Indeed, essentialist biases are inherently reductionistic. Perhaps ironically, any notions of absolute "feminism" and "masculinism" are most likely taught to children by women (who still comprise the majority of primary caregivers in this country). It is, therefore, rather myopic to pin the "tale" on the patriarchy, as women continue to participate in the perpetuation of traditional conceptions of feminine and masculine. Clearly, any attempt to promote sexual egalitarianism must include both sexes taking responsibility for the acculturation of children and dispensing with the tendency to classify characteristics and traits as male or female.

36. For example, a 1989 Time/CNN poll revealed that twice as many women supported the goals of the women's movement as were willing to call themselves feminist (Wolf 1993). Friend (1994) reports that a Time/CNN poll shows that 94 percent of Americans believe in the "movement's leading issue" of equal pay for equal work, but that another Time/CNN poll reveals that only 37 percent of American women consider themselves feminists (and according to still another poll, only 16 percent of college women "embraced the term") (52). These statistics indicate that more people are feminists politically than they are rhetorically. Many women, especially, may believe in core "feminist" principles but fear being typed as a humorless man-hater if they call themselves feminists.

Even the phrase "core feminist principles" is problematic, however; as Fox-Genovese (1991) points out: "Today, as in the past, feminists divide over whether women should be struggling for women's rights as individuals or women's rights as women—whether women need equality with men or protection for their difference from men. . . . This debate over equality versus difference lies at the core of contemporary feminist thought, not merely because of the way in which it divides feminist theorists, but, perhaps more important, because of its ability to link theory and practice" (56). Wolf (1993) addresses the same issue, distinguishing between "victim feminism," which employs "an exaggerated assertion" of female "innocence and powerlessness," and "power feminism," which encourages women to "identify with one another through the shared pleasures and strengths of femaleness" (224).

Asserting that the strongest objection women have to contemporary feminism is its lack of a "line-item veto" (276), Wolf maintains: "If feminism is a specific agenda rather than a conviction of female worth, then we are left with a political movement that has defined itself as of the minority, by the minority, and for the minority" (277). By Wolf's definition, "feminism means, on one level, nothing more complicated than the willingness of women to act politically to get what they need" (276). Broadening this notion even further, Wolf concludes that "any woman who believes in women's right to self-definition and self-respect is a feminist in my book" (278).

37.   Building on Bem's recent work on sexual inequality, Sullivan and Turner point out that both men and women forget that the differences they see as natural and inevitable were, in fact, created by humans. Sullivan and Turner discuss Bem's three "lenses of gender" (androcentricism, gender polarization, and biological essentialism) and concur with Bem that we must look at rather than through these lenses in order to expose sexual inequities in both private and public life. If we do not engage in this type of scrutiny, Sullivan and Turner maintain, "cultural assumptions about gender . . . are 'naturalized' and presented under the cloak of science or 'objective' fact" and "emerge as immutable" (14).

Androcentrism offers male experience as the norm and female experience as a deviation from that norm. Gender polarization rests on the assumption that men and women "naturally" perform opposite roles and views variations on these roles as deviant. Biological essentialism promotes the infamous "biology is destiny" argument, using genetic explanations to legitimize and reproduce gender differences in both public and private spheres. (Biologist E. O. Wilson, for example, argued that women are naturally more passive because they need to wait for the most genetically "fit" mate, and that men are naturally aggressive because they need to spread their seed around.)

38.   Although many feminists consider the normalization of traditional gender roles a key issue, feminism itself continues to be plagued by definitional confusion and stigmatized by the media. Some critics seek to end all debate by proclaiming that we are living in a "postfeminist" era. (For a detailed discussion of "postfeminism," see Modleski's *Feminism without Women* (1991). Esquire (1994) reports that of the one thousand women (between eighteen and twenty-five) polled, 54.3 percent would rather "get run over by a truck" than "gain 150 pounds" (65). Has the "beauty myth" discussed by Wolf and others consumed young women, precluding any possibility of a next generation of feminism? Not according to Friend (1994), who calls the ideology of contemporary young feminists like Wolf "do-me" feminism, noting that: "The do-me feminists are choosing locker-room talk to shift discussion from the failures of men to the failures of feminism, from the paradigm of sexual abuse to the paradigm of sexual pleasure. They want to return sex from the political realm to the personal. In short, they want to have fun" (50).

39. The belief that ideology and fun are mutually exclusive is illustrated in the now-dated joke: Question: How many feminists does it take to change a lightbulb? Answer: That's not funny!

CHAPTER 2

1. The *Komos* was "a communal ritual carouse" similar to contemporary Mardi Gras celebrations. The *Komos* frequently included masks, costumes, and occasionally "the phallos: an imitation penis, often too large for one person to lift with ease, carried on a pole or cart." The primary purpose of the *Komos* was "to promote fertility by honoring or encouraging the gods (and driving away spirits of blight) through a boisterous display of health, prosperity, and virility." (Porter 2002).

2. Kaplan (2002b) considers the so-called sick humor of the 1990s Bruce's legacy:

> Turning the tables on the politically-correct mindset of the '90s, comedians like Dave Attell and radio "shock jocks" like Howard Stern—both Jewish—transformed taboo into titillation. Equal opportunity offenders, they smashed sacred cows of the right and left wings with equal fervor. "Sometimes, for lack of a better word, people call [this comedy] 'sick,'" says humor writer Tom Leopold, "but, in fact, it's just so purely honest it's hilarious, because it says what we all think, but can't say. Lenny Bruce did that." (15)

3. Describing the life of medieval professional fools, Zijderveld (1982) notes that: "Even such an accomplished and successful jester as Will Sommer who sat next to the king during dinners, would at night sleep in the kennel among the spaniels" (113).

4. An "early form of organized adult education," the enormously popular lyceums featured "debates and lectures on topics of current interest," and ultimately included notable speakers such as Ralph Waldo Emerson, Frederick Douglass, and Susan B. Anthony (Lyceum Movement, 2003).

5. Perhaps not surprisingly, Pips has remained a heavily male-dominated club. When I performed there in the mid-1980s, the audiences were challenging, not having been exposed to many female comics

6. However, in 1995, The Improv closed its clubs in New York, San Diego, and Chicago.

7. In fact, it was Cathy Ladman who told me, "Go to New York City—go down to SoHo to a club called Comedy U, ask for Bert, and tell him that Cathy sent you." I followed her directions and became a regular at a weekly "Woman's Comedy Night" at that club.

8. Borns (1987) notes the phenomenal success of comedy club franchises like Catch a Rising Star, Funny Bones, and Punchline. Catch a Rising Star went public in 1987, the year it began opening its twenty-five projected franchises.

9. One of the first times I was ever heckled (at Charlie Goodnight's in Raleigh, North Carolina), I pointed to the offender and said, "Look at this guy—voted most likely to stand on top of a tall building and fire at random into a crowd." The audience roared; I had won. And winning is the essence of stand-up comedy. In order to succeed, a comic must take control from the moment she or he steps onstage and

maintain that control throughout the set. Like a racehorse, an audience senses instinctively when a slackening of reins occurs, and (to extend the equine metaphor) once a comic loses control, it is about as difficult to regain as it is to remain atop a wildly bucking bronco.

10. Comics are the best and worst audience for comedy. If a comic writes a brilliant new line or delivers an old one particularly well, other comics usually laugh and respond appreciatively (although there are those who never acknowledge anything funny unless they thought of it). Conversely, however, if a comic is truly terrible—not just having a bad night or playing a tough room, but downright rotten and displaying a shameless disregard for the art (for example, by performing dated, inappropriate, or stolen material or assuming an extremely arrogant attitude) other comics will withdraw their loyalty in an instant and often become as openly hostile as any heckler.

On the other hand, comics can be extremely supportive of one another. Because the same faces appear night after night, enduring interminable hours of "open mike" horrors, waiting sometimes until 2:00 AM while twenty-six other comics each perform five minutes of material, comics become very familiar with each other's acts. Favorite "bits" are like favorite songs, sometimes requested by comic audience members. More than once as I did my "Bloomingdale's lady" character, for example, I heard anticipatory giggles and whispers of "I love this bit" or "This is her best bit" from comic colleagues in the audience.

11. These are the so-called male rhythms that some feminist critics disparage—the "build-punch" dynamic that most comics use. I used these rhythms because as an audience member I had been conditioned to expect them. Does that mean I was simply a pawn of patriarchy? Are these rhythms distinctly "male" because stand-up comedy has always been male dominated? Would the same rhythms have evolved if women had dominated the industry? Clearly, this point is open to debate. One certainty, however, is that any comic—female or male—who deviates from this expected rhythm or formula stands out from the rest. Steven Wright and Wendy Liebman are two good examples of comics whose popularity rests upon precisely this difference from the rest. These performers and others like them face a difficult challenge; they must literally "teach" the audience their unique rhythms so that laughter occurs at the right time.

12. Beginning comics learn early that even their entrance into the sanctified halls of a top showcase club requires considerable adaptability. For example, the first time I auditioned at Catch a Rising Star, one of the two premier showcase clubs in New York City, David Brenner walked in, unannounced (this type of occurrence is not uncommon as well-established comics often use these clubs as a proving ground for trying out new material prior to televised or high-profile live performances). Brenner performed for thirty minutes, much to the delight of the audience and dismay of the other comics (as we would all now be pushed back to a later or possibly nonexistent spot). I spoke with Mr. Brenner before my audition and found him very warm and encouraging. The audience, however—that wonderful, easily amused bunch—trickled out as the night wore on, and by the time I got onstage (about 1:15 AM), it was reduced to my two friends, a couple of strays, and three or four comics in the back of the room.

I'll never forget the way the MC introduced me: "And now, ladies and gentlemen, I'd like to introduce our last act of the evening. She's a funny lady and I think you're gonna like her a lot. Please, give a warm welcome to [she turned to me, waiting offstage] what's your name again? [she turned back to the audience] Oh, Jo Gilbert!" Unbelievably, this was a comic I had actually worked with at another club! Despite her introduction, however, and the fact that I was exhausted from waiting for four hours, the tiny audience responded incredibly well. The club booker pulled me aside and said, "Look, I want to be honest with you. Tonight was so crazy with Brenner coming in and all. I really wasn't listening to your set. Call me next week and we'll set up another time."

After a month of trying to reach this man, I finally scheduled another audition. Again, it was after 1:00 in the morning, and the crowd had dwindled to a masochistic few. My set, though not as good as the first, was well received. The booker said, "I think you would do really well here—the crowd likes you and you make them laugh—but if I passed you now, I wouldn't be able to give you any spots—I just don't have any openings right now. Call me in three months." When I dolefully reported the outcome to my comic friends, they were ecstatic. "Three months—that's terrific," they said. "He tells most people six!"

13. Clearly, comics must engage in continual audience analysis. I remember complaining to another comic in the mid-1980s that contemporary audiences were totally unreceptive to intellectual humor—that they wanted to feel smart for getting the jokes but did not want to work terribly hard to do so. My friend responded, "You've got to understand that when Woody Allen was making Gertrude Stein references in the sixties and audiences were falling all over themselves, everyone was a liberal arts major. Now, everyone's a business major, and to be funnier you don't have to read more, you have to watch more TV."

14. It is interesting to note the lack of a particular constraint within the genre of stand-up comedy—the absence of costume. Whereas in centuries past, "To insure that nothing the clown said would be taken seriously, the clown always had to dress distinctively and carry distinctive props"(Nilsen 1993, 44), contemporary comics— with the few exceptions who enjoy wearing unique, even bizarre, fashions—dress exactly like their audiences. Comics today have eschewed the motley of fools and it is now simply technical and formal constraints that distinguish comic from audience. This fact raises some compelling questions: what happens when the fool looks just like the king? If no distinctive costume is worn, does the contemporary comic's marginality serve as rhetorical motley? What implications does "passing" (by looking just like the audience) have for the performance of marginality? And how does this phenomenon affect audience identification (given that most audiences are at least partially composed of members of marginalized groups)?

15. Although her analysis predates the national recognition of comics like Roseanne and Judy Tenuta, these and other so-called feminist comics were performing material in 1986 that includes attacks on other women.

16. Kramarae's perspective is based on the "muted group theory" of anthropologists Edwin Ardener and Shirley Ardener. Kramarae (1981) explains muted group theory in these terms: "The language of a particular culture does not serve all its speak-

ers equally, for not all speakers contribute in an equal fashion to its formulation. Women . . . are not as free or as able as men are to say what they wish, when and where they wish, because the words and the norms for their use have been formulated by the dominant group, men. So women cannot as easily or as directly articulate their experiences as men can. . . . Women are thus 'muted'" (1).

17.   The mere fact that you, the reader, probably smiled at the preceding dick joke illustrates this point. As a comic myself, I experienced the unfortunate truth of Freud's assertion countless times. For example, in 1987, I performed at an anniversary celebration of Pip's Comedy Club in New York. I had been told by the club's manager that the audience for this special performance would be elderly and Jewish; consequently, I performed my best Jewish material and received a fairly good response. The performer who followed me, however, Jackie "the Joke Man" Martling, did his signature filthy act—a string of dick jokes—and literally had the audience (a number of whom were in wheelchairs) rolling in the aisles. These and other experiences as a comic taught me that in the arena of stand-up comedy, dick jokes reign supreme—a hard lesson (so to speak), to be sure.

CHAPTER 3

1.   Even female comics who are not noticeably heavy sometimes comment on their dissatisfaction with their body image. For example, Paula Poundstone (1991) looks down at her physical position during her act and says, "If you have huge, fat thighs, you'll want to sit on your legs to get the full spread." Another example is Margaret Smith (1993) who comments on her own slight build, noting, "I want to build a butt—I'm like a couple of saltines back there . . . friends say, 'How do you stay on the toilet? Your thighs?'"

2.   I base my claims not on statistical evidence but on years of experience, as a member of both the professional comic performance community and the audience for live and televised (cable and network) comedy.

3.   When I performed stand-up comedy in New York City in the mid-1980s, for example, sources of my material included family ("My mom got so excited when I told her I'm going to Club Med—she thought that's where you go to meet doctors!"), religion/ethnicity ("If Joan of Arc had been Jewish, she would have said, 'Sure—I've got visions, I've got voices, but do they call? Do they write?'"), relationships ("I heard on the radio that you can tell when your child is ready for kindergarten because he can manage a scissors easily and knows the names of common animals . . . this scared me because the last three guys I've dated have not met these criteria!"), and random observations ("New York is a great place to live—where else do people sleep on the streets and the dogs wear sweaters?").

4.   For a full discussion of this phenomenon, see chapter 5.

5.   Certainly, male comics may perform proctological humor, but they do not seem to do this nearly to the extent that female comics perform gynecological humor. Both female and male comics, however, perform material related to pregnancy and childbirth; in fact, some of the classic material on these topics was performed by Bill Cosby and Robin Williams.

6. This type of violation and vulnerability is one men simply do not experience at the hands of the medical (or any other) profession. Because they have no referent for such an experience, it is sometimes difficult for them to understand the trauma women may undergo during this annual ritual.

7. Adams's book *The Sexual Politics of Meat* is a fascinating exploration of the way both animals and images of women are objectified, fragmented, and consumed in contemporary culture. Her "feminist-vegetarian theory" suggests that both eating meat and victimizing women are constructs that reify and reinscribe patriarchal ideology.

8. It should be noted that not all of the monologues in Ensler's play are humorous. They all address aspects of women's experience, however; whether a Bosnian rape victim or a Scarsdale antique dealer, the speakers articulate views with which many women can identify.

9. This issue is discussed in considerable detail in chapter 5.

CHAPTER 4

1. Here and throughout this investigation, the words "threatening" and "nonthreatening" refer to audience perception. Because this is not a study that measures audience response, my assumptions about the threat potential in female comedic performance is based on my experience as both performer and audience member in this context. Generally, an overtly sexual female comic is potentially threatening—even intimidating—to both sexes. She is, after all, foregrounding a societal taboo (flagrant female sexuality)—which may make audiences uncomfortable at the very least. Male comics, on the other hand, are almost expected to be overtly sexual; unlike female sexuality, (heterosexual) male sexuality has never been culturally constructed as aberrant but as "normal" and "healthy."

2. Although DeGeneres does not always perform long story monologues such as the example discussed here, her kid style is evident even in shorter bits. DeGeneres also portrayed the kid as the star of her popular sitcom, *Ellen*. Although her own and her character's sexuality were foregrounded from her famous "coming out" episode in 1997 onward, DeGeneres's diction and playful physical comedy continued to adhere to the kid persona—a mask that made the issue of lesbianism less threatening to mainstream audiences.

3. It is small wonder that Poundstone relates to children exceptionally well. In a 1999 appearance on Garrison Keillor's *A Prairie Home Companion Joke Show*, for example, Poundstone deftly played with a young audience member:

> How old are you? You're seven? And what did you have for dinner last night? Pizza soup? Your mom is one heck of a cook . . . maybe I just don't cook well—it never occurred to me to combine the pizza and the soup that way. That is absolutely brilliant. You had pizza? Was it pizza your mom made or did they call out for it? It was just soup? As it turns out, there was no pizza involved. You were just trying to impress me. . . . What kind of soup was it? Noodle soup? Was there any kind of a broth in there or was it just noodles? It had broth? You never hear a seven-year-old say "broth." You have a very mature vocabulary, are you aware of that? What grade are you in? First? . . . We're long beyond that, and if we each told you something we

knew from the first grade, you could just pretty much take the rest of the year off. [To his mom:] Ma'am, wouldn't you like to have him home during the day more? "Mother, where's my broth?"

4. Recent (2002) media accounts of Poundstone's alcoholism and allegations of problematic behavior toward her foster children may have sullied her reputation as "safe," but she remains a popular kid comic nevertheless.

5. Rosie O'Donnell's recent (2002) crusade for gay and lesbian foster parents' rights and concomitant coming out as a lesbian have garnered a great deal of media attention; however, much like DeGeneres, O'Donnell has maintained the kid persona, keeping her comic presence decidedly nonsexual. It is interesting to note that although they publicly self-designate as lesbians, DeGeneres, Poundstone, and O'Donnell all ignore their relational lives onstage and in so doing have become three of the most successful contemporary kid comics. Unlike lesbian "bitch" comics Lea Delaria and Robin Tyler, DeGeneres, Poundstone, and O'Donnell have enjoyed a mainstream popularity that could only occur by remaining tightlipped about their sexuality.

6. Although this investigation focuses on American comics, Tanguay, a Canadian, was an important influence and is thus included in this discussion.

7. Kibler points out that although Shaw's and Elinore's performances challenged gender norms in their use of bawdy, physical comedy, they simultaneously reinscribed social hierarchies like ethnicity and class.

8. Jewell (cited in Sullivan and Turner 1996), for example, describes four cultural depictions of African American women: Mammy (submissive to the Master and happy with her domestic career), Aunt Jemima ("cantankerous version of Mammy," as in *Gone with the Wind*), Sapphire (as in *Amos 'n' Andy*—engages in verbal duels with men and berates them), and Jezebel (attractive by Eurocentric standards but possesses "masculine" traits of independence, aggressiveness, and so on and is criticized by dominant white culture for these). I am also grateful to Dr. Dana Cloud of the University of Texas at Austin for her insights regarding this matter. Like the tradition of Jewish comic performance, the tradition of African American comic performance is fruitful for study but beyond the scope of this investigation.

9. The only mention of Noel, Williams, and Robinson is in Smith's discography, *Comedy on Record* (1988). Although they were obviously not major comic celebrities, these women are good examples of the 1960s bawd (and good examples of the many little-known comics who released comedy albums as part of the bawd trend).

10. The phrase "stock jokes" refers to unoriginal material repeated by comics (and others) over the years until it is public domain. Widely recognized by audiences and often condemned by comics, stock jokes are considered easy and even thought to be a form of cheating.

11. One reason for the prevalence of explicitly sexual material in the 1960s was the cultural climate of the decade. Another reason for the decline in graphic sexual bawdiness (with the exception of videos like *Comedy's Dirtiest Dozen,* which focus exclusively on this type of material) is obviously the increased reliance on television as a vehicle for comic performance. Even cable TV has parameters that preclude the use of excessively blue humor.

12.   The comic tradition continued by Vidale is that of the "lustful" African American female. Mabley's conflation of the bawd and "Mom" personas was unique in female comic performance.

13.   Several years ago, Snow was quite heavy and typically began her act with jokes like, "I'm fat, but I'm hot." After losing a good deal of weight, she now performs "bawdier" material (still, she does not physicalize her comedy nearly as much as do performers like Scott and Hodge). Snow is not the only female comic to alter her act along with her body shape/image. Roseanne is perhaps the most famous recent example of a woman who reinvented herself physically (with the help of cosmetic surgery) and changed her material along with her image.

14.   In the performance discussed, Scott also constructs her persona as distinctly African American by her attire, specifically her cowrie jewelry. (I am grateful to Dr. Joni Jones of the University of Texas at Austin for her observations about this aspect of Scott's performance.) Scott also performs material (see chapter 3) related to issues of race and racism.

15.   Undoubtedly, many feminist critics would balk at labeling Hodge's bit "feminist" and prefer to consider it a reinscription of patriarchal stereotypes (for example, the femme fatale). Still, this material comprises one of very few examples of female comic performance—in fact, one of very few examples of marginal humor—that purportedly seeks to transform economic conditions (chapter 5 discusses the issue of rhetorical vs. political subversion in detail). This bit could just as easily be called sexist, however, as its implied message is that men are easily duped by female sexuality.

16.   Rivers's larger than life persona makes her a favorite of impressionists, specifically female impersonators.

17.   Jews have long played the insider/outsider in comedy—according to Horowitz (1997), estimates suggest that Jews comprise a mere 2 percent of the U.S. population but over 60 percent of the American comedy industry.

18.   In terms of grating vocal quality, Roseanne's bitch persona resembles Rivers's, but here the comparison ends as Rivers generally attacks other women (celebrities or audience members) whereas Roseanne tends to attack men (both specifically and generally).

19.   Indeed, men's response toward blatant sexism directed toward them through humor often seems appreciative. Perhaps this is because, as members of the dominant culture, they do not perceive jokes at their expense as truly threatening (this issue is discussed in chapter 5). Certainly, they might laugh for a number of reasons—discomfort, peer pressure, enjoyment—but the reason they laugh is not as important as the act of laughing—an act that legitimizes discourse such as Tenuta's as humor (laughter as legitimation is discussed in chapters 2 and 5).

20.   Other "out" lesbian comics, like Kate Clinton, Marga Gomez, and Suzanne Westenhoefer present much "softer" personas, usually assuming the reporter posture.

21.   See chapter 5 for a detailed discussion of self-deprecation as subversion.

22.   The fact that self-deprecatory jokes are often discussed by critics as truths rather than jokes is addressed at length in chapter 5.

23.   Some of her material has also featured put-downs of her fictitious husband, "Fang"; when telling these jokes, Diller has assumed the bitch persona.

24. For an extensive discussion of the way comics use "what works" and the implications of comics' material "working" with different audiences, see chapter 5.

25. Horowitz (1997) compares Rivers to Woody Allen and notes that they both portray sexual losers comedically. She wonders, "Is the comedy of men and women interchangeable? Or is there a difference related to the fact that she is a woman?" (100). Clearly, the difference is that despite an underdog persona, a male comic is still a member of the dominant culture (Woody Allen's Jewishness marginalizes him, but Horowitz is commenting only on gender differences here). Unlike her male counterparts, when a female comic performs self-deprecation, she is echoing cultural sentiment; this is precisely the reason many feminist critics interpret this type of material literally, failing to see the subtle and subversive cultural critique such discourse offers.

26. Roseanne (1987) mandates, "If you're fat, just be fat and shut up, and if you're thin—fuck you!" Instead of assuming the whiner posture, Roseanne maintains the bitch persona, fueling her words with overt anger. Implicit in her material on this subject is the message, "I don't like being fat," but her vitriolic delivery precludes any notion of Roseanne as a whiner. Instead of saying, "Look at how fat I am," as other whiner comics might, Roseanne seems to dare her audience to make weight an issue (and, in daring, of course, proceeds to make it an issue, engaging in self-objectification—a point addressed in chapter 5).

27. Perhaps it is not surprising that in a culture that simultaneously promotes the image of the "waif" as female fashion ideal and sanctions potentially damaging breast implants, comics—like many other women—feel compelled to become ever thinner and/or bigger breasted. Of course, we must consider that, as always in comic discourse, Rudner's and Wise's remarks are performed as jokes. The humor of their material may lie in identification with feelings of inadequacy or it may lie in the critique of cultural values such jokes imply (that is, audience members may laugh at the comic-as-butt or they may laugh at society-as-butt; this issue is addressed in chapter 5).

28. Although I do not rely on statistical data for this claim, even a cursory glance at the discourse of contemporary comics (of both genders) reveals a substantial amount of material that can be called "emotional self-deprecation." Perhaps the so-called New Age has made the psyche as much a target of humor as the body. This emotional self-deprecation is especially interesting in the context of contemporary male comic performance, as male comics (with the exception of heavy comics performing "fat" jokes) have not traditionally used much physical self-deprecation in their acts.

29. Despite her occasional whiner and bitch lines, Boosler most often assumes the posture of the reporter.

30. This comic persona has long been employed by performers of both genders. Male reporters include Bill Cosby, David Brenner, Jay Leno, Jerry Seinfeld, and Bill Maier.

31. Despite Diller's claim to the title, Carroll predates her as the first female stand-up comic. Indeed, in the 1950s, Carroll and her male contemporaries were the first comics to perform what present-day audiences recognize as stand-up comedy (observations in monologue form).

32. Important female comics whose focus is character are not included in the above typology because these women do not perform traditional stand-up comedy.

Still, it is important to acknowledge their influence. Beginning in the early decades of the twentieth century with figures like British monologist Beatrice Hereford and the legendary Ruth Draper, the tradition of female "character" comics continued to flourish in performances by Lily Tomlin (included in this investigation by virtue of her reporter material and the popularity of her kid, Edith Ann) and Gilda Radner in the 1970s and Danitra Vance and Whoopi Goldberg in the 1980s. Today, comics Sandra Bernhard and Judy Tenuta frequently (though not exclusively) perform characters. As previously mentioned, this places them on the somewhat slippery brink between stand-up comedy and performance art. Also worth mentioning is comic Judy Toll's parody of Andrew "Dice" Clay in a twelve-minute video called *Lips Only.* In the persona of Andrea "Dice" Clay, Toll hurls abuse at male audience members and discusses her sexual activities in lurid detail, focusing on various descriptions of men servicing her. Assuming exaggerated versions of both the bawd and bitch postures, Toll alternately amuses and intimidates her audience, replicating Clay's belligerent style.

33. The word "strategic" is problematic in this context. I do not presume to know the intent of female comics. In my own experience of writing and performing stand-up comedy, I certainly did not consider my material rhetorically strategic. Rather, like most performers, I used what worked. I discuss the self-presentation of female comics as strategic here in order to explore further the ways in which rhetorical marginality appears to be constructed onstage. Clearly, whether a comic intends to intimidate or simply writes material that happens to work by intimidating, the end result is the same.

34. In fact, it is precisely the lack of apparent strategy that makes the reporter so popular. Certainly, like all performers, the reporter wants the audience to like her (at least at the level of needing laughter to legitimize her humor and receive her paycheck), but she does not employ ingratiation in the same way as does the kid. Hence, the reporter does not appear overtly strategic and is therefore omitted from this particular discussion.

35. Perhaps more interesting than the fact that female comics assume particular postures onstage is the reason(s) they find it necessary. Why do some audiences laugh at the bitch but not the whiner? Why do some audiences laugh at both postures? These questions are part of the politics of performing marginality discussed in chapter 5.

36. As mentioned earlier in this chapter, although she primarily assumes the whiner posture, Diller occasionally plays the bitch as well. She is most commonly associated with the former, however; critics who wish to dismiss Diller as "simply" self-deprecatory fail to consider all of the material she has performed about Fang (and others, especially other women) throughout her career.

37. In my own act, I combined the bitch and whiner personas, occasionally becoming the reporter when dealing with the random observations category. The reporter is neutral and hence well suited to this particular topical category; what unites the bitch and the whiner, as mentioned earlier, is anger.

38. The issue of aggression and the development of the bitch persona is discussed further in chapter 5 and the conclusion.

39. The bitch/whiner dichotomy is discussed in detail in chapter 5.

CHAPTER 5

1. Gruner (1997) claims that even wordplay (puns, riddles, and the like) is about winning and losing because the teller is a winner, telling the riddle or pun in order to "best" the ignorant audience. Hence, the teller "wins" the "contest of wit" (150). This argument seems specious at best because it could apply to any interaction—we are always sharing information and therefore there is always a "winner" who understands vs. a "loser" who does not or who is just learning the information for the first time.

2. Some comics, of course, do believe at least part of the material they present. For example, Mo Gaffney, former host of *Women Aloud,* a comedy/talk show on HBO in the 1990s, believes that "Couched in comedy, you can tell a lot of truth" (cited in Horowitz 1997, 159). There is a big difference, however, between the blatant cultural critique of Lenny Bruce or Roseanne and the self-deprecatory veneer of Phyllis Diller or other whiner comics. Regardless of what whiners truly feel about their own inadequacies, the personas they present onstage are highly exaggerated versions of these flaws, designed both to elicit laughter and, at times, to present a subtle and subversive critique of a culture that judges individuals by such superficial characteristics.

3. In fact, according to the website of the Women's International Center, which honored her with its 1990 Living Legacy Award, Diller "was recently honored by the American Academy of Cosmetic Surgery for having the courage to publicly bring plastic surgery 'out of the closet.'"

4. In fact, in April 2001, Diller performed a cameo role as herself in *Kiss My Act,* an ABC television movie about an aspiring female stand-up comic (played by Camyrn Manheim).

5. Within the last several years, Roseanne has lost a good deal of weight, constructed a newly coiffed image, and has even appeared on the cover and inside photo layout of *Vanity Fair.* Critics like Auslander believe that some of Roseanne's anger (and hence her bitingly funny persona) has been lost along with her weight. In a *20/20* interview (1994), Roseanne explained that she changed her image not to conform to conventional standards but for her own developing self-esteem—a product of confronting her abusive past. Still, she continues to objectify herself and others through humor.

6. As mentioned in chapter 4, the line is from Barr's 1987 HBO special: "Like a lot of people come up to me all the time. . . . They go, ' . . . Roseanne, you're not very feminine,.' . . . So I say, 'Well, suck my dick!'"

7. Note that Roseanne's size continues to be an issue in the popular press. The use of the phrase "Roseanne-size stardom" is an obvious double entendre, playing on both Roseanne's physical size and the magnitude of her success. Despite her new image, it seems that the objectification of Roseanne as a "fat" comic still holds.

8. Boosler made this comment in 1976. Her later material certainly often reflects basic "feminist" principles, but to my knowledge, she has never publicly called herself a feminist comic or even a woman's comic.

9. DeGeneres's much-publicized 1996 television first as the network prime-time sitcom character Ellen (on the show of the same name) who comes out as a

lesbian and the equal attention the media gave to DeGeneres's acknowledgment of being gay in real life reframed her as a sexual—and therefore not innocent or child-like—being. Ironically, her television character continued to be portrayed as sexually naive after coming out; it was the coverage of her personal life focusing on her relationship with her female partner that reconfigured this autobiographical performance.

10.　Comic Robin Tyler provides the following response to those who see stand-up comedy as a male province: "When male comics are talking about stand-up being phallic, what they're talking about is aggressively controlling an audience, and women aren't supposed to be allowed this. My answer to that is, 'Tough shit!' They think somehow, the prick is the most aggressive thing, and that's not true; the mind is much more powerful than the prick—and the mind doesn't go down in two minutes" (cited in Horowitz 1997, 160).

11.　In so doing, marginal comics may educate their audiences by insisting that they "confront persistent prejudices and question received truths" (Kaplan 2002b, 19).

12.　The controversy surrounding a 1980 *Saturday Night Live* sketch for "Jewess jeans" illustrates Cohen's point. According to Kaplan (2002a): "[Jewess jeans was] a faux ad for jeans with Jewish stars emblazoned on the posterior, modeled by Gilda Radner's gum-chewing Jewish shopaholic. Rabbi Bob Alper criticizes the sketch for giving 'permission to those who engage in negative Jewish stereotypes.' Robert Smigel defends it as simple observational comedy. 'Jewess Jeans doesn't bother me,' he says, 'because there are girls like that. That's what comedy is about. You're pointing things out. If there wasn't an element of truth to it, the sketch wouldn't have been such a big hit. It worked because it struck a chord. I'm not saying all stereotypes are born out of truth, because there are stereotypes that are total nonsense. But I think a lot of the time the audience is going to tell you what's appropriate'" (4).

13.　Morreall (1987) maintains that the superiority theory, popular for over two thousand years, does not account for many types and instances of humor. The relief theory developed by Freud, Morreall suggests, is limited as well. The incongruity theory currently in vogue, Morreall asserts, "seems more promising than its two competitors, simply because it attempts to characterize the formal object of amusement" (6). In the context of marginal humor, however, superiority theory is most relevant as it deals explicitly with targets and consequently subject-object relationships.

14.　A contemporary version of superiority theory is Gruner's (1997) belief that all humor is a game—in the sense of being fun/leisure/entertainment and also in the sense of competition, keeping score, and producing winners and losers. In Gruner's opinion, laughing = winning (which is the same as "getting what you want"), and suddenness is key. Hence, in Gruner's world, successful humor = winning suddenly. Gruner further argues that there is no such thing as "innocent" humor—that even humor that is relatively nonaggressive cannot be totally innocent. Ultimately, he maintains that those who feel superiority theory cannot explain all humor, such as "play" humor, ignore the "contest nature of 'play'" (76). Within his schema, Gruner always considers the audience to be the "winner." I take issue with this point because laughing does not always equal winning (for example, when we identify with the butt of the joke).

15. Although her assertion is based on the depiction of women in film, Mulvey's notion of "to-be-looked-at-ness" applies to women in any form of cultural representation. As noted in chapter 3, female comics tend to talk about weight and body image more than do male comics. Of course, as discussed in chapter 4, both male and female comics may assume a variety of postures, some (whiner, bawd, stud) more likely to focus on physical appearance than others. Still, some of the most popular male comics of the twentieth century (Hope, Cosby, Seinfeld) tend to de-emphasize physical appearance, while some of the most popular female comics (Diller, Rivers, Roseanne) focus on it.

16. The point of view of the performer should not be confused with the various points of view she or he performs during a single act. Both male and female comics perform male and female point of view (usually performing the opposite gender parodically), but the performer's own point of view (shaped by a constellation of factors including race, gender, sexual orientation, and life experience) is clearly the determining factor—the unitary "voice" and ideological foundation behind the multiple masks that she or he may employ.

17. For the purposes of this investigation, the term "marginal humor" refers to humor created and performed by members of marginal groups. The popularity of ethnic/racist and sexist jokes told by members of the dominant culture are not included.

18. Shapiro (1999) comments on the inversion and potential subversion inherent in Jewish humor: "There is much in Jewish humor that works in that Bakhtinian way to turn the (oppressive) world upside down; the victim becomes a winner, the fool the smart one, the most pathetic the one with wisdom. In all of this, laughter provides an emotional transcendence of the world; what appeared fixed and immutable suddenly seems arbitrary and changeable. Such humor deconstructs a world which moments before appeared so unalterable. We do not simply see the world in a new and fluid light, but perhaps more importantly, we feel it in our bellies" (25). Like the humor of all marginalized groups, the Jewish comic tradition makes use of the topsy-turvy "carnival" notion discussed in chapter 2.

19. It is interesting to note that Nevo's studies of Israeli Jewish and Arab students suggest that "when laughing at 'their group,' individuals appeared to be laughing at other individuals in the group and not necessarily at themselves" (cited in Gruner 1997, 105). An example of this is my own enjoyment of Jewish humor (as a Jew) being at least partly attributable to my lack of complete identification with all of the characteristics (for example, neurotic, overly concerned with money) lampooned in typical Jewish jokes.

20. Davies responds: "This [Grotjahn's] is a vivid but misleading image, for the point of getting hold of the dagger is not only to demonstrate superior dexterity but to switch daggers, so that an innocuous rather than a potentially envenomed weapon is used. This is a tactic that has both frustrated and infuriated anti-semites—who see Jewish humor as humanizing those whom they wish to demonize and as making a people whom they seek to represent as a malign threat appear comically harmless" (Cited in Gruner 1997, 99).

21. Supplication is one of Jones and Pittman's self-presentation strategies discussed at length in chapter 4.

22. Mintz offers a taxonomy of stages of Jewish humor that may well apply to the humor of other marginal groups: (1) critical—targets the outgroup; (2) self-deprecatory; (3) realistic; and (4) critical—targets the ingroup (cited in Nilsen 1993, 220). Although Mintz's schema identifies important types of marginal humor, it suggests that the development of such humor is a linear process. The data for this investigation, however, indicate that in the five postures delineated in chapter 4, self-deprecation, and attack on the hegemonic culture are present simultaneously in the marginal humor of contemporary female comics (for example, Haber's dating material and Roseanne's impotence jokes)—indeed, sometimes even within a single act. Certainly, the same is true of Jewish, African American, and other types of marginal humor as well. Although attack on self may precede attack on others in the historical development of marginal humor, in contemporary comedic discourse, Mintz's types can perhaps best be seen as a constellation of stages existing concurrently.

23. Field is speaking specifically of British audiences. She later notes that her comedy trio, Sensible Footwear, likes living and performing in Canada because "We're just not marginalized here. We're allowed to just join in nicely with everybody and our difference is our Britishness rather than our femaleness" (cited in Hengen 1998, 259). What Field does not discuss is that she and her partners are still marginalized by ethnicity if not by gender (obviously, this type of "difference" does not present a problem, and is consequently unnoticed).

24. Little (1983) maintains that "individuals, in order to shake off some doubt about behavior or attitude, will ridicule their own misgivings and laugh themselves back into the community of belief which their group of friends accepts" (9). From Little's perspective, then, self-deprecatory humor may function as a way for comics to voice their own insecurities and reaffiliate with a group identity; this belief, however, like so much work on "women's humor," rests on the unfounded assumption that the joketeller is articulating truths rather than jokes—that she or he truly believes everything she or he says onstage.

25. Saper proposes a model from cognitive behavioral psychology in order to address "laughing at" vs. "laughing with." This model features a stimulus; a response; organismic variables such as tastes, attitudes, and so on; and consequences (SROC). Gruner applies the SROC model to a Jewish joke in which "S" is the joke containing "Jewish elements," "O" is who tells it to whom, "R" is the attitude and behavioral response of the listener, and "C" refers to any lasting effects of the telling (cited in Gruner 1997, 100–101). Saper's SROC model may prove useful in future studies of marginal humor as a way to assess victims and butts of jokes as well as audience identification and attitude.

26. To my knowledge, Roseanne has never performed this particular joke as part of her act. In the *Playboy* interview, Tom and Roseanne discussed it as a "line" she had used during another interview. Perhaps she never performed it onstage due to its potentially offensive and controversial content. Given Roseanne's tendency to push the envelope of social acceptability (for women) onstage, however, it seems likely that

it may have been precisely the backlash potential and consequent condemnation from other feminists that she feared.

27.   Freud speculates that the need to tell another person a joke in order to legitimize it might be connected to the joke's end product—laughter. As he notes, "When I make the other person laugh by telling him my joke, I am actually making use of him to arouse my own laughter" (156).

28.   For discussion of the "Two Culture Hypothesis," see Tannen (1990) and Hopper (1992).

29.   Certainly, the reasons mentioned are not the only reasons a man or woman might laugh at a female comic's use of self-deprecation. What is significant here is that different people may laugh for different reasons.

30.   Fraiberg (1994) notes that Ellen DeGeneres "manages to practice a coercive form of identification and displacement that actually inverts what could be seen as the self-deprecatory humor usually found in women's stand-up routines" (321). Illustrating the way DeGeneres gets the audience to identify with her as the main character in embarrassing stories rather than simply laughing at her, Fraiberg describes this as an empowering strategy. Indeed, DeGeneres's ability to win the audience's affection is integral to her kid persona.

31.   Perhaps this is the reason that Margaret Smith found the last line of the male comic preceding her ("I like to fuck women with no legs, 'cause I put 'em on the end of my dick and spin 'em'") particularly unnerving—his description of an act of violence toward women is representative of actual violence toward women.

32.   Norman Holland (1982) notes that "Nobody 'makes' anybody laugh (except by tickling or laughing gas)" (175). According to Holland's identity theory, laughter is always volitional.

CONCLUSION

1.   As noted in chapter 3, male comics from Bill Cosby to Robin Williams perform material about pregnancy and childbirth, but obviously, their perspective is that primarily of an observer—a participant only in the broadest sense. Williams even performs material to this effect, noting that men cannot actually share the experience of childbirth because "Unless you've passed a bowling ball—I don't think so . . . unless you've had an umbrella opened up your ass, I don't think so . . . you're along for the ride!"

2.   Indeed, even the choice to perform "not-woman" brings woman into the equation. To perform "person" totally outside of biological sex and gendered behavior is, of course, impossible. Audience perception of biological sex plays a part in the interpretation of a comic's material and, like any factor that shapes messages, cannot be ignored. Because it is obvious to the audience that a comic is female, even if she performs the kid or reporter persona, a comic (like any woman) cannot help but perform her sociological marginality at all times.

3.   See, for example, Auslander 1993; Barreca 1991; Merrill 1988; Walker 1988.

4.   Indeed, for a woman merely to speak in public may be interpreted as a rhetorically subversive act when viewed in the context of patriarchal traditions. As Kalcik

(1975) notes, "A woman once told me that she never got to speak in a seminar because she kept waiting to make sure the male students were finished talking; they never were" (4–5). Perhaps stand-up comedy is one way for a woman not to wait but to take her turn in the cultural conversation.

5. Throughout this investigation, the term "feminist" potentially includes both genders. Because my definition of feminism (gender egalitarianism) can certainly be espoused by both women and men, the term "feminist" is not limited to women. Most feminists (including feminist critics), however, are female (given the number of women unwilling to call themselves feminists, it is certainly not surprising that most men do not use the term as a self-designation). Regardless of gender, feminists who seek to replace patriarchy with an equally oppressive matriarchy are merely crying, "The king is dead! Long live the queen!"

6. Arguing that postmodern feminism has lapsed into "ludic" or discursive politics, Ebert calls for a "materialist" feminist politics of "resistance"—one that seeks to transform social conditions.

7. Kibler is referring to scholarship specifically focused on the subversive nature of "female comedy."

8. My conception of politics as economically driven and as distinct from rhetoric is, in large part, the result of extensive discussion with Dr. Roderick Hart of the University of Texas at Austin.

9. The present investigation is necessarily limited in scope but raises questions for future research. Future issues for critical and interpretive studies of humor might include exploration of rhetorical marginality in the context of comic costume. As noted in chapter 2, the notion of "passing" vs. assimilation into the dominant culture is relevant to the way comics dress. Whereas the traditional fool wore motley, contemporary comics dress in much the same manner as does the establishment. What does it mean when the fool looks just like the king? Is marginality a form of rhetorical motley? Is "passing" a matter of survival or selling out?

Another area of investigation is the comparison and contrast between the modern humor of put-down or tendentious jokes (the material used in this investigation) and the postmodern humor of puns and other types of wordplay. What are the rhetorical features and functions of postmodern humor? What are the political implications of a humor based on shifting subject positions?

In order to eradicate essentialist assumptions about male and female humor (and communication in general), the discourse of comics of both genders (including gay and lesbian comics) can be studied in order to examine issues such as the rhetorical construction of romantic relationships and metacommunication (that is, how they talk about how they talk). Additionally, cross-cultural studies of stand-up comics would provide a template for investigating the above issues as well as those related to rhetorical and political marginality (who performs overtly "political" humor and why?).

Finally, empirical research may be useful to test the assumptions commonly made about the attitudes of audiences and joketellers alike. Nietz (1980), for example, maintains: "Men and women find different kinds of jokes funny, and may laugh at the same joke for different reasons. In addition, the gender of the joker may make a difference in whether or not an individual finds a joke funny, as may the presence of others of the same or different gender in the audience. Finally, men and women may tell different kinds of jokes and they may tell them to different audiences" (218). Clearly, audience-centered studies are needed to test the above and other assertions, such as the continued appeal of dick jokes.

As discussed in chapter 5, comics use what works. And asking which material works to entertain contemporary audiences is fundamental to understanding the relationship between humor and power. Even in this era of "isms," amid the political correctness controversy and the increasing cacophony of New Right rhetoric, it is that reliable standard, the dick joke, that guarantees laughs. (This is hardly surprising in a country where two of the news items receiving the most coverage and generating more humor than many others in recent years—Lorena Bobbitt's and Bill Clinton's "crimes"—were, in fact, the ultimate dick joke.) Pipkin (1994), for example, reports that two hours into a Comic Relief concert in Los Angeles, thirty-eight Lorena Bobbitt jokes had already been told. In 1994, I performed stand-up comedy for an audience of several hundred at Southwest Missouri State University; of course, it was not my carefully crafted material that got the biggest laugh but my observation (referring to a pipe organ onstage, as the performance was held in a recital hall) that "I'm onstage with the largest organ I've ever seen."

Ultimately, gathering statistical data regarding the demographic composition of comedy club audiences would be useful in determining the percentage of "always already marginal" individuals attending live comic performances in America today. Empirical research should also survey comics themselves to determine the percentage of marginal comics and to explore issues such as comics' perception of "difference" and the extent to which their self-presentation is "strategic."

There are more working comics in America today than at any other time in history. This would seem to bode well for women and other marginalized aspiring comics. In 1994, Pipkin observed that although the "comedy boom" suggested a bright future for the comedy industry in this country, comedy as an art might suffer: "The explosion of comedy in the past ten years has been both good and bad for the form. While there are now more comics in America than ever before (many desperately looking for work as hundreds of comedy clubs succumb to a stand-up glut), the material unfortunately has become terminally topical . . . the search for the broadest common denominator has resulted in a narrowing of the form, a sort of comedy inbreeding" (40).

Hence, although female comics today have more opportunities to perform, they also have more competition and more potential for exposure to wider markets before they have fully refined their acts.

Vocabulary remains a problem as well. When introducing female comics, even the most seasoned veterans sometimes falter. When introducing comic Carol Siskind on a 1994 *Tonight Show* appearance, for example, Jay Leno began to say "comedienne," then caught himself and told the audience, "No—it's comedian . . . I don't know why we say 'comedienne' . . . it's a comedian who just happens to be female . . . she's very funny and attractive. . . ." Leno's flustered metatalk is not anomalous; many male talk show hosts and MCs are at a loss for a label when it comes to female comics (and not a one has ever yet introduced a male comic as "attractive").

As a unique and powerful rhetoric/antirhetoric, humor affects us daily through personal interaction, professional relationships, and exposure to media. Clearly, the field of humor studies provides fertile ground for future scholarship.

WORKS CITED

PRINT MATERIALS

Abrahams, R. D. 1968. Trickster, the outrageous hero. In *Our living traditions: An introduction to American folklore,* edited by T. P. Coffin, 170–79. New York: Basic Books.

Adams, C. J. 1991. *The sexual politics of meat: A feminist-vegetarian critical theory.* New York: Continuum.

Adler, R. B., L. B. Rosenfeld, N. Towne, and R. F. Proctor. 1998. *Interplay: The process of interpersonal communication.* 7th ed. Ft. Worth: Harcourt Brace.

Apte, M. L. 1985. *Humor and laughter: An anthropological approach.* Ithaca: Cornell University Press.

———. 1987. Ethnic humor versus "sense of humor." In *Humor, the psyche, and society,* edited by A. A. Berger (special issue of *American Behavioral Scientist*), 30 (1): 28–30.

Aristotle. 1984. *Rhetoric.* In *The rhetoric and poetics of Aristotle,* translated by R. Roberts. New York: Random House Modern Library College Editions.

Auslander, P. 1993. Brought to you by "Fem-Rage": Stand-up comedy and the politics of gender. In *Acting out: Feminist performances,* edited by P. Phelan and L. Hart, 315–36. Ann Arbor: University of Michigan Press.

Barreca, R. 1988. Introduction to *Last Laughs: Perspectives on women and comedy,* edited by R. Barreca, 3–23. New York: Gordon and Breach.

———. 1991. *They used to call me Snow White . . . but I drifted: Women's strategic use of humor.* New York: Penguin.

Bauman, R. 1977. *Verbal art as performance.* Prospect Heights, Ill.: Waveland Press.

Beatts, A. 1975. Can a woman get a laugh and a man too? *Mademoiselle,* November, 140+.

Bellafante, G. 1996. A league of her own. *Time,* 24 June, on-line edition.

Bentley, E. 1971. The life of the drama. In *Comedy: A critical anthology,* edited by R. W. Corrigan, 767–75. Boston: Houghton Mifflin.

Berger, A. A. 1987. Introduction to *Humor, the psyche, and society,* edited by A. A. Berger (special issue of *American Behavioral Scientist*), 30 (3): 6–15.

Bergson, H. 1956. Laughter. In *Comedy,* edited by W. Sypher, 3–93. New York: Doubleday Anchor Books.

Bernstein, R. 1990. "Just kidding"—but at whose expense? *New York Times,* 8 April, H1+.

Bier, J. 1984. The rise and fall of American humor. In *Critical essays on American humor,* edited by W. B. Clark and W. C. Turner, 99–107. Boston: G. K. Hall and Co.

Black, E. 1976. The sentimental style as escapism, or the devil with Dan'l Webster. In *Form and genre: Shaping rhetorical action,* edited by K. K. Campbell and K. H. Jamieson, 75–87. Falls Church, Va.: Speech Communication Association.

Boal, A. 1985. *Theatre of the oppressed.* New York: Theatre Communications Group.

Borman, E. 1976. Rhetorical criticism and significant form: A humanistic approach. In *Form and genre: Shaping rhetorical action,* edited by K. K. Campbell and K. H. Jamieson, 165–85. Falls Church, Va.: Speech Communication Association.

Borns, B. 1987. *Comic lives: Inside the world of American stand-up comedy.* New York: Simon and Schuster.

Boskin, J. 1979. *Humor and social change in twentieth-century America.* Boston: Trustees of the Public Library of the City of Boston.

Boskin, J., and J. Dorinson. 1987. Ethnic humor: Subversion and survival. In *American humor,* edited by A. P. Dudden, 97–18. New York: Oxford University Press.

Brodzinsky, D. M., K. Barnett, and J. R. Aiello. 1981. Sex of subject and gender identity as factors in humor appreciation. *Sex Roles* 21:561–73.

Brooks, D. E., and W. R. Jacobs. 1996. Black men in the margins: Space Traders and the interpositional strategy against b(l)acklash. *Communication Studies* 47(4): 289–302.

Bunkers, S. L. 1985. Why are these women laughing? The power and politics of women's humor. *Studies in American Humor* 4(1–2): 82–93.

Burke, K. 1945. *A grammar of motives.* New York: Prentice-Hall.

———. 1950. *A rhetoric of motives.* Berkeley: University of California Press.

Butland, M. J., and D. K. Ivy. 1990. The effects of biological sex and egalitarianism humor appreciation: Replication and extension. *Journal of Social Behavior and Personality* 5:353–66.

Butler, J. 1990. Performative acts and gender constitution: An essay in phenomenology and feminist theory. In *Performing feminisms: Feminist critical theory and theatre,* edited by S. E. Case, 270–83. Baltimore: Johns Hopkins University Press.

Campbell, K. K., and K. H. Jamieson. 1976. Introduction to *Form and genre: Shaping rhetorical action,* edited by K. K. Campbell and K. H. Jamieson, 9–33. Falls Church, Va.: Speech Communication Association.

Campbell, M. 1999. Carlin finds beauty in simple words well said. *Saginaw News,* 18 December, B4.

Cantor, J. 1976. What is funny to whom? The role of gender. *Journal of Communication* 26:164–72.

Chafe, W. 1987. Humor as a disabling mechanism. In *Humor, the psyche, and society,* edited by A. A. Berger (special issue of *American Behavioral Scientist*) 30 (1): 18–20.

Chaikin, J. 1977. *The presence of the actor.* New York: Atheneum.

Chapman, A. J., and N. J. Gadfield. 1976. Is sexual humor sexist? *Journal of Communication* 26:141–53.

Clair, R. P. 1998. *Organizing silence: A world of possibilities.* Albany: SUNY Press.

Clay, R. A. 1997. Why are knock-knock jokes so funny to kids? *APA Monitor* 28 (9): 17.

Cohen, T. 1999. Jokes: *Philosophical thoughts on joking matters.* Chicago: University of Chicago Press.

Collins, P. H. 1986. Learning from the outsider within: The sociological significance of black feminist thought. *Social Problems* 33:514–32.

Conquergood, D. 1991. Rethinking ethnography: Towards a critical cultural politics. *Communication Monographs* 58:179–95.

Coser, R. L. 1960. Laughter among colleagues: A study of the social functions of humor among the staff of a mental hospital. *Psychiatry* 23:81–95.

Cottom, D. 1989. *Text and culture: The politics of interpretation.* Minneapolis: University if Minnesota Press.

Crossen, C. 1997. Funny business. *Wall Street Journal,* 31 January, 1, A6.

Davies, I. 1990. Lenny Bruce: Hyperrealism and the death of Jewish tragic humor. *Social Text* 22:90–110.

de Lauretis, T. 1987. *Technologies of gender: Essays on theory, film, and fiction.* Bloomington: Indiana University Press.

Dets de Vries, M. F. R. 1990. The organizational fool: Balancing a leader's hubris. *Human Relations* 43:751–70.

Dolan, J. 1992. Gender impersonation onstage: Destroying or maintaining the mirror of gender roles. In *Gender in performance: The interpretation of difference,* edited by L. Senelick, 3–13. Hanover, N.H.: University Press of New England.

Dolan, M. A. 1989. Today's women comics—knock-down funny, knock-down serious. *Los Angeles Times,* 2 January, pt. II, p. 5.

Dorinson, J., and J. Boskin. 1988. Racial and ethnic humor. In *Humor in America: A research guide to genres and topics,* edited by L. E. Mintz, 163–95. New York: Greenwood Press.

Douglas, M. 1975. Jokes. In *Rethinking popular culture: Contemporary perspectives in cultural studies,* edited by C. Mukerji and M. Schudson, 291–309. Berkeley: University of California Press.

Dresner, Z. 1988. Women's humor. In *Humor in America: A research guide to genres and topics,* edited by L. E. Mintz, 137–63. New York: Greenwood Press.

———. 1991a. Domestic comic writers. In *Women's comic visions,* edited by J. Sochen, 93–115. Detroit: Wayne State University Press.

———. 1991b. Whoopi Goldberg and Lily Tomlin: Black and white women's humor. In *Women's comic visions,* edited by J. Sochen, 179–93. Detroit: Wayne State University Press.

Dudden, A. P., ed. 1987. *American humor.* New York: Oxford Press.

Ebert, T. L. 1993. Ludic feminism, the body, performance, and labor: Bringing materialism back into feminist cultural studies. *Cultural Critique* (winter): 5–50.

Ensler, E. 2001. *The vagina monologues: The v-day edition.* New York: Villard.

Esquire. 1994. Would one thousand young American women rather increase the size of their income, political power, or breasts? February, 65–67.

Finney, G. 1994. Unity in difference? An introduction. In *Look who's laughing: Gender and comedy,* edited by G. Finney, 1–14. Amsterdam: Gordon and Breach.

Flora, C. B. 1977. Working-class women's political participation: Its potential in developed countries. In *A portrait of marginality*, edited by M. Githens and J. L. Prestage, 75–96. New York: David McKay.

Forte, J. 1990. Women's performance art: Feminism and postmodernism. In *Performing feminisms: Feminist critical theory and theatre*, edited by S. E. Case, 251–70. Baltimore: Johns Hopkins University Press.

Fox-Genovese, E. 1991. *Feminism without illusions: A critique of individualism*. Chapel Hill: University of North Carolina Press.

Fraiberg, A. 1994. Between the laughter: Bridging feminist studies through women's stand-up comedy. In *Look who's laughing: Gender and comedy*, edited by G. Finney, 315–35. Amsterdam: Gordon and Breach.

Franklin, J. 1979. *Joe Franklin's encyclopedia of comedians*. New York: Bell Publishing Co.

Freud, S. 1960. Jokes and their relation to the unconscious. In *The standard edition of the complete psychological works of Sigmund Freud*, vol. 8, edited and translated by J. Strachey. London: Hogarth Press.

Friend, T. 1994. Goddess, riot grrrl, philosopher-queen, lipstick lesbian, warrior, tattooed love child, sack artist, leader of men: Lock up your sons—the 21st-century woman is in the building. *Esquire*, February, 47–56.

Fry, C. 1971. Comedy. In *Comedy: A critical anthology*, edited by R. W. Corrigan, 753–60. Boston: Houghton Mifflin.

Fry, W. 1987. Humor and paradox. In *Humor, the psyche, and society*, edited by A. A. Berger (special issue of *American Behavioral Scientist*), 30 (3): 42–71.

Gagnier, R. 1991. Between women: A cross-class analysis of status and anarchic humor. In *Feminisms: An anthology of literary theory and criticism*, edited by R. Warhol and D. Price Herndl, 927–44. New Brunswick, N.J.: Rutgers University Press.

Gallo, H. 1991. *Comedy explosion: A new generation*. New York: Thunder Mouth Press.

Gifford, D. J. 1979. Iconographical notes toward a definition of the medieval fool. In *The fool and the trickster: Studies in honour of Enid Welsford*, edited by P.V. A. Williams, 33–41. Cambridge: D. S. Brewer.

Gilbert, J. 1989. "That's not funny . . . ": Feminism in stand-up comedy. Paper presented at the meeting of the Speech Communication Association, November, San Francisco.

————. 1996. Last laughs and final words: Humor and power in the Hill/Thomas hearings. In *Outsiders looking in: A communication perspective on the Hill/Thomas hearings*, edited by P. Siegel, 186–221. New York: Hampton Press.

Gilligan, C. 1982. *In a different voice*. Cambridge: Harvard University Press.

Gindele, K. C. 1994. When women laugh wildly and (gentle)men roar: Victorian embodiments of laughter. In *Look who's laughing: Gender and comedy*, edited by G. Finney, 139–61. Amsterdam: Gordon and Breach.

Githens, M., and J. L. Prestage, eds. 1977. *A portrait of marginality*. New York: David Mckay.

Goffman, E. 1959. *The presentation of self in everyday life*. New York: Doubleday Anchor Books.

Goldsmith, R. H. 1955. *Wise fools in Shakespeare*. Minneapolis: University of Minnesota Press.

Graham, E. E., M. J. Papa, and G. P. Brooks. 1992. Functions of humor in conversation: Conceptualization and measurement. *Western Journal of Communication* 56:161–83.

Gray, J. 1992. *Men are from Mars, women are from Venus: A practical guide for improving communication and getting what you want in your relationships.* New York: Harper Collins.

Greenblatt, S. 1989. Towards a poetics of culture. In *The new historicism,* edited by H. A. Veeser, 1–15. New York: Routledge.

Grotjahn, M. 1987. Dynamics of Jewish jokes. In *Humor, the psyche, and society,* edited by A. A. Berger (special issue of *American Behavioral Scientist*), 30 (1): 95–104.

Gruner, C. R. 1997. *The game of humor: A comprehensive theory of why we laugh.* New Brunswick, N.J.: Transaction Publishers.

Handelman, D. 1988a. Funny bizness. *Rolling Stone,* 3 November, 55.

Handelman, D. 1988b. Comedy index. *Rolling Stone,* 3 November, 101–9.

Harbage, A., ed. 1969. *William Shakespeare: The complete works.* New York: Viking.

Harman, L. D. 1988. *The modern stranger: On language and membership.* Berlin: Mouton de Gruyter.

Hart, R. P. 1997. *Modern rhetorical criticism.* 2d ed. Boston: Allyn and Bacon.

Havelock, E. 1963. *A preface to Plato.* Cambridge: Belknap Press.

Hegde, R. S. 1996. Narratives of silence: Rethinking gender, agency, and power from the communication experiences of battered women in south India. *Communication Studies* 47 (4): 303–17.

Hendra, T. 1987. *Going too far.* New York: Doubleday.

Hengen, S. 1998. "Raised by poodles": An interview with Sensible Footwear. In *Performing gender and comedy: Theories, texts, and contexts,* edited by S. Hengen, 244–66. Amsterdam: Gordon and Breach.

Holland, N. 1982. *Laughing: A psychology of humor.* Ithaca, N.Y.: Cornell University Press.

hooks, b. 1984. *Feminist theory: From margin to center.* Boston: South End Press.

Hopkins, E. 1990. Who's laughing now? Women. *New York Times,* 16 September, sec. 2, pp. 1, 5.

Hopper, R. 1992. Genderlects and powerless speech. Paper presented at the meeting of the International Communication Association, May, Miami.

Horowitz, S. 1997. *Queens of comedy: Lucille Ball, Phyllis Diller, Carol Burnett, Joan Rivers, and the new generation of funny women.* Amsterdam: Gordon and Breach.

Inge, M. T. 1985. Preface to *Studies in American Humor* 4 (1–2): 5–6.

Innes, C. 1981. *Holy theatre: Ritual and the avant garde.* Cambridge: Cambridge University Press.

Ivanov, A. J. 1994. Mae West was not a man: Sexual parody and genre in the plays and films of Mae West. In *Look who's laughing: Gender and comedy,* edited by G. Finney, 275–99. Amsterdam: Gordon and Breach.

Janus, S. S. 1981. Humor, sex and power in American society. *American Journal of Psychoanalysis* 41 (2): 161–67.

Jenkins, M. M. 1986. What's so funny? Joking among women. In *Proceedings of the Berkeley women and language conference, 1985,* edited by N. C. Brenner and B.

Moonwomon, 135–51. Berkeley: Linguistics Department, University of California, Berkeley.

Jones, E. E., A. Farina, A. H. Hastorf, H. Markus, D. T. Miller, and R. A. Scott. 1984. *Social stigma: The psychology of marked relationships.* New York: W. H. Freeman.

Jones, E. E., and T. S. Pittman. 1982. Toward a general theory of strategic self-presentation. In *Psychological perspectives on the self,* edited by J. Suls, 1:231–61. Hillsdale, N.J.: LEA.

Jung, C. G. 1959. On the psychology of the trickster figure. In *The collected works,* edited by H. Mead, M. Fordham, G. Adler, and W. McGuire, vol. 9, pt. 1, 255–75. New York: Bollingen.

Kalcik, S. 1975. "... like Ann's gynecologist or the time I was almost raped": Personal narratives in women's rap groups. In *Women and folklore,* edited by C. R. Farrer, 3–11. Austin: University of Texas Press.

Kaplan, A. 2001. Wizards of wit: How Jews revolutionized comedy in America, part I. *Reform Judaism* (winter). http://uahc.org/rjmag/1101ak.html.

———. 2002a. Wizards of wit: How Jews revolutionized comedy in America, part II. *Reform Judaism* (spring). http://uahc.org/rjmag/302ak.html.

———. 2002b. Wizards of wit: How Jews revolutionized comedy in America, part III. *Reform Judaism* (summer): 11–19.

Kibler, M. A. 1998. Nothing succeds like excess: Lillian Shaw's comedy and sexuality on the Keith vaudeville circuit. In *Performing gender and comedy: Theories, texts, and contexts,* edited by S. Hengen, 59–81. Amsterdam: Gordon and Breach.

King, S. 2000. Comedy Central lineup growing. *Saginaw News,* 19 June, D4.

Klapp, O. E. 1962. *Heroes, villains, and fools: The changing American character.* New Jersey: Prentice-Hall.

Klein, J. 1984. The new stand-up comics, *Ms,* October, 116–21.

Kolbert, E. 1993. Why late-night TV is a man's world. *New York Times,* 22 August, sec. 2, pp. 27–28.

Korsmeyer, C. 1981. The hidden joke: Generic uses of masculine terminology. In *Sexist language: A modern philosophical analysis,* edited by M. Vetterling-Braggin, 116–31. Totowa, N.J.: Littlefield Adams.

Koziski, S. 1984. The standup comedian as anthropologist: Intentional culture critic. *Journal of Popular Culture* (fall): 57–76.

Kramarae, Cheris 1981. *Women and men speaking: Frameworks for analysis.* Rowley, Mass.: Newbury House.

Krupp, C. 1993. Meet *Grace under fire's* Brett Butler. *Glamour,* November, 185–86.

Lakoff, R. 1975. *Language and woman's place.* New York: Harper.

Laughtrack. 1989. 1 (June), no. 4.

Lee, C. I., and T. Gura. 1992. *Oral interpretation.* 8th ed. Boston: Houghton Mifflin.

Le Guin, U. K., ed. 1989. *Dancing at the edge of the world: Thoughts on words, women, places.* New York: Harper and Row.

Levine, J. B. 1976. The feminine routine. *Journal of Communication* 26:173–75.

Levine, L. W. 1977. *Black culture and black consciousness: Afro-American folk thought from slavery to freedom.* New York: Oxford University Press.

Levy, B. 1997. *Ladies laughing: Wit as control in contemporary American women writers.* Amsterdam: Gordon and Breach.

Limon, John. Heller, S. 2000. Interview with John Limon, author of *Stand-Up comedy in theory, or, abjection in America. Chronicle of Higher Education* (18 August 18).

Little, J. 1983. *Comedy and the woman writer: Woolf, Spark, and feminism.* Lincoln: University of Nebraska Press.

————. 1991. Humoring the sentence: Women's dialogic comedy. In *Women's comic visions,* edited by J. Sochen, 19–33. Detroit: Wayne State University Press.

Long, B. W., and M. F. Hopkins. 1982. *Performing literature: An introduction to oral interpretation.* Englewood Cliffs, New Jersey: Prentice-Hall.

Lorde, A. 1983. The master's tools will never dismantle the master's house. In *This bridge called my back: Writings by radical women of color,* edited by C. Moraga and G. Anzaldua, 98–102. New York: Kitchen Table: Women of Color Press.

Los Angeles Daily Variety. 1991. Cannes film festival reviews of *Wisecracks.* 16 May.

Love, A. M., and H. D. Lambert. 1989. Humor appreciation as a function of sexual, aggressive, and sexist content. *Sex Roles* 20:649–54.

Lutfiyya, M. N. 1990. Critical street theorizing: A case study of ladies against women or comedy as political policy development. Paper presented at the meeting of the Speech Communication Association, November, Chicago.

MacCambridge, M. 1992. Female humor stands up. *Austin American-Statesman,* 2 October, 11.

Margolis, H. 1998. Sneaky re-views: Can Robert Townsend's taste for stereotypes contribute positively to identity politics? In *Performing gender and comedy: Theories, texts, and contexts,* edited by S. Hengen, 199–219. Amsterdam: Gordon and Breach.

Marks, P. 2000. Fear and joking on the late-night campaign trail. *New York Times,* 7 May, AR 31+.

Martin, L., and K. Segrave. 1986. *Women in comedy.* Secaucus, New Jersey: Citadel Press.

Martineau, W. H. 1972. A model of the social functions of humor. In *The psychology of humor,* edited by J. H. Goldstein, 101–11. New York: Academic Press.

McManus, B. K. 1976. Literary comedy to concert comedy: The achievements of Artemus Ward, Petroleum V Nasby, and Josh Billings. Ph.D. diss., University of Texas, Austin.

McMullen, D. 1970. The fool as entertainer and satirist on stage and in the world. *Dalhousie Review* 50:10–22.

McNamara, B. and R. Schechner. 1982. Introduction to the Performance Studies series. In *From ritual to theatre: The human seriousness of play,* edited by V. Turner. New York: Performing Arts Journal Publications.

McWhirter, D. 1994. Feminism/gender/comedy: Meredith, Woolf, and the reconfiguration of comic distance. In *Look who's laughing: Gender and comedy,* edited by G. Finney, 189–205. Amsterdam: Gordon and Breach.

Mellencamp, P. 1986. Situation comedy, feminism, and Freud: Discourses of Gracie and Lucy. In *Studies in entertainment: Critical approaches to mass culture,* edited by T. Modleski, 80–95. Bloomington: Indiana University Press.

Meredith, G. 1971. An essay on comedy. In *Comedy: A critical anthology,* edited by R. W. Corrigan, 738–44. Boston: Houghton Mifflin.

Merrill, L. 1988. Feminist humor: Rebellious and self-affirming. In *Last laughs: Perspectives on women and comedy,* edited by R. Barreca, 271–81. New York: Gordon and Breach.

Michael, Shayne. 2001. The rise and fall of standup comedy. Http://shayne-michael.com/risefall.htm.

Midwinter, E. 1979. *Make 'em laugh: famous comedians and their words.* London: George Allen and Unwin.

Miller, C. R. 1984. Genre as social action. *Quarterly Journal of Speech* 70:151–67.

Miller, H. 1991. *On the fringe: The dispossessed in America.* Lexington, Mass.: Lexington Books.

Mintz, L. E. 1987. Standup comedy as social and cultural mediation. In *American humor,* edited by A. P. Dudden, 85–97. New York: Oxford University Press.

———, ed. 1988. *Humor in America: A research guide to genres and topics.* New York: Greenwood Press.

Mitchell, C. 1978. Hostility and aggression toward males in female joke telling. *Frontiers* 3:18–27.

Mizruchi, E. H. 1983. *Regulating society: Marginality and social control in historical perspective.* New York: Free Press.

Modleski, T. 1991. *Feminism without women: Culture and criticism in a "postfeminist" age.* New York: Routledge.

Moore, T. E., K. Griffiths, and B. Payne. 1987. Gender, attitudes toward women, and the appreciation of sexist humor. *Sex Roles* 16:521–31.

Morreall, J., ed. 1987. *The philosophy of laughter and humor.* Albany: State University of New York Press.

Mulvey, L. 1991. Visual pleasure and narrative cinema. In *Feminisms: An anthology of literary theory and criticism,* edited by R. Warhol and D. Price Herndl, 432–43. New Brunswick, N.J.: Rutgers University Press.

Mundorf, N., B. Azra, D. Zillman, P. Lester, and S. Robertson. 1988. Gender differences in humor appreciation. *Humor: International Journal of Humor Research* 1–3:231–43.

Neve, M. 1988. Freud's theory of humor, wit and jokes. In *Laughing matters: A serious look at humour,* edited by J. Durant and J. Miller, 34–45. Harlow, England: Longman Scientific and Technical.

Nietz, M. J. 1980. Humor, hierarchy, and the changing status of women. *Psychiatry* 43:211–23.

Nilsen, D. 1993. *Humor scholarship: A research bibliography.* Westport, Conn.: Greenwood Press.

Olsen, L. 1990. *Circus of the mind in motion: Postmodernism and the comic vision.* Detroit: Wayne State University Press.

Olson, S. K. 1988. Standup comedy. In *Humor in America: A research guide to genres and topics,* edited by L. E. Mintz, 109–37. New York: Greenwood Press.

Ortner, S. B. 1996. *Making gender: The politics and erotics of culture.* Boston: Beacon.

Pearson, J. C., G. R. Miller, and M. Senter. 1983. Sexism and sexual humor: A research note. *Central States Speech Journal* 34:257–59.

Pearson J. C., West, R. L., and Turner, L. H. 1995. *Gender and communication.* 3rd ed. Dubuque: Brown and Benchmark.

Pelias, R. J. 1992. *Performance studies: The interpretation of aesthetic texts.* New York: St. Martin's Press.

Pershing, L. 1991. There's a joker in the menstrual hut: A performance analysis of comedian Kate Clinton. In *Women's comic visions,* edited by J. Sochen, 193–236. Detroit: Wayne State University Press.

Phillips, L. 1989. Venus envy. *Laughtrack,* June, 14–17.

Pipkin, T. 1994. Onstage. *Austin Chronicle,* 11 February, 40–41.

Phyllis Diller: Comedienne and humanitarian. Women's International Center. Retrieved May 2, 2003 from http://www.wic.org/bio/pdiller.htm

Porter, John. Aristophanes and Greek old comedy. Retrieved April 29, 2003 from http://duke.usask.ca/~porterj/coursenotes/Aristophanes/html.

Pulliam, G. J. 1991. Stock lines, boat-acts, and dickjokes: A brief annotated glossary of standup comedy jargon. *American Speech* (smmer): 164–70.

Reeder, H. M. 1996. A critical look at gender difference in communication research. *Communication Studies* 47 (4): 318–30.

Roseanne. 1993. Interview with Roseanne and Tom Arnold. *Playboy,* June, 66–74.

Rosenblatt, R. 1991. What brand of laughter do you use? *New York Times,* 17 November, H5+.

Rosmarin, A. 1985. *The power of genre.* Minneapolis: University of Minnesota Press.

Rowe, K. 1995. The unruly woman: Gender and the genres of laughter. Austin: University of Texas Press.

Said, E. 1978. *Orientalism.* New York: Vintage Books.

Schechner, R. 1974. From ritual to theatre and back: The structure/process of the efficacy-entertainment dyad. *Educational Theatre Journal* 26:455–82.

———. 1977. Drama script, theatre, and performance. In *Essays on performance theory,* edited by R. Schechner, 99–110. New York: Drama Book Specialists.

Schuler, C. 1990. Spectator response and comprehension: The problem of Karen Finley's *Constant state of desire. Drama Review* 34:131–46.

Schutz, C. E. 1977a. *Political humor: From Aristophanes to Sam Ervin.* Cranbury, N.J.: Associated University Presses.

———. 1977b. The psycho-logic of political humor. In *It's a funny thing, humor,* edited by A. J. Chapman and H. C. Foot, 60–69. Oxford: Pergamon Press.

Sella, M. 2000. The power and prejudice of political comedy: The stiff guy vs. the dumb guy. *New York Times Magazine,* 24 September, 72–80+.

Senelick, L., ed. 1992. *Gender in performance: The interpretation of difference.* Hanover, N.H.: University Press of New England.

Shapiro, S. 1999. A life on the fringes: My road to critical pedagogy. *Tikkun* 14 (1): 23–27.

Sheppard, A. 1986. From Kate Sanborn to feminist psychology: The social context of women's humor, 1885–1985. *Psychology of Women Quarterly* 10:155–70.

———. 1991. Social cognition, gender roles, and women's humor. In *Women's comic visions,* edited by J. Sochen, 33–57. Detroit: Wayne State University Press.

Sheppard, R. W. 1983. Tricksters, carnival and the magical figures of Dada poetry. In *Forum for modern language studies,* xix: 116–26.

Simmel, G. 1921. The sociological significance of the "stranger." In *Introduction to the science of sociology,* edited by R. E. Park and E. W. Burgess, 322–27. Chicago: University of Chicago Press.

Simon, S. 2001. Interview with Kelly Leonard, executive producer of Second City Theater Company. National Public Radio: NPR weekend edition (January).

Simons, H. 1976. Genre-alizing about rhetoric: A scientific approach. In *Form and genre: Shaping rhetorical action,* edited by K. K. Campbell and K. H. Jamieson, 33–51. Falls Church, Va.: Speech Communication Association.

Smith, R. L. 1988. *Comedy on record: The complete critical discography.* New York: Garland.

Sochen, J. 1991. Slapsticks, screwballs, and bawds: The long road to the performing talents of Lucy and Bette. In *Women's comic visions,* edited by J. Sochen, 141–58. Detroit: Wayne State University Press.

Sonkowsky, R. P. 1983. Oral performance and ancient Greek literature. In *Performance of literature in historical perspectives,* edited by D. W. Thompson, 1–31. Lanham, Maryland: University Press of America.

Stallybrass, P., and H. White. 1986. *The politics and poetics of transgression.* Ithaca, N.Y.: Cornell University Press.

Stewart, L. P., P. J. Cooper, A. D. Stewart, and S. A. Friedley 1996. *Communication and gender.* 3d ed. Scottsdale, Ariz.: Gorusch Scarisbrick.

Stillion, J. M., and H. White. 1987. Feminist humor: Who appreciates it and why? *Psychology of Women Quarterly* 11:219–32.

Stone, L. 1996. Rosie complexion. *Village Voice,* 9 July, on-line edition.

Stonequist, E. V. 1937. *The marginal man: A study in personality and culture conflict.* New York: Charles Scribner's Sons.

Strauss, D. 1988. The clubbing of America: Today's comedy is in chains. *Rolling Stone,* 3 November, 89+.

Sullivan, P. A., and L. H. Turner. 1996. *From the margins to the center: Contemporary women and political communication.* Westport, CT: Praeger.

Swortzell, L. 1978. *Here come the clowns: A calvalcade of comedy from antiquity to the present.* New York: Viking.

Tannen, D. 1990. *You just don't understand: Women and men in conversation.* New York: Random House.

Toth, E. 1984. A laughter of their own: Women's humor in the United States. In *Critical essays on American humor,* edited by W. B. Clark and W. C. Turner, 199–217. Boston: G. K. Hall.

Turner, V. 1982. *From ritual to theatre: The human seriousness of play.* New York: Performing Arts Journal Publications.

———. 1988. *The anthropology of performance.* New York: PAJ Publications.

Unterbrink, M. 1987. *Funny women: American comediennes, 1860–1985.* Jefferson, North Carolina: McFarland.

USA Today. 1990. Comedy at women's expense isn't funny. January, 8–9.

Veeser, H. A. 1989. Introduction to *The new historicism,* edited by H. A. Veeser, ix–xvi. New York: Routledge.

Villanueva, F. M. 1982. Jewish "fools" of the Spanish fifteenth century. *Hispanic Review* 50:385–409.

Walker, N. 1987. Humor and gender roles: The "funny" feminism of the post–world war II suburbs. In *American humor,* edited by A. P. Dudden, 118–38. New York: Oxford Press.

———. 1988. *A very serious thing: Women's humor and American culture.* Minneapolis: University of Minnesota Press.

———. 1991a. Nineteenth-century women's humor. In *Women's comic visions,* edited by J. Sochen, 85–93. Detroit: Wayne State University Press.

———. 1991b. Toward solidarity: Women's humor and group identity. In *Women's comic visions,* edited by J. Sochen, 57–85. Detroit: Wayne State University Press.

———. 1998. Afterword to *Performing gender and comedy: Theories, texts, and contexts,* edited by S. Hengen, 267–68. Amsterdam: Gordon and Breach.

Ware, V. 1992. *Beyond the pale: White women, racism, and history.* London: Verson.

Warhol, R., and D. Price Herndl. 1991. *Feminisms: An anthology of literary theory and criticism.* New Brunswick, N.J.: Rutgers University Press.

Waters, H. F. 1993. Three stars are born. *Newsweek,* 25 October, 70.

Weiss, P. 1988. 100 characters in search of an offer: Welcome to the first American comedy convention. *Rolling Stone,* 3 November, 56+.

Weisstein, N. 1973. Why we aren't laughing anymore. *Ms,* November, 79–81+.

Welsford, E. 1935. *The fool: His social and literary history.* New York: Faber and Faber.

White, C. L. 1988. Liberating laughter: An inquiry into the nature of feminist humor. In *Women communicating: Studies of women's talk,* edited by B. Bate and A. Taylor, 75–90. Norwood, New Jersey: Ablex.

Whitfield, S. J. 1988. Political humor. In *Humor in America: A research guide to genres and topics,* edited by L. E. Mintz, 195–212. New York: Greenwood Press.

Wilde, L. 1968. *The great comedians talk about comedy.* New York: Citadel.

Williams, E. A. 1991. Moms Mabley and the Afro-American comic performance. In *Women's comic visions,* edited by J. Sochen, 158–79. Detroit: Wayne State University Press.

Willie, C. V. 1975. Marginality and social change. *Society* 12 (5): 10–13.

Wilt, J. 1980. The laughter of maidens, the cackle of matriarchs: Notes on the collision between comedy and feminism. In *Gender and literary voice,* edited by J. Todd, 173–97. New York: Holmes and Meier.

Wisse, R. R. 1971. *The schlemiel as modern hero.* Chicago: University of Chicago Press.

Wolf, N. 1993. *Glamour,* November, 221+.

Yeats, W. B. 1977. *The collected poems of W. B. Yeats.* New York: MacMillan.

Yudice, G. 1988. Marginality and the ethics of survival. In *Universal abandon? The politics of postmodernism,* edited by A. Ross, 214–37. Minneapolis: University of Minnesota Press.

Zehme, B. 1988. Who's afraid of Sandra Bernhard? Hey—nobody said reinventing comedy would be pretty. *Rolling Stone,* 3 November, 76+.

Zijderveld, A. C. 1982. *Reality in a looking-glass: Rationality through an analysis of traditional folly.* London: Routledge and Kegan Paul.

Zillman, D., and S. H. Stocking. 1976. Putdown humor. *Journal of Communication* 26:154–63.

NONPRINT MATERIALS

Audio

Benson, B. B. *Bea Bea Benson lets it all hang out.* Laff Records.

Clinton, K. *Live in Austin, TX.* Audiocassette.

Diller, P. 1960. *Are you ready for Phyllis Diller?* Verve.

———. 1961. *Phyllis Diller laughs.* Verve.

Edwards, Tony. 1991. *Live from The Improv,* comedy club series #5. Audiocassette.

Hodge, Stephanie. 1991. *Live from The Improv,* comedy club series #5. Audiocassette.

Live from the Improv: Dating. 1991. Wood Knapp.

Mabley, M. 1960. *The funniest woman in the world.* Chess.

———. *The best of Moms Mabley.* Chess.

Nickman, Bob. *Live from The Improv,* comedy club series #5. Audiocassette.

Poundstone, Paula. In *A prairie home companion joke show.* NPR.

Rivers, J. 1983. *What becomes a semi-legend most?* Geffen.

Seinfeld, 1991. *Live from The Improv,* comedy club series #5. Audiocassette.

Shydner, Rich. 1992. *Live from The Improv,* comedy club series #5. Audiocassette.

Tomlin, L. 1972. *"And that's the truth."* Polydor.

———. 1975. *Modern scream.* Polydor.

Warren, R. *Knockers up!* Jubilee.

Film

Singer, G., dir. 1991. *Wisecracks.* Zinger Films in association with the National Film Board of Canada's Studio D.

Video

Unless otherwise noted, all comedy shows were on the Comedy Central channel.

Behar, Joy. 1988. *Women of the night.* HBO

———. 1989. *Rascal's.*

———. 1992. *One night stand.*

Boosler, Elayne. 1984. *Party of one.* HBO.

———. 1988. *Broadway baby.* HBO.

Butler, Brett. 1992a. *Stand up New York.*

———. 1992b. *Women aloud.*

———. 1993. *The late show with David Letterman.* CBS.

Carter, Judy. 1990. *Comedy express.*

Carroll, Jean. 1959. *The very best of Ed Sullivan, vol. 2*

Chappell, Cassie. 1991. *Evening at The Improv.* A&E.

Cho, Margaret. 1992. *Ladies of laughter.* NBC.

Cleghorne, Ellen. 1990. *Caroline's comedy hour.*

———. 1991. *Retaining laughter.* Lifetime.

DeGeneres, Ellen. 1992. *The tonight show with Jay Leno.* NBC.

Delaria, Lea. 1993. *Gay and lesbian march on Washington.*

Digiulio, Janine. 1993. *Women aloud.*

Diller, Phyllis. 1969. *The very best of Ed Sullivan, vol. 2*
———. 1993. In *20/20*. ABC.
Dumbrowski, Louise. 1993. *Two drink minimum.*
Eaton, Cindy. 1993. *Evening at The Improv.* A&E.
Essman, Susie. 1988. *Women of the night.* HBO
Fields, Totie. 1967 *The Ed Sullivan Show.*
Ford, Diane. 1992. *Women of the night.* HBO
Foster, Amy. 1990. *Stand up New York.*
Fraser, Casey. 1993. *The Jane Whitney show.* KBC
Garofalo, Janeane. 1993. *Stand up New York.*
———. 2001. *Comics come home.*
Glass, Todd. 1993. Cable appearance (no specific show)
Haber, Karen. 1985. *Girls of the comedy store.* Playboy channel.
———. 1990a. *Comedy express.*
———. 1990b. *London underground.*
Hemphill, Shirley. 1985. *Girls of the comedy store.* Playboy channel.
Henry, Carol. 1990. *Women of the night.* HBO
Hodge, Stephanie. 1992. *Two drink minimum.*
Jordan, Diana. 1993. *Evening at The Improv.* A&E.
Kamenoff, Wendy. 1992. *Evening at The Improv.* A&E.
Karam, Jann. 1990. *Two drink minimum.*
———. 1991. *Two drink minimum.*
———. 1992. *Evening at The Improv.* A&E.
Kightlinger, Laura. 1991. *Retaining laughter.* Lifetime.
———. 2001. *Comics come home.*
Kolinsky, Sue. 1992. *The tonight show with Jay Leno.* NBC.
Krinsky, Leah. 1991. *Retaining laughter.* Lifetime.
———. 1993. *Evening at The Improv.* A&E.
Ladman, Cathy. 1992a. *A-list.*
———. 1992b. *Women aloud.*
———. 1993a. *Girls' night out.*
———. 1993b. *USO comedy tour.*
Leifer, Carol. 1990. *Comedy spotlite.* Showtime.
———. 1992. *The late show with David Letterman.* CBS.
———. 1993. *London underground.*
Liebman, Wendy. 1992a. *Ladies of laughter.* NBC.
———. 1992b. *The tonight show with Jay Leno.* NBC.
———. 2001. *The late show with David Letterman.* CBS.
Lowks, Suzy. 1990. *Women of the night.* HBO
Lynch, Nora. 1993. *Stand-up spotlite.*
Madigan, Kathleen. 1990. *Women of the night.* HBO
———. 1992. *Ladies of laughter.* NBC.
Maier, Bill. 1993. *Sunday comics.*
Mantel, Henriette. 1992. *Women aloud.*
Matteson, Pam. 1992. *A-list.*

Nichols, Diane. 1990. *Women of the night.* HBO
———. 1993. *Evening at the Improv.* A&E.
Piper, Monica. 1990. *Comedy spotlite.* Showtime.
Poundstone, Paula. 1987. *Women of the night.* HBO
———. 1991. *Women of the night.* HBO
———. 1992. *One night stand.*
Rhea, Caroline. 1991. *Comic strip.*
———. 1993. *Women aloud.*
———. 2001. *Comics come home.*
Rivers, Joan. 1968. *The Ed Sullivan Show*
———. late 1970s ("TV appearance"); *History of stand-up comedy.*
———. 1981. *The tonight show with Johnny Carson.*
Roseanne. 1987. *The Roseanne Barr show.* HBO.
———. 1992. *Roseanne Arnold: Live from Trump Castle.* HBO.
———. 1994. In *20/20.* ABC.
Rudner, Rita. 1987. *Women of the night.* HBO
———. 1991. *Rita Rudner: BBC special.*
Scott, Angela. 1992. *Women aloud.*
Siskind, Carol. 1992. *Ladies of laughter.* NBC.
———. 1993. *The tonight show with Jay Leno.* NBC.
Smith, Linda. 1992. *Women aloud.*
———. 1993. *Women aloud.*
Smith, Margaret. 1992. *A-list.*
———. 1993. *Stand-up spotlite.*
Snow, Carrie. 1985. *Girls of the comedy store.* Playboy channel.
———. 1991. *Retaining laughter.* Lifetime.
———. 1992. *A-list.*
Soro, Suzy. 1992. *Women aloud.*
———. 1993. *Igby's.*
Stein, Abby. 1991. Cable appearance (no specific show).
Stillson, Jeff. 1993. *Stand up New York.*
Stone, Pam. 1992. *Sunday comics.*
———. 1993. *Stand-up spotlite.*
Swisher, Deborah. 1993. *Igby's in L.A.*
Sykes, Wanda. 2001. *Comics come home.*
Tenuta, Judy. 1987. *Women of the night.* HBO
———. 1992. *Sunday comics.*
Toll, Judy. 1991 *Lips Only.*
———. 1992. *Women aloud.*
Tolsch, Adrienne. 1993. *Women aloud.*
Tyler, Robin. 1993. *Gay and lesbian march on Washington.*
Warfield, Marsha. 1987. *Paramount comedy theatre.*
Westenhoefer, Suzanne. 1992. *Women aloud.*
———. 1993. *Gay and lesbian march on Washington.*
Winstead, Lizz. 1988. *Women of the night.* HBO

————. 1990. *Caroline's comedy hour.*

————. 1993. *Women aloud.*

Wise, Anita. 1991. *Improv, L.A.*

————. 1992. *Ladies of laughter.* NBC.

A & E's evening at the improv. A & E.

The a-list. Comedy Central.

Best of the big laff off. Comedy Central.

Bob Hope: Ladies of laughter. 1992. NBC.

Caroline's comedy club. Comedy Central.

Comedy express. WGN.

Comedy tonight. Comedy Central.

Comics come home. Comedy Central.

Comic strip live. Comedy Central.

The Ed Sullivan show. 1967. 16 April. KBC.

Gay and lesbian march on Washington. 1993.

Girls night out. HBO.

Girls of the comedy store. Playboy Channel.

History of stand-up comedy.

History of television: Comedy. 1988. PBS.

The Jane Whitney show. 1993. KBC.

The late show with David Letterman. CBS.

Lips only. 1991.

London underground. Comedy Central.

One night stand. Comedy Central.

Retaining laughter. 1991. Lifetime.

Short attention span theater. Comedy Central.

Showtime comedy spotlight. Showtime.

Stand-up/sitdown comedy. Comedy Central.

Stand-up spotlite. VH-1.

Stand-up/stand-up. Comedy Central.

Sunday comics. MTV.

The tonight show with Jay Leno. NBC.

The tonight show with Johnny Carson. NBC.

20/20. ABC.

Two drink minimum. Comedy Central.

USO comedy tour. Comedy Central.

The very best of Ed Sullivan. Vols. 1 and 2.

Women aloud. Comedy Central.

Women of the night. HBO.

INDEX

Abrahms, M. H., 174
accommodating strategy, 130, 131
Ace, Jane, 96
Adams, C. J.: *The Sexual Politics of Meat*, 92, 192n7
A&E, 53
African American comics, 158
African American women: both maternal and hypersexualized in popular culture, 103; cultural depictions of, 193n8; marginalized by both race and sex, 25, 33
Albrecht, Chris, 57
Allen, Gracie, 96
Allen, Tim, 134
American humor: marginal traditions, 18–19; objectification of women, 156
androcentrism, 187n37
And That's the Truth, 97
antirhetoric, 10, 12, 172, 177
Ardener, Edwin, 181n7, 184n18, 190n16
Ardener, Shirley, 190n16
Are You Ready for Phyllis Diller?, 118
Aristotle, 45, 154, 182n1
Arnold, Tom, 142
asexual innocence, 97–99
As You Like It, 47
audience: identification, 161; interruption, 55; laughter, 2, 13; paying for abuse, 22; response, 55; role of in comic performance, 1, 13, 57, 162–67; as ultimate arbiter of humor, 13, 15, 178

Auslander, P., 182n9; on creation of community, 156–57; on empowerment of women in audience, 167; on humor as feminist tool, 147; on role of microphone, 69; on Roseane, 60; on self-deprecating humor, 140; on women comics' risks, 70
autobiographical self, 51–52

baby boom generation, antiestablishment humor, 23
Baby Snooks (character), 96, 97
Bakhtin, Mikhail, 59, 61, 158–59
Ball, Lucille, 49, 63, 96, 115–16
Barreca, Regina, xv, 9, 21, 26, 27, 29, 35; on aggression in humor, 31; on comedy and carnival, 59; definition of feminism, 39; on feminist criticism's avoidance of comedy, 27, 40; on male laughter, 156; paradox in feminist criticism, 139; on self-deprecating humor, 130; on women's humor, 65, 137; on women's humor as feminist humor, 33
Barth, Belle, 104
Bauman, R., 3
bawd persona, 100–108, 129, 170
Beatts, A., 27, 34
Behar, Joy: bitch persona, 110; on feminism, 87; gynecological jokes, 84; on relationships, 77; on self-help books, 88–89; on weight, 79–80; *Wisecracks*, 35

Bellafante, Ginia, 99
Belly Room, 69
Bem, Sandra, 187n37
Benson, Bea Bea, 103
Bergson, H., 8; on complicity among laughers, 15; on laughter as suspension of sympathy, 12–13, 155; notion of a "secret freemasonry," 162
Berle, Milton, 68
Bernhard, Sandra, 69, 133, 196n32
Bier, J., 19
biological essentialism, 187n37
birth control, as source of material for female comics, 75
bitch persona, 108–14, 170; intimidation, 129; more common than any other persona, 133–34, 170; often labeled "feminist comic," 114, 135; overt expression of anger, 117
Black, E., 39
black humor, 66
Boal A., 61
Bobbitt, Lorena, 203n9
body image humor, 79–81, 90, 117–22, 191n1
Bogosian, Eric, 152
"Boomer humor," 23
Boosler, Elayne, 53, 85; on advertising, 88; disavowal of feminist label, 148; reporter persona, 49, 125–26, 138, 195n29; sexual humor, 75–76; on weight, 79; whiner persona, 123
"borderlands," 4
Borns, Betsy, 54, 188n8; on aggression in humor, 173; on the comedy club, 60–61; Comic Lives: Inside the World of American Stand-Up Comedy, 36, 181n5; on heckling, 56; on impact of television on stand-up comedy, 53; on "writing onstage," 55
Boskin, J., 18, 154, 155, 158, 164
Brenner, David, 36, 52, 189n12, 195n30

Brice, Fanny, 96, 97
Broadway follies, 46
Brooks, G. P., 8
Brown, Charles ("Artemus Ward"), 50
Bruce, Lenny, 23, 49; congruence between real and stage selves, 48, 51; on Jewish humor, 183n15; legacy, 48, 188n2; on rhetorical power of racial epithets, 109
buffoons, 45
Bunkers, 140
Burke, K., 13, 154, 155
Burnett, Carol, 49, 63, 96, 115, 116, 186n32
Butler, Brett, 81, 83, 86, 145–47
Butler, Judith, 6, 8
butt: required by all humor, 153; and victims, 160–62

cable, 53
Campbell, K. K., 42, 43
Canova, Judy, 96, 115
Carey, Jim, 49
Carlin, George: on antirhetoric, 10, 12; any topic fair game for humor, 57–58; censure for obscenity by the FCC, 23; on role of audience, 15, 162; on violent language of humor, 13
carnival: inversion, 172; officially sanctioned chaos, 160; and stand-up comedy, 59–61
carnivalesque atmosphere, 176
Caroline's, xiii
Caroline's Comedy Hour, 53
Carroll, Jean, as the first female stand-up comic, 124, 195n31
Carson, Johnny, 36, 119
Carter, Judy, 109
Catch a Rising Star, 52, 53, 188n8, 189n12
censorship, 23
Chafe, W., 12
Chaikin, J., 7
Channing, Carol, 115

Chappel, Cassie, 79
character comics, 195n32
Charlie Goodnight's, 54
Chase, Chevy, 49
Cho, Margaret, 82
Clair, R. P., xvii, 6, 175
Clay, Andrew "Dice," 23, 48, 49, 163, 166
Cleghorne, Ellen, 24–25, 74, 76, 82, 166
Clinton, Kate, 34, 85, 87, 148, 194n20
closeted gays and lesbians, 6
clown, 44, 45–46
Coca, Imogene, 115
coffeehouse, 52
Cohen, T., 9, 18, 58, 151, 198n12
Collins, P. H., 5, 153
comedy. See humor
comedy albums, 36
"comedy boom," xiii–xiv, 203n9
Comedy Central, xiii, xix, 35, 53, 182n10
Comedy Central Presents, xiii
comedy clubs, xiii, xix, 46, 181n4; audience marginality, 166; context for "trying out" subversive rhetoric, 176; officially sanctioned disorder, 60; origins of, 52–54; women comics in, 35
"comedy condos," 49
Comedy's Dirtiest Dozen, 105, 193n11
The Comedy Store, xix, 52
comic activism, 164
comic egalitarianism, as an oxymoron, 172
Comic Relief concert, 203n9
Comic Strip, 52
commodification, 16, 182n3
concert comedy, 50, 52
confronting, 130, 131
Conquergood, D., xvi
Cosby, Bill, 191n5, 195n30, 201n1
Cottom, D., 12
court fool/jester, 17, 21, 44, 45
Crystal, Billy, 53

cultural values, and shaping of responses to humor, 163

Dahl, Arlene, 120
The Daily Show, 49
Davies, Joan, 151, 152
Davis, Joan, 115
DeGeneres, Ellen, 37, 97–98; coercive form of identification and displacement, 201n30; ingratiation, 128; kid style, 192n2; reframed as a sexual being, 198n9; self-designation as lesbian, 193n5; specific performances of marginality, 181n3; view of humor as a genderless phenomenon, 148
Delaria, Lea, 87, 113–14, 193n5
demonization, 60
denying, 130, 131
Dets de Vries, M. F. R., 12
dick jokes: as view of stand-up comedy as inherently male, xiv, 68; female comics use of, 75; male comics' frequent use of, 90; reliable standard, 191n17, 203n9; vs. sexual jokes, 181n5
Digiulio, Janine, 75
Diller, Phyllis, 48, 63, 96; bitch persona, 196n36; Kiss My Act, 197n4; "loser" persona, 95; rapid-fire delivery, xiv; self-deprecatory humor as cultural critique, 140–42; substitution of self for society, 162; transitional rhetoric, 176; whiner persona, 116–19, 139
discursive power, and political power, 164, 167
disidentification, 155, 163
Dolan, M. A., 140, 149
Dollimore, Jonathan, 164
domestic activities, as category of women's humor, 85
Dorinson, J., 18, 158
Douglas, M., 10–11, 17
Draper, Ruth, 96, 196n32

Dresner, Z., 28, 30, 184n23
Dressler, Marie, 96, 114–15
"dumb blonde" stereotype, 115, 116
Dumbrowski, Louise, 76, 84, 92

Eagleton, 160
Ebert, Teresa, 171, 178
Edith Ann (character), 96, 97, 125, 196n32
The Ed Sullivan Show, 118, 120, 124
Edwards, Tony, 134
Elinore, Kate, 100, 193n7
Ellen, 35, 192n2, 197n9
emotional self-deprecation, 195n28
Ensler, Eve, 92–93, 192n8
entertainment, 182n2
Ephron, Nora, 183n15
Ernestine (character), 125
Essman, Susie, 65, 75, 182n11
exemplification, 128

Faludi, Susan: *Backlash: The Undeclared War against American Women,* 40
family, as category of women's humor, 83–84
Faranda, Louis, xiii–xiv
fashion, as category of women's humor, 81
"fat" jokes, 114, 121
feature act, 54
female comics, stand-up, 31–40, 61–71; accession to male-defined industry standards, xiv; addressing of "universal" concerns in order to entertain widest possible audience, 169; audience resistance to "authority," 32–33; combining of personas, 131–32; comedic personas, 96–128; degrading introductions by male MCs, 34; "dick jokes," 75; "double text" of self-deprecatory jokes, 29; existing scholarship on, 67; extent of involvement in industry, 35–37; feminist cultural criticism of, 70;

influenced by the conditions feminism has produced, xix; intimidation of men, 34–35; little difference from male comics, 173; marginality, 2, 16–17, 173; opportunities to perform, xix; perceived as threatening, xiv; power relations inherent in performance of marginality, xviii; response to hecklers, 132–33; self-presentation strategies, 128–31; style, 65; topical categories in performances of, 73; traditions of, 95–96; weight and body image humor, 90
female humor, 25–40; as definable genre, 137; and feminist humor, 63–68; five types of, 66; problematic label, 170–71; regarded as worthy of analysis, xvii; regarded with fear and suspicion, 28; scholarly research on, 27–31; self-deprecating, 65; as subversive, xiv–xv, 65, 66; very seldom performed by women, 93–94. *See also* feminist humor; humor; marginal humor
female subjectivity, 155
feminism, xvii; defined as gender egalitarianism, 40, 93, 138, 202n5; difficulty of defining, 38–40, 187n38; disavowal of label by American women, 148–49, 186n36; and "fun," 40; view of as humorless, 164
feminist critics, failure to recognize difference between victims and butts, 162
feminist humor, 137; definitions of, 31, 66–67; differences from marginal humor, 71; Martin and Segrave on, 32; men as butts of, 153–54; perceived as less abusive than traditional male humor, 147–48; popular perception of, 135; problematic label, xx, 25–26, 93,

170–71; problems with studies in, 138–50; and women's movement, 30
"festival" fools, 45
Field, Alison, 34, 159, 185n31, 200n23
Fields, Totie, 120–21
Finley, Karen, xi
Finney, G., xv, xix, 66, 67, 70–71, 158
Fisher, Rhoda, xvi
Flora, C. B., 5
fool makers, 161, 184n19
fools/jesters: "festival," 45; "mythical," 45; "natural," 45; professional, 17, 21, 22–23, 44, 45, 160–61, 169, 188n3; wise, 18, 45, 46–50
fool societies, 45
Ford, Diane, xiv, 74
Foster, Amy, 89, 110
Fox-Genovese, 186n36
Fraiberg, A.: "Between the Laughter: Bridging Feminist Studies through Women's Stand-Up Comedy," xvi–xvii, 67, 70, 98, 174, 201n30
Franklin, Irene, 97
Fraser, Casey, 82–83
Freud, Sigmund: on joking, 9–10, 11, 156, 162, 183n10, 201n27; notion of mini-rebellions, 158; notion of tendentious humor, 68, 91; relief theory, 8, 198n13
Friedan, Betty: The Feminine Mystique, 40
Friedman, Budd, 52, 53
Friedman, Silver, 52
Friend, T., 148, 186n36
Friganza, Trixie, 115
The Funniest Woman in the World, 102
Funny Bone, 54, 188n8

Gaffney, Mo, 157, 159, 197n2
Gagnier, R., 65
Gallo, Hank: Comedy Explosion, 36, 52
Garofalo, Janeane, 88, 126
gays and lesbians, 6. See also lesbian comics

Gelbart, Larry, 183n14
gender: as social construction separate from biological sex, 6; sociolinguistic nature of, 62
gender differences, in humor, 27
gender egalitarianism, feminism as, 40, 93, 138, 201n5
genderlect hypothesis, 62
gender polarization, 187n36
gender roles, 39
generic criticism, 42–44
genre, 42–44
Gentlemen Prefer Blondes, 115
Gindele, K. C., 67
Girls Night Out, 35
Glass, Todd, 165
Goldberg, Whoopi, 35, 69, 96, 196n32
Goldthwait, "Bobcat," 51
Gomez, Marga, 194n20
Gore, Al, xii, 181n1
Gottfried, Gilbert, 134
Gould, Stephen J., 39
Grace under Fire, 35, 145
Graham, E. E., 8
Greenblatt, Stephen, 16
Gregory, Dick, 48, 159
Gridiron dinner, 13
Griffiths, K., 185n26
Grimaldi, Joseph, 46
Grotjahn, M., 158
group laughter, 15
Gruner, C. R., 58, 197n1, 198n14
gynecological humor, 84–85, 169–70, 191n5; as metaphor, 89–93

Haber, Karen, 78; ethnic humor, 81–82; family humor, 83; relationship humor, 76; reporter persona, 126; self-deprecation, 130, 131, 177; sexual humor, 74; whiner persona, 122–23, 160
Half-Hour Comedy Hour, 53
Handelman, D., 22
Harlequin, 46
Hart, Roderick, 182n12, 202n8

HA! The TV Comedy Network, 53
Hawn, Goldie, 96, 116
HBO, 53
headliner, 54
heckling, 55–56, 58–59, 188n9; responding to, 132–33, 162
Hegde, R. S., xviii
hegemonic humor, co-option of, 21, 175
Hello Dolly, 115
Hemphill, Shirley, 112
Hendra, T., 23
Henry, Carol, 74
Hereford, Beatrice, 196n32
hierarchy, essential to most humor, 156
Hobbes, Thomas, 8, 154
Hodge, Stephanie, 76, 194n15; bawd persona, 105, 107, 122, 129; body-focused humor, 121–22; portrayal of both bawd and whiner, 122, 132
Holland, Norman: on laughter, 13, 57, 155, 163, 201n32; on laughter as social corrective, 9; on social function of humor, 11
Holliday, Judy, 115
"hook," 109
hooks, bell, 5, 25, 39
Hope, Bob, xiv, 117, 118, 142
Hopkins, E., 21, 38
Hopper, Robert, 62
Horowitz, S., xv, 155; on Burnett, 116; comparison of Joan Rivers to Woody Allen, 195n25; on Diller, 118; on historical personas of women comics, 94, 95–96; on Jewish comics, 194n17; on Joan Rivers, 109; on male and female comedic style, 65; *Queens of Comedy*, 63; on social potential of humor, 172
humor: aggressive, 10, 158, 159, 172–73, 183n11; alienating, 11; as an antirhetoric, 172, 177; bending or breaking of rules, xviii; breach of social norms, 59–60, 61; as

catharsis, 10; as cathexis, 10; as communication, 9; critical function in society, 169; defined, 8; democratizing function, 14; economic dimension of, 15–17; as a form of social control, 9; gender differences in, 63; and hierarchy, 156, 172; in-group/out-group distinctions, 14; as inherently social, 15; legitimization by laughter, 13, 162; not inherently gendered, 94; and objectification, 150–62; of oppression, 18; and power, xv, 9, 13, 69–70, 177–79; psychological dimension of, 9–12; as rhetorical weapon, xv, 3, 12–15, 164; as socially constructed phenomenon, 64; sociocultural critique as "entertainment," xii; transitional rhetoric, 176. *See also* female humor; feminist humor; marginal humor
humor studies, 8
hybridization, as resistance to patriarchal norms, 60

identification, 11, 155, 163, 167
Improv, 52, 53, 182n10, 188n6
incongruity theory, 8
inductive and deductive generic analysis, 44
Inge, M. T., 70
ingratiation, 128
"in one" persona, 51
intimidation, 128, 129
inversion, 60, 172
Irwin, May ("Madame Laughter"), 114
Ivanov, A. J., 101

The Jack Paar Show, 116
Jamieson, K. H., 42, 43
Janus, Samuel, 19, 169, 170, 184n16
Jenkins, M. M., 63–64
Jewel, 193n8
Jewish American Princess ("JAP") jokes, 58

Jewish American Princess persona, 109
Jewish comics, 184n16, 184n17, 185n29
Jewish female comics, 33
Jewish humor, 18–19, 20, 66, 199n19, 199n20; function of in culture, 157–58; inversion and subversion in, 199n18; relationship to "American" humor, 183n15; relationship to oppression, 183n14; taxonomy of stages of, 200n22
jokes: Freud on, 9–10, 11, 156, 162, 183n10, 201n27; as "mini-rebellions," 158
Jones, E. E., 128, 129, 130
Jordan, Diana, 74, 80
Joyner, Mario, 24

Kalcik, S., 201n4
Kamenoff, Wendy, 83, 88
Kane, Helen ("Betty Boop"), 97
Kant, Immanuel, 8
Kaplan, A., 185n29, 198n12
Karam, Jann, 80, 126
Karlin, Ben, 49–50
Kauffman, Donna, 147–48
Kaufman, Gloria: Pulling Our Own Strings: Feminist Humor and Satire, 71, 154
Kay, Karyn, 115, 166
Keith, Benjamin, 46
Kibler, M. A., xvii, 32, 100, 174, 193n7
kid persona, 97–100, 128, 170, 192n2, 193n5
Kightlinger, Laura, 75, 83, 89, 126
Kings of Comedy, 36
Kinison, Sam, 51
Klapp, O. E., 47
Klein, Robert, 48, 52
Knockers Up, 103
Kolinsky, Sue, 79, 88, 127
komoidos, 45
Komos, 187n1
Koziski, S., xvi, 181n6

Kramarae, Cheris, 27, 64, 181n7, 190n16
Krinsky, Leah, 76, 77, 84, 86, 113, 129

L.A. Improv, 52
Ladies of Laughter, 35
Ladman, Cathy, 54, 188n7; family humor, 73, 83; gynecological humor, 84; relationship humor, 78; response to heckler, 132; self-deprecation, 130; shopping humor, 81; whiner persona, 123
Lakoff, Robin: Language and Woman's Place, 62
Lapiduss, Maxine, 37
Late Night, 53
late-night comedy shows, political candidates' appearance on, xii
The Late Show with David Letterman, xii, xiii, xiv, 121
Laugh-In, 97, 116, 125
laughter: group, 15; as legitimation, 13, 162; male, 156; nervous, 163; as suspension of sympathy, 12–13, 155
"laughter in the kitchen," 29, 65
Legman, Gershon, 156
Le Guin, U. K., 174
Lehane, Chris, xii
Leifer, Carol, 21, 53, 88; marriage/divorce humor, 78; reporter persona, 49, 126, 127; sexual humor, 74; on working out, 80–81
Leno, Jay, xii, 36, 184n21, 195n30, 202n9
Leonard, Kelly, 169
lesbian comics, 113–14, 192n5, 193n5
Letterman, David, xii, 21–22, 184n20
Levine, Emily, 19, 34, 38; on alternate versions of reality, 94; on marginal humor, 157; on power in stand-up comedy, 70; subversive humor, 151
Levy, B., 34
Lewis, Jerry, 186n32
Lewis, Richard, 134

Liebling, Deborah, xiii
Liebman, Wendy: body-image humor, 121; family humor, 83; gynecological humor, 85; popular culture humor, 87; relationship humor, 78; unique rhythm, 189n11; whiner persona, 123
"liminoid" phenomena, 3
Limon, John, 57
Lincoln, Erik, 158
Lips Only, 196n32
Little, Judy, xv; *Comedy and the Woman Writer,* xiv, 27–28; double-voiced discourse, 158; on liminality of women's humor, 60, 70; on potential of marginal humor, 172, 178; on self-deprecatory humor, 200n24
Live at the Improv, 53
Locke, David ("Petroleum V. Nasby"), 50
Lord of Misrule, 47
Lorenz, Konrad, 14
Lotta Crabtree (character), 96, 97
Lowks, Suzy, 78, 79, 109–10
lyceum, 50–52, 188n4
Lynch, Nora, 80

Mabley, Jackie "Moms," 36, 96; as bawd persona, 102–3, 194n12
MacCambridge, Michael: "Female Humor Stands Up," 37–38
Madigan, Kathleen, 76–77, 82, 83, 84, 126
Madonna, 139, 184n20
"Madonna question," 139
maiden, 95
Maier, Bill, 134, 195n30
Malaprop, Mrs., 96
male comics: comedic style, 65; little topical difference from female comics, 173; material on sports, politics, and substances, 90; personas, 134–35; reporters, 195n30
Manheim, Camryn, 197n4

Mantel, Henriette, 121, 161
marginal humor, xvi, 17–25; as aggressive, 158, 159, 183n11; defining characteristics, 135, 199n17; lack of subject-subject relationship, 154; as means of legitimizing alternate versions of reality, 94; modern, 178; paradoxical nature of, 157, 177; as performing culture, 175–76; as performing power, 177–79; as performing transition, 176–77; politics of, 137–38; as resistance to hegemonic strictures, 21, 175; rhetorical strategies of subversion, 171, 178; as social criticism, 14; studies of focusing on Jewish and/or African American humor, 157; and tendentious jokes, 10, 12; and transformation of social conditions, 164–65; types of, 200n22; underscoring power imbalances in American culture, 178
marginality: defined, 3, 4–5; essential societal function, 4; sociological *vs.* rhetorical, 5
margins, shifting, 7–8
Margolis, H., on stereotypes, 151–52
Marks, P., xii
Martin, Linda: on comedy as a weapon, 9; on development of American comedy, 52; on early female comics, 32; on Eva Tanquay, 100; on Fanny Brice, 97; on gynecological humor, 90; on Jean Carroll, 125; on Mae West, 101; on victimization, 91
Martin, Steve, 49
Marx Brothers, 48
mass entertainment, 52
masturbation, as topic of humor, 76
matriarch, 95
Matteson, Pam, 110
McCawley, Jim, xiv
McGhee, Paul, 66
McMahon, Ed, 54
McManus, B. K., 50–51, 52

McNamara, B., 1
McWhirter, D., 67, 111
Mead, Margaret, 120
Mellencamp, P., 156
Mendoza, John, 134
Meredith, G., xv, xviii
Merrill, L., 31, 153, 156, 162
meta-self-deprecation, 133
Meyrowitz, Joshua, 166
Michaels, Shayne, xix, 182n10
microphone, 69, 70
Midler, Bette, 104–5
The Mike Douglas Show, 120
Miller, C. R., 44
Mindless, Harvey, 9
minorities: defined, 5; self-deprecating
    humor, 20; subversion through
    humor, 20
Mintz, L. E., xv–xvi, xvii, 18, 200n22
misogynistic humor, 154
Mitchell, C., 185n26
mock sermon, 47
Modern Scream, 125
Modleski, T., 31, 153
monologue, xii, 70
Montgomery, Carol, 34
Moore, T. E. K., 185n26
Morreall, J., 198n13
Morton, Bob, xiv
MTV, 23, 53
Muggeridge, Malcolm, 9
Mulligan, Gerry, xii, 50
Mulvey, Laura, 156, 199n15
"muted group theory," 64, 184n18,
    190n16
"mythical" fool, 45

National Lampoon, 36
"Natural" fools, 45
Nelson, Christine, 36
"nervous laughter," 163
Neve, M., 9
Nichols, Diane, 74, 77, 88
Nickman, Bob, 134
Nietz, M. J., 155–56, 202n9

Nilsen, D., 8, 9
Noel, Hattie, 103, 193n9

objectification, 92; humor and, 150–62
observational humor, 49, 89, 138, 150,
    183n11
O'Donnell, Rosie, 35, 54, 99–100;
    ingratiation, 128; kid persona,
    193n5; self-designation as lesbian,
    193n5; specific performances of
    marginality, 181n3
Olsen, L., 174, 178
one-liner, 14
opener, 54
Ortner, S. B., 4, 174–75

Page, La Wanda, 105
Papa, M. J., 8
Parker, Dorothy, 29, 96
Parks, Tom, 53
"passing," 6
Payne, B., 185n26
Pearl, Minnie, 96, 115
penis size, as common source of
    material for female comics, 75
performance: defined, 1, 2; persuasive, 2
performative speech act, as "feminist,"
    171
performers, rhetorical power and
    marginal status, 3
Pershing, L., 34
phallus, preeminent power of in
    Western culture, 111
Phillips, Emo, 134, 148
Phyllis Diller Laughs, 118
physical comedy, 115–16
physical size, and female comic
    bawdiness, 100–102
Pierrot, 46
Piper, Monica, 79, 85
Pipkin, T., 203n9
Pip's Comedy Club, 52, 188n5, 191n17
Pitchford, H. G., 9
Pittman, T. S., 128, 129, 130
Pitts, Zasu, 115

platform humorists, 50–51
Plato, 23, 154
political constraints, 57
political correctness, 12, 152, 166, 182n10
political humor, 14–15, 85–87
popular culture phenomena, as category of women's humor, 87–89
Porges, Paul P., 19
postmodernism: humor, 202n9; marginality in, 5; notion of a destablized center, 6
Poundstone, Paula, 55, 89, 192n3, 193n4; body image humor, 191n1; ingratiation, 128; kid persona, 97, 98–99, 170; observational humor, 37; self-designate as lesbian, 193n5; view of humor as a genderless phenomenon, 148
power, 38, 139; discursive, and political power, 164, 167; and humor, xv, 9, 13, 69–70, 177–79; rhetorical, 3
powerless speech hypotheses, 62
power of powerlessness, 137, 138, 159
premarginalization, 165
Premium Blend, xiii
presidential election of 2000, xii
Private Benjamin, 116
Professional Comedians Association, xix
professional fools, 188n3; as "fool-makers," 160–61; Greek origins, 45; as licensed social critics, 22–23; professional comics as analogues of, 17, 21, 44, 169
prop comics, 57
Pryor, Richard, 36
Pulcinella, 46
Punchline, 54, 188n8
punchlines, 57
put-down humor, 26, 44, 108, 148, 154–55, 202n9

Radner, Gilda, 196n32, 198n12
random observations, as category of women's humor, 89

Raskin, Victor, 163–64
Raye, Martha, 115
Reeder, H. M., xviii
Reiner, Carl, 183n14, 184n17
relationships, as category of women's humor, 76–79
relief/arousal theory, 8, 9, 198n13
religion/ethnicity/region, as category of women's humor, 81–83
reporter persona, 124–28, 170, 196n34
revisioning, 130–31
Rhea, Caroline: bawd persona, 105, 107, 129; body image humor, 80; on cultural differences, 82; relationship humor, 77; sexual humor, 74, 76
rhetoric: defined, 182n1; of social criticism, in stand-up comedy, 2; subversive, 135, 171, 176, 178; transitional, 176; of victimage, 135, 137, 138, 171
rhetorical marginality, 6, 21, 170, 175–76, 183n5
Rivers, Joan, 36, 48, 63; "bitch" comic posture, 108–9; as a feminist, 120; gynecological humor, 92; "loser" persona, 95; portrayals of both the bitch and the whiner, 132; self-deprecatory humor, 140; whiner persona, 119–24
road clubs, 53–54
roasts, 13
Robinson, Lynn, 103, 193n9
Rock, Chris, xi
Rogers, Will, 48
role-transformative humor, 66
role-transgressive humor, 66
Roseanne, xix, 35, 48, 49, 92; aggression, 65; on birth control, 75; bitch persona, 111–12, 195n26; change of material along with physical image, 194n13, 197n5; characterization of humor as "women's point-of-view jokes," 149; considered as feminist comic, 143–45, 148; on domestic

activities, 85; gynecological jokes, 84; on homophobia, 87; hybridization of male "dick" joke, 60, 143–44; intimidation, 129; marriage/divorce humor, 78; objectification as a "fat" comic, 197n7; on parenting, 83; regional jokes, 83; and Rivers, 194n18; self-objectification, 142–43; sexual humor, 75; transitional rhetoric, 176; "wall" joke, 141, 161, 200n26; weight/body image humor, 79

The Roseanne Barr Show, 142

Rosenblatt, R., 11

The Rosie O'Donnell Show, xiii

Rosmarin, A., 42–43, 44

Rudner, Rita, 24, 89, 157; domestic humor, 85; on marriage, 78–79; relationship humor, 77; reporter persona, 126, 127; on shopping, 81; whiner persona, 122

sacred cows, 57

Said, E., 153

Sanborn, Kate: *The Wit of Women,* 28

Saper, Bernard: SROC model, 200n25

Saturday Night Live, 53, 198n12

Schechner, R., 1, 2, 58, 182n2

Schlafly, Phyllis, 156

schlemiel, 44

Schopenhauer, Arthur, 8

Schuler, C., 70

Schutz, C. E., 14–15, 15, 58

Scott, Angela, 86–87, 105, 106, 194n14

"screwball" comics, 115

Second City Theater, 169

Segrave, Kerry, xiv; on comedy as weapon, 9; on development of American comedy, 52; on early women comics, 32; on Eva Tanguay, 100; on Fanny Brice, 97; on gynecological humor, 90; on Jean Carroll, 125; on Mae West, 101; on victimization, 91

Seinfeld, Jerry, 10, 48, 55, 134; on laughter, 164; reporter persona, 49, 124, 138, 195n30

self-deprecation: critical condemnation of, 139–40, 141; as cultural critique, 140; disarming function, 130; echoing of cultural sentiment, 194n25; in ethnic humor, 19–20; and marginality, 20, 135, 171; in relation to body image, 117–22; in relation to issues of self-esteem, 122–24; "safe" entertainment, 160; as subversive, 21, 138, 158–60; of whiner persona, 114; by women comics, 194n25

"self-heckling," 133

self-marginalization, 165–66

self-objectification, 139, 142–43, 163

self-promotion, 128

"self-uglification," 116

Sella, M., xii

"sense of humor," 184n22

Sensible Footwear, 34, 159, 200n23

sensitive New Age guy (SNAG), 134

"set-up, pause, and pay-off," 116–17

sex and sexuality, 181n5; material for both the bitch and the bawd comics, 106–8, 112; as topic of women's humor, 73–76

sexist jokes, 163, 185n26

Shapiro, S., 157–58, 199n18

Shaw, Ann Howard, 28

Shaw, Henry ("Josh Billings"), 50

Shaw, Lillian, 100, 193n7

Sheppard, Alice, 28, 66

Shore, Mitzi, 69

Showtime, 53

Shydner, Rich, 134

Simmel, G., notion of the stranger, 182n4

Simons, H., 43

Singer, Gail, 37

Siskind, Carol, 76, 78, 126, 203n9

Smith, Linda, 79, 82

Smith, Margaret, 170; body image

Smith, Margaret, (*continued*)
humor, 191n1; "dick joke"
experience, 68–69, 201n31; political
jokes, 85–86; relationship humor,
77; reporter persona, 124, 127
Smith, Ronald: *Comedy on Record: The
Complete Critical Discography,* 36–37,
186n33, 193n9
Snow, Carrie, 87, 177; bawd persona,
105–6, 194n13; bitch persona, 110;
fat jokes, 121; intimidation, 129;
parenting humor, 83; self-heckling,
133
Sochen, June, xv, 33
social critics, comics as, 14, 18, 22,
23–24, 48, 221
sociological marginality, 6, 170, 175
Solon, 23
Soro, Suzy, 77, 78, 85
Spencer, Gary, 58
"squelches," 132–33
Stallybrass, P., 59, 60, 160, 167
stand-up comedy: abhors ideological
purity, 179; absence of costume,
190n14; as an aggressive genre,
172–73; as an autobiographical art
form, 94; audience participation, 1,
14, 15; boom era of, 182n10;
brevity, 56; as carnival, 59–61;
cumulative nature of performed
marginality, 24; as a democratic
enterprise, 178; evolution of,
44–52; generic features and
constraints of, 54–59; as genre, 43,
44–61; highly adaptive, 55;
interactive nature of, 162; lack of
"feminist" humor within, 172; as a
"male-defined" genre, xiv, 68–71;
and objectification, 154; and power,
xi–xii, 69–70; public context within
which women can wield rhetorical
power, xv; as rhetorical act, 2; as a
self-correcting genre, 55; as solo art,
54; taboo topics, 10; and tradition
of wise fool, 46, 48–50; unique

forum in which cultural values are
both affirmed and interrogated, xvi;
violent language of, 13; as a
vocabulary for discussing societal ills,
176–77
stand-up comics: as anthropologists,
xvi; as cultural barometers and
cultural critics, xiii; as
ethnographers, xvi; impact of
television on, xiii, 53; as licensed
social critics, 18, 48; marginality, 17,
24. *See also* female comics, stand-up
Stand-Up Spotlight, 53
Star Search, 54
Stein, Abby, 74
stereotypes: controversy over intent in
stand-up comedy, 58; currency of
stand-up comedy, 151–52
Stillion, J. M., 41
Stillson, Jeff, 134
Stocking, S. H., 185n26
stock jokes, 193n10
Stone, Laurie, 99
Stone, Pam, 77, 80, 81, 133
Stonequist, Everett, 3–4
strategic self-presentation, 128–35,
196n33
Strauss, D., 22
subjectivity, and marginality, 153
subversion: in Jewish humor, 199n18;
rhetorical, 135, 171, 176, 178; self-
deprecation as, 21, 138, 158–60;
through marginal humor, 20–21;
women's humor as, xiv–xv, 65, 66
Sullivan, P. A., 130–31, 187n36
superiority theory, 8, 9, 154–55, 172,
178, 198n13, 198n14
supplication, 128, 129–30, 130, 134,
159
Swisher, Deborah, 112, 175
Swortzell, L., 47
Sykes, Wanda: bitch persona, 110; on
friendships, 79; relationship humor,
77–78; sexual humor, 74–75; on
unfair cultural expectations for

female attractiveness, 80; variation on the whiner persona, 122

taboo topics, 91, 175–76
Tanguay, Eva, 100, 193n6
television, impact on stand-up comedy, xiii, 53
television talk shows, 13
Telushkin, Rabbi Joseph, 19
tendentious humor, 10, 68, 91
Tenuta, Judy, 54, 65, 161; bitch persona, 110, 113; character comedy, 51, 196n32; controversial persona, 23, 48, 49, 65; family jokes, 84; intimidation, 129; jokes about the pope, 82; relationship humor, 76
Thersites, 45
Thompson, Robert, 38
time limits, 56
timing, 57
Toll, Judy, 89, 196n32
Tolsch, Adrienne, 105, 106–7
Tomlin, Lily, 96, 97, 125, 196n32
The Tonight Show, xiii, xiv, 35–36, 119, 127
"toomlers," 46
Torres, Liz, 82
Toth, E., 28
traveling comedy variety shows, 52
"trickster" comic personalities, 44, 49
Truth, Sojourner, 28
Tucker, Sophie, 100
Turner, V., 3, 130–31, 182n3, 187n37
TV Guide, 36
Tyler, Robin, 36, 37; bitch persona, 114, 193n5; jokes about the pope, 82; political humor, 86, 87; on stand-up comedy as male province, 33, 198n10

Unterbrink, M., 25

The Vagina Monologues, 92–93
Vance, Danitra, 196n32

Van Dyke, Dick, 49
vaudeville, 46
V-Day Campaign, 93
Veeser, H. A., 177
VH-1, 53
victims and butts, 160–62, 176
Vidale, Thea, 105, 129, 194n12
The View, 110

Waldoks, Moshe, 183n15
Walker, Nancy, xv, xviii, xix, xx, 21, 29; on double text of women writers, 29; on humor and the women's movement, 40, 184n25; on paradox of women's humor, 27; on self-deprecating humor, 33, 141, 158; on subversion of women's humor, 159; on women's humor and feminist humor, 30–31, 32, 137
Ware, V., xviii, 29
Warfield, Marsha, 75, 88, 109, 126, 185n32
Warren, Rusty, 36–37, 103–4
Waters, H. F., 147
weight/body image, as category of women's humor, 79–81, 117–22, 191n1
Weinstock, Lotus, 69
Weiss, P., xiv, 68
Welsford, Enid: The Fool: His Social and Literary History, 45, 47
West, Mae, 96, 100–102
Westenhoeffer, Suzanne, 87, 194n20
What Becomes a Semi-Legend Most?, 108
whiner persona, 114–24, 160, 170, 197n2
White, C. L.: on carnival, 59, 160; on feminist humor, 31, 41, 71, 154; on politically transformative humor, 167; on sex role delineation in humor, 27; on symbolic processes in humor, 60
Whitfield, S. J., 14
Williams, Elsie, 102, 193n9
Williams, Pearl, 103

Williams, Robin, xix, 53, 191n5,
201n1
Wilson, Marie, 116
Wilson, Midge, 38
Wilt, Judith, 95
Winstead, Lizz, 75, 88, 112, 157
Wise, Anita, 75, 122, 157
Wisecracks, 33, 37–38
wise fools, 45, 46–50
Wolf, N., 148, 150, 186n36
women: cultural identification with
subordination, 29; male accusation
of lack of sense of humor, 64; as a
"marginalized majority" in the
United States, 5
Women Aloud, 157, 197n2
Women and Cinema (Kay, ed.), 115

Women of the Night, xiv, 35
women's movement, and humor, 30,
40, 184n25
women's point of view jokes, 94
women's speech, powerlessness of, 62
women's studies, xvii
women writers, double text, 28, 29
wordplay, 138, 150, 183n11, 197n1,
202n9
Wright, Steven, 189n11

Yudice, G., 5

Zanies, 54
Zijderveld, A. C., 17, 21, 188n3
Zillman, D., 185n26